WITHDRAWN

JEAN DE MURAT

THE GREAT EXTIRPATION OF HELLENISM
AND CHRISTIANITY
IN ASIA MINOR

THE HISTORIC AND SYSTEMATIC DECEPTION OF WORLD OPINION
CONCERNING THE HIDEOUS CHRISTIANITY'S UPROOTING OF 1922

MIAMI, FLORIDA, U.S.A.
FEBRUARY 1999

Edited and published in February 1999 by the writer JEAN DE MURAT
Literary Pseudonym of DR. MENANDER PHOEBUS ACADEMUS

ISBN 09600356-7-2

The author's Declared Literary Pseudonym (pen name) is Dr. Menander Phoebus Academus and publishes some of his works under this pen name.

Dr. John Murat is honorary member of Asian, European and American Libraries with granted accesibility to certain former U.S.S.R. famous Libraries as well.

The book is protected by the Universal Copyright Convention of 16 September 1995 and the Bern Convetnion on 1 March 1989 for the Protection of Literary and Artistic Works. Greece belongs to «Bern Union» and the Greek Constitution provides for any person who does any unauthorised act in relation to this publication may be liable to criminal prosecution and civil claims for damages.

Author
© Dr. John Murat 2132 N.W. 11th Avenues Miami, FLORIDA

Printed in Athens by A. TRIANTAFILLIS
7, Mavromichali str.
Tel.: 36.36.325 - 36.25.849

PUBLISHED
BY A NON-PROFIT
COMPANY OF
HISTORICAL
RESEARCH

ESTABLISHED AND BASED IN ATHENS, GREECE
13, Ippocratous str., 1st floor, N° 11

All the historical sources of this book had meticulously been checked-up and verified for accuracy, by the author's persistent criss-crossing corresponding historical works attainable in European and other world's Liabraries.

The present historical material has been historically checked over and approved by specialized university professors of History, members of a Special Service elected by the Department of Education and Culture of the U.S.A. Covernment, Washington D.C.

"Kemal celebrated his triumph by transforming Smyrna into ashes and by slaughtering the whole of the indigenous Christian population"

WINSTON CHURCHILL

"... tens of thousands of (Greek) men, women and Children were expelled and dying. It was clearly a deliberate extermination. 'Extermination' is not my word. It is the word being used by the American mission".

LLOYD GEORGE British Prime Minister
(House of Commons. The Parliament
Debates, Fifth series, vol. 157)

"The Turks seem to be acting based on a premeditated plan for the elimination of the minorities...."

Letter of Sir HORACE RUMBOLD,
British High Commissioner, in
Constantinople, to CURZON,
the British Minister of Foreign Affairs

Biographical Outline

He entered this world with the twentieth century. After receiving his primary schooling, he continued into further and advanced education up the gradually unfolding stages of the educational ladder. The pattern of this learning process was as follows: Preparatory, Primary, Secondary and High Schools. (a) Athens University, Greece (b) Columbia University, New York City, USA (c) Post-graduate courses at the Sorbonne University, Paris and at Heidelberg University, Baden, Germany. His strenuous and incessant efforts were rewarded both morally and in terms of his position by his reaching a high mental plateau within his work; he was also recognised by his fellow-humans and was bestowed with acclaims and accolades by several High Educational Institutions and Academies.

He began in his new environment in the USA by doing various jobs on a temporary basis. As time went on, he again took up his old profession of Attorney-at-Law and, possessing the necessary knowledge, he was subsequently appointed by the Court to be a trustee to handle legal cases involving intricate financial matters. He went on to serve as the State's Criminal District Prosecutor and later as a District Judge and tried to dispense justice fairly and with evenhanded impartiality.

The constant intervention and pressure exerted upon him by powerful politicians and the disgusting double-dealing of many practising lawyers and judges who had also obviously succumbed to the political pressure exerted upon them, enraged him to the point where he could bear it no longer and, on his own initiative and determination, he withdrew from the legal profession and retired from it for good.

There now followed the last thirty and most productive years of his life when he spent his time in the quest of man's primordial history by persistently and tirelessly digging out, tracing and bringing to the fore some of the factual events of man's history on this planet which have still not been completely traced. He has written several copyrighted historical books - most of them develop this subject and can be found on numerical cards in the historical sections of the famous USA Congress Library, and also in the Libraries of most European and other countries.

Republished in March 1999 by JEAN DE MURAT

THIS BOOK IS DEDICATED

TO THE MEMORY OF THE FORGOTTEN MILLIONS OF GREEKS AND ARMENIANS, WHICH HAS FADED AWAY AND BEEN FORGOTTEN BY THE PASSAGE OF TIME EVEN FROM LIVING MEMORY TO THE OUTSTANDING HISTORIC ACTION OF THEIR EXISTENCE TO THOSE WHO OVER THE CENTURIES WERE BUTCHERED AND DESTROYED BY THE TURKS WITH BRUTAL, BLOODY AND EXCRUCIATING SAVAGERY. ALSO TO THE GREATEST PHILHELLENE OF THE TWENTIETH CENTURY

GEORGE HORTON

WHOSE MEMORY HAS BEEN FORGOTTEN AND WHO FOR 13 WHOLE YEARS DID HIS UTMOST ON BEHALF OF HELLENISM AND WHO SHOWED HIS LOVE FOR GREECE AND ESPECIALLY FOR THE MILLIONS OF ENSLAVED AND VICTIMISED GREEKS OF ASIA MINOR IN THE MOST IRREFUTABLE WAY, SAVING HUNDREDS OF GREEKS AND ARMENIANS FROM THE CLUTCHES OF THE TURKS; ALSO FIGHTING, WITH HIS SIGNIFICANT DIPLOMATIC INFLUENCE, FOR AN IMPROVEMENT IN THE TERMS (SO INHUMAN FOR GREECE) OF THE PEACE TREATY WITH TURKEY AT «MOUDANIA», WHICH THE GREAT NATIONS WHO WERE VICTORIOUS IN THE FIRST WORLD WAR OF 1914-18, WITH INHUMAN PRESSURE FORCED GREECE TO ACCEPT, ON BEHALF OF THE DISGRA-CEFUL PROFIT-SEEKING INTERESTS WHICH THEY WANTED TO GAIN FROM TURKEY - A GREECE DEFEATED BY THE TURKS, IMPOVERISHED AND IN A MISERABLE CONDITION, WITH ONE AND A HALF MILLION STARVING, SICK AND UPROOTED REFUGEES WHO HAD BEEN THROWN ONTO HER INFERTILE SOIL

January 1999
The Author
JEAN DE MURAT

GEORGE HORTON

PORTRAIT OF AN UNSUNG HERO

As the tragic history of humanity unfolds, with its inhuman wars, the savage burning of great cities and villages and its innumerable other catastrophes, there are always unknown heroes who come into the limelight; they are spiritually brave and courageous men who, with a conscientious spontaneity, sacrifice their own lives to save others from death.

George Horton was such a man. He was the US General Consul in Smyrna, Turkey, during the Greek-Turkish War of 1922.

George Horton's heroism came to the fore during the most terrifying moments of the ghastly holocaust of the once beautiful city of Smyrna, when he made a brave attempt to save its Christian population of Greeks and Armenians from mass slaughter at the hands of the Turkish murderers. These are substantiated historical facts which have been recorded in the official documented annals of an irrefutable historical reality.

George Horton, upset by the tragic disaster which befell the Christian population of Greeks and Armenians, did what he could by taking appropriate action under the circumstances to save the lives of hundreds of the fiercely percecuted of innocent Greeks and Armenians. As US Consul, he helped the Greeks right up to the dramatic end, despite all the obstacles which he met at every step and despite the strong reaction of the political leaders of the Great Powers who had already initiated a rapaciously gainfue profit-seeking Turkophile political stance which was diametrically opposed to what he was doing.

George Horton was an honorable man who had moral principles and who was a great humanitarian. He despised the political profiteering expediency of the Great Nations who were willing to sacrifice the lives of innocent Greeks at the altar of economic interest. He worked tirelessly without stopping, risking his own life, supplying the refugees with the appropriate documents which were aimed at ensuring their escape under the tragic circumstances. At one point he even offered the great and unforgettable Archbishop Chrysostomos the opportunity of saving his life and of escaping the anticipated cruel and bloody handling of the Turks - but Chrysostomos, as the pastoral head of the Christians, refused to save himself by abandoning his Christian flock at that most critical hour and remained subsequently to meet a savage death at the hands of the brutal and fanatical Muslims.

At the same time that George Horton was doing his utmost, exposing himself to the evil which threatened and risking his diplomatic career and his official position as General Consul of a US which had already taken a different political direction, the Great Powers were looking on ruthlessly, indifferently and totally unmoved at the same tragic time that the systematic slaughter of thousands upon thousand of unprotected Greeks and Armenians was being perpetrated by the bloodthirsty Turks.

Even when the actual Consulate building was burning after being set on fire by the Turks, George Horton continued with his philanthropic action, not abandoning his office until, with his own life in immediate danger, he was forced by the responsible for his life american local naval head at the time, and against his will to leave the burning Consulate building, which was ablaze.

George Horton's personal and objective opinion concerning the tragic events during those lamentable days in September 1922 has been precisely recorded in his notes, in the diaries which he kept and in his books, reports and other publications in which he sets out the great betrayal and the cold indifference of the Great Powers at the time these dramatic and horrible events were taking place - even though these same powers who were victorious in the First World War could have prevented the brutal killing and extermination of a few million innocent Christians (Greeks and Armenians) who were the remains of an Asia Minor which was once Greek, and the total destruction of the beautiful and prosperous Smyrna. Both in the diaries and notes and in the reports, books and supplements which he wrote, George Horton sets out the true history of vicious politics in its worst colours. With an incredible lack of conscience, the foreign policy reversal of the United States of America, which was influenced by her interests in Turkey, led the then makers of US foreign policy not only to a full and unscrupulous profit-seeking expediency but also to villainy which contributed to the true facts being distorted in a way which, by turning reality on its head, accused the Greeks and Armenians of being the cause of the fire and destruction of Smyrna.

George Horton, on that fateful day in September 1922, was forcibly grabbed and taken against his will out of the burning and rapidly collapsing Consulate building in a violent kidnap by the naval crew of the US battleship Litchfield, by order of Captain J Hepburn, the commander of the battleship, who was concerned for the life of the Consul. Horton just had time to grab and save the necessary diplomatic files, leaving behind him his rare collection of priceless antiques which he had collected during his travels around the world and which had cost him considerable expense.

The moment of his departure from Smyrna was a very depressing one for George Horton and one which he felt deeply as he left; it was a moment full of extreme emotion mingled with a dramatically strong despair. He climbed the rope ladder of the battleship S.S. Litchfield with difficulty and, arriving on the deck of the ship, looked back at the voracious flames of the fire which reached up to the sky with a horrid roar and which had already encircled his beloved city of Smyrna together with all its inhabitants who were inside.

His final words show for then, for now and for always the true feelings of this truly great-hearted, brave man with his adamantine character when he voiced this immortal phrase:

« I feel ashamed to belong to the human race ».

January 1999

The Author
Jean de Murat

Supplementary Portrait
of George Horton
US Consul General in Smyrna

In his books «*The Blight of Asia*» and «*Recollections Grave and Gray*», George Horton analyses with penetrating depth the Turkish curse in Asia.

Horton lived among the Turks from 1911, he knew their language well, he watched them every day as they went about their business and he studied their psychology for thirty years.

He was the only Consul to have a classical education and he had an excellent knowledge of both the ancient Greek language (he could recite by heart verses in the ancient text from Homer's *Odyssey* and *Iliad*) and of the modern Greek language, in which he communicated very well indeed with the Greeks in Asia Minor, and he knew how they were victimised by the Turks. He was also the only one of all the diplomats from the European Nations who spoke fluently not only Greek but also Turkish, French, German and Italian.

Yet, and despite of this actuality (that in his love for the ancient literary classical works of the great Greek philoshophers and Greece) Horton had never let his intellectual and thoroughly independent mind to be influenced by partiality in his pursue to find out and tell the truth. Hence he's presenting always the found and truthfully expressed facts.

SKETCH
OF THE PATRILINEAL DESCENT
OF THE TURKS

To which race of all those which are distinguished by the characteristic instinct of a wild brutality, do the Turks belong?

They have been intermingled with many other races but what is their origin?

Where, how and when were they first brought to light by the shining brilliance of human history?

This Turano-Mongol primeval race of Turks, so intermingled with other races and with their odious and antipathetic deformity, their primitive and brutal savagery and their bestial instincts, appears for the first time on the stage of human history in around 2200 to 2150 BC, according to the only preserved sources from that period (see Book of Chinic Odes in French translation) of the wise men of the ancient Sino Empire which went by the old name of China Chang-Hua Mi-Kuo. According to these Sino sources, the blood-thirsty and anthropomorphic race of the Turkish ancestors, who lived like animals, who were named Hun-Yu and whose population was put by ancient Sino sources at around 180,000 to 210,000 people (at dates BC), lived in the uplands of the South-Eastern side of the huge Ural-Altaic mountain range. Chinese historians later changed their name from Hun-Yu to Hien-Yun or Hiung-Nu, a name which prevailed. The people of this race, naked or crudely dressed in skins of wild animals for warmth, lived by eating nuts and tree-roots and hunted small animals with slings and large stones and they also had battles to the death with large wild animals which had fallen into holes which they had dug in the ground and slyly covered with grasses and fruits; they depended for their food mostly on wild animals which they often killed by desperately strangling them with their wild, strong fingers, hands and arms, even though they themselves were covered in blood, wounds and lacerations.

With the fall and dethronement of the Chinese Emperor of the first great Imperial Dynasty of «HIA», the dethroned last imperial descendant of the «HIA», in order to save himself, resorted to the human gathering in the north of China, where the beast-men of the race of the Hun-Yu lived and from whom he asked for asylum. The beast-men of this race, whose only weapons were clubs made from tree-trunks and pointed stones, seeing for the first time in their lives a man dressed ostentatiously and clad in a gold-embroidered suit of armour, riding a tall, white horse, also showily decorated, took him, with the prejudice of their tribe, for a god and fell at his feet, paying him homage and making him their leader when they realised that he was coming to live with them.

With the power which he acquired as their leader and with the diplomatic mastery which the clever wise men of ancient China possessed and applied with adroitness, he slowly taught the wild men of this tribe the skill, unknown to them, which was necessary to win a war. He managed to organise them into a battle team by managing to impose blind obedience upon them, as their leader and by ignoring the wild and instinctively bestial characteristics of their tribe; with very studied and wise, uncomplaining Chinese meditation and in order to avoid a mass reaction, he pretended that these characteristics originated from distant tribal customs which he did not care about and which he was unwilling to involve himself in. From that time on there were expansionary raids and the boundaries of his state were enlarged with the final result that he dominated almost all of the geographical area of Central Asia and nearly conquered Europe as well. With the passage of time, this race successively took on various names which went down in history. In most of the Asiatic peoples the name of «Hunni» (from the originally Hun-Yu) finally prevailed and remained (and this name was also adopted by the Byzantines, as is written by the historian Prokopios in the sixth century) which the Europeans peoples abbreviated to the name «Huns». The Greeks were influenced by the simplified and lazy tonic system of pronunciation (because the ancient and more methodical system of rising and falling tones in words depended on the short or long vowels which came before or after the consonant in the word in agreement with the Iambic tonal system - a method which demanded knowledge which however, during the Hellenistic period, the disparate Asiatic and peasant northern population which then too had inundated the geographical area of ancient Greece did not have the ability to absorb) and they changed the «dasi» consonant «H» of the Latin alphabet of the Byzantines to the «dasia» breathing-mark, which was established by the Alexandrian tonal system and the word *Hunni* changed to *Ounni*.

This Turano-Mongol race remained for years on the Siberian Steppes of Kirk-Ghiz from where, setting off in around 500 to 650 AD, now with the name of Turkman or Turkomani, they made invasions from the passes of Kazakstan to the southern areas of Asia in groups, wild «blood-thirsty» incoherent, hungry hordes, bringing with them (as history reports) wherever they set foot, destruction, devastation and death. In 404 AD, under their General Attila, they tried to conquer the whole of Europe with an army composed of peoples who had been defeated and enslaved by them - around 600,000 to 660,000 - and they would have been successful if the Roman General Aetios (meaning keen sighted man) had not succeeded in uniting the Roman legions, which were few then, and the independent army units of Teutons, Gauls and Celts and in cutting off Attila's progress with this joint army.

Today's Turks accept this without hesitation and, on the contrary, they consider it something to boast about that they are the descendants of the blood-thirsty Attila. In a description in 409 AD, the Gothic bishop and historian Jordanes, who was Attila's contemporary, wrote that Attila was a short, ugly and flat-faced man with his head stuck onto his body almost without a neck, with two holes for eyes, as if they had been opened up with a nail, and with an unimaginable cruelty which showed in his features. But he was exceptionally agile, farsighted and he had a diabolic intuition for the targets which the other man was trying to achieve. On Attila's death and the fight between his sons for the leadership, his limitless dominions collapsed quickly with their successive deliverance from the yoke of slavery under which most of the submissive countries were suffering (for more analytical details about Attila, see the book «The Extermination of Hellenism» by the same author and historian). The forefathers of today's Turks, over the centuries which have passed from the time when the ancient Chinese first found them, have taken the names of Patzinaks, Cumans, Kazaks, Tadzhiks, Uigurs, Seljuks, Osmanli, Uzbek and others, under the great empires which subjugated them (like the Romans, uncontrollable invading hordes of Mongols and Arabs and Soviets), without however changing their wild and brutal instincts. The degree of the savagery which their brutal animalism reached, also showed itself in 1078-1086 AD in the historically confirmed fact of the cannibalism which was a tradition of their tribe.

When they killed their enemy, they showed the innate blood-thirsty instinct of the wildest carnivorous beast of the jungle. Their first act was to fall onto their victim, to cut his throat through the deep artery (the aorta) and to drink with delight the still warm blood; then they cut open the chest of their dead enemy with their swords, pulled out his heart and devoured it while it was still warm, sitting side-saddle on their small horses. They believed that, with this tribal custom, which was innate and deeply-rooted in their brains, they would acquire the strength of their defeated enemy.

S O U R C E S : Vernadsky, 25, Series 1, 1940-41, Cambridge Medieval History IV. 1.13. E Franjius, 1967, p 316, and many Asiologist historians in their works in the libraries of the world which are accessible to everybody.

An Extra Historical Revelation

In the official Minutes, written in the Minutes Book as a record of what took place at the memorable Conference of 1919 in Paris, the capital of France, as a settlement for the provisions of the Peace Treaty:

...... *The Prime Minister of the Empire of Turkey,* then known as the «Ottoman Empire», whose seat was at Constantinople, *the Grand Vizier Damad Ferid, approached humbly: He made an appeal to the Council, beseeching the Councillors to help with military reinforcements the official imperial government of Turkey to defeat and neutralise the revolutionary guerilla army (then small in size) of the rebel Kemal* (as the Sultanic factors of the government Authority in Constantinople then called him).

To an observation of a Councillor that Turkey's terrible crimes weighed heavily against them on the scales, Damad Ferid, with bowed head and humbly apologising, pronounced clearly the phrases of this regret which are written into the Minutes of the Council: «For and on behalf of Turkey, the Grand Vizier Damad Ferid expressed deep regret at Turkey's crimes which, he admitted, had been such as to make the conscience of mankind shudder with horror for ever». In rejecting his apology, the Council countermoved with this statement: «Turkey could not evade the consequences of having entrusted her affairs into the hand of men who, utterly devoid of the principle of pity, could not even command success». He was summarily dismissed. Records from the Board Meeting of the Peace Treaty of 1919 in Paris, France. *Smyrna Affair*, Marjory Housepian, pp 72, 74; and several other sources.

The Grand Vizier, Damad Ferad, returned to Turkey empty-handed and with reduced prestige over the very humbling behaviour shown to him by the Peace Conference, which refused to accept the apology which Turkey had put forward so humbly by submitting an impressive written appeal to the delegates at the Council, but which rejected the regret for her crimes, expressed in this very delayed and hypocritical act; they also unanimously rejected the appeal by the imperial government of the Sultan for urgent military aid which was necessary in its attempt to quash Kemal and his guerillas.

All these unfortunate and dishearteningly negative consequences of his efforts at the Peace Conference in Paris made the Grand Vizier Damad Ferid resign from the Prime Ministership of Turkey. The elections which were proposed by the Allies to appoint a new government brought the Kemalist rebels to power and they arrested Damad Ferid and executed him with the same cruel methods of torture which they used against the Christian, because they considered him reactionary and also because he dared to humiliate Turkey by accepting all the horrible crimes which the Turks had committed.

The Great Allies had all begun, either secretly or openly, to support Kemal's nationalist movement, openly giving arms and ammunition against a promise given by Kemal that he would grant them monopolies in Turkey and in particular the oil monopoly, which all the Allies desired at that time; it was the target of them all and, with underhand, infernal action and subversive counteraction, each Ally tried to supplant the other. Kemal, aware of the rivalry between the Allies, played his part with mastery and succeeded with his proverbial Eastern cunning to gain what he wanted.

Introduction

For a full understanding of the dramatic events which took place during the period 1919-1922, unknown details of which are revealed here, it is considered necessary to give a short historical introduction, the contents of which is the real foundation on which this book is based and the point at which we start unravelling the narrative of the three-year period. The historical events which happened during the period immediately preceding this three-year period and which are referred to in this introduction constitute a closely connected, sustained and uninterrupted historical continuity, a historical period which is linked to the consequences of the deep meaning .... contained in the whole historical analysis.

February 1911

History of the Standard Oil Co., volume II, page 272, Gibb, G.S. Knowlton, E.H., «The Regent Years 1911-1927».

John D. Rockefeller, founder and chief shareholder of the Standard Oil Co., turned the attention of his company to the discovery and exploitation of crude oil wherever it could be found on earth. He began with the oil-wells of the United States of America. His company's refineries even refined oil brought for this purpose by foreign companies. The enterprises of this company gradually spread throughout the world. Historians note in their writings with abundant frankness something which political diplomacy has tried to conceal from the general public: "all the stages involved in the actions of this company in foreign countries inevitably became caught up in the web of international intrigue and foul play in the interests of acquiring oil».

March 1912

Smyrna Affair, pp 65-66, see Marjory Housepian, U.S.A.

The United States of America, with the two oceans which flank it and with its consequent essential shipping needs, perceived very early on the technical advantages of using oil to power ships. In the interests of the most important factor of speed and the many other benefits which oil offered, they set to work immediately to convert their coal-powered ships into oil-powered ones. Well before they entered the First World War, their shipyards had built a significant oil-powered merchant and battleship fleet.

1914-1918

One single shooting was the pretext for the First World War of 1914-18. (It was called a world war because it drew into itself almost the whole world). This shooting was the crucial spark which was needed to set off a bomb and which, in this case, almost blew up nearly the whole of the world. It was in other words the underlying reason for the outbreak of this terrible war which drew into itself most of the world's nations.

28 June 1914

On 28 June 1914 in Sarajevo, Serbia, this fateful shooting killed the heir to the throne of the Austro-Hungarian Empire, Francis Ferdinand, Archduke of the House of Hapsburg (which bore at that time the worldwide recognised title of «Holy Roman Empire») «and heir presumptive to the (then) Glorified Austrian Throne». This world war escalated successively as the days unfolded between 1 July and 4 August 1914, drawing in most of the nations of the world, one after the other. Nations were drawn-in in approximately the following order: Because of the fateful assassination of the heir to the Austro-Hungarian Empire, Austria-Hungary declared war on Serbia and their armies invaded its territory. Russia, tied into an alliance for the protection of the small Slav state of Serbia, declared war on Austria-Hungary. France and Britain, tied with Russia into the Entente Cordiale, as they had then called their tripartite war alliance, went into the war against Austria-Hungary. The then Kaiser of Germany and King of Prussia, William II Hohenzollern, who had many reasons to seek war against France but who lacked the necessary pretext to begin it and who was tied into an alliance with the Austro-Hungarian Empire, grabbed the chance he had been waiting for and which was suddenly presented to him (on the pretext of that fateful shooting and its consequences) and declared war on France and also on her ally, Britain.

4 August 1914

On 4 August 1914 - approximately one month after the fateful shooting which was the spark which brought about the explosion, that is the underlying motive - Germany invaded Belgium and then France. Japan, opportinistically and having with Germany an «antent cordial» like the one France had with Russia, grabled the chance and entered the war to materialize its nationalistic designs by incorporating in her hegemony some territorial lands neighboring to her island». The Ottoman Empire, later named Turkey allied with the warring Germany, which it began to supply with oil, food and everything else necessary to Germany and which it was able to provide. Turkey was at that time swamped with German secret agents and military personnel, who helped her with strategic advice to repel a British naval attack in the Dardanelles. And, as the months passed, various national enmities and old racial hatreds found a convenient way out; and these pretexts pulled the nations into war so that they could sort out their hostile differences, allying themselves according to their sympathies or antipathies in order to profit or to gain their own ends, or according to their forecasts of the final victory, either on one side or the other of these multiple alliances.

At the beginning of this global conflict, the German alliance group won victories on all fronts, which brought the allies fighting on the opposing side to a terrible condition. The precarious and uncertain position in which this side found itself, in mass retreat, made it turn for help to the neutral United State of America. But since there was no essential national motive to prompt the US government and the Congress to abandon its neutrality and become involved in this international conflict, the British and French, who were in a terrible condition - having urgent need of reinforcements from the US - sought to pull this neutral country into the war against Germany by fiendish subterfuge and underhand means. The US political system however was one which restrained every important decision by the control of the statutory constitutional balancing of the political and military consequences of that decision, and the abandonment of the country's neutrality was seen to be undesirable. However, the majority of the people inclined with great favour towards the Anglo-French alliance, which had sustained the barbarous German attack and invasion of its territory. This spirit of popular support pushed the US government, with the approval of Congress, to finance the allies with the equivalent of the market value of the food, medicines and other necessary goods with which they supplied them, sending them by sea, the only method of transport then in existence. But not weapons; neutral countries were strictly forbidden by the commonly recognised international law «concerning sea transport» to transport these by sea to any of the warring parties. This gesture by the Americans, favourable to the British and the French (the Russians had already been defeated by Germany and Japan and found themselves in a state of internal anarchy and Marxist revolution), angered the German Kaiser and dictator, William II, to such a degree that, in a fit of manic passion, he announced merciless measures against American shipping, ordering the commanders and naval leaders of all German submarines to torpedo US ships without discrimination. This was the worst move that the despotic German Kaiser had ever made in his life, a mistake which cost him lifelong imprisonment under strict supervision, as well as the defeat and humiliating surrender of Germany.

6 April 1917

In the beginning, the US tried to avoid war by making diplomatic protests concerning the transgression of its neutrality, but to no avail. Finally, due to the indiscriminate sinking by torpedo even of the passenger ships in her fleet - among these was the luxury ocean liner the «Lusitania», which was full of American passengers (the «Lusitania», a miracle of shipbuilding skill in speed and in stability, was the twin ship of the ill-fated ocean liner the «Titanic» which sank a few years earlier, in the middle of the ocean with hundreds of its passengers after hitting an iceberg) - the US declared war on Germany on 6 April 1917. It was the beginning of the end, because the US threw into the battle the weight of its great power and productivity, and this decided the outcome of World War I.

11 November 1918

On 11 November 1918 at - as the declaration document shows - eleven o'clock in the morning, a totally crushed and defeated Germany surrendered unconditionally. The document was signed and delivered, inside a French military vehicle parked on the road to the south-west French township of Compiegne, to the French Commander-in-Chief, Marshal Ferdinand Foch, supreme commander of the united Allied Forces. Since then and every year, this date, 11 November, is celebrated by the great nations of the alliance as «Armistice Day». The conditions of the Treaty with Germany were extremely harsh and exceptionally humiliating for the proud Germans. This humiliation was never forgotten by them but on the contrary became fertile ground on which to cultivate hatred and a feeling of revenge among young Germans; this eventually showed itself and broke out unexpectedly with the sudden support for and predominance of the bloody dictatorship of the inhuman and bloodthirsty tinsmith, Adolph Hitler.

30 October 1918

The Ottoman Empire, also overwhelmed by the Allies in battle and completely routed on all its war fronts, capitulated, also unconditionally, by surrendering on 30 October 1918 - just one month before the Germans - and by signing a treaty which abolished it as an empire. The official ceremony of surrender and signing by the defeated party of its submission to the Treaty document took place on the British battleship «Agamemnon» which was anchored off the Aegean island of Mytilini to the Allies' deputy, British Vice-Admiral Gough-Calthrope, commander of the Mediterranean Fleet. The conditions of this treaty had a wide perspective which provided for the break-up of the Ottoman Empire, the partition of its territories and the sharing-out of these among the victorious allies based on a division of the lands which would be settled later in a special agreement, and the sovereign exploitation of the region acquired by each beneficiary ally from then on.

The First World War of 1914-1918 and the events which followed in 1919-1922, were a terrible tragedy for mankind with their tens of millions of dead, wounded and crippled (both physically and mentally) and their unimaginable destruction, which in total exceeded all previous wars put together.

However depressing or cruel and ruthless such a prediction may seem, yet there is no doubt that given the well-known hunger of the profit-seeking greed which lies inside the human «being», the future will see endless recurrences of these horrible precedents. Depressing for mankind but nonetheless real as the means of human destruction become increasingly sophisticated; the deadly upward escalation of these destructive means will increase in an arithmetical progression but the casualties which they will cause will multiply in a geometrical progression.

It is at approximately this point that this chronological account and introductory briefing comes to an end. It is the vital link in the chain of history which connects the preceding events with those that followed in a united sequence. It also makes it easier to understand the historical events which appear later in the narration.

Introduction
The Intervening Events

9 April 1917

It was on this day that the Treaty of «St Jean de Mauriene» was signed. The three great Allies of the First World War, the Russians, the British and the French, in order to entice Italy to enter the war against the German alliance of the Central European powers and also to unite her military strength in an alliance with them, proposed that, in the event of their winning the war, to proceed to concede Symrna and its surrounding hinterland to her; and that, if she agreed, they were willing to ratify this agreement by an official Treaty. Italy, who had always coveted and needed the fertile, productive land of Asia-Minor to spread out its large hungry population, accepted this proposal and the agreement was signed and sealed in the town of St Jean de Mauriene on 9 April 1917. In exchange, Italy declared war on Germany and fought on the side of the three other allies.

30 July 1917

Approximately four months after the signing of the Treaty of St Jean de Mauriene, Greece, whose Prime Minister was Eleftherios Venizelos, entered the war on 30 July 1917 as an ally of Britain and France and declared war on Germany. Venizelos had correctly foreseen that the Sea Powers would win, but the most important reason for pitching Greece into the war was the committed but hypocritical (since they had already conceded the same lands to Italy) promise of the two great allies that they would allow him to liberate the Greek populations of Smyrna and its surrounding area. They assured him, repeatedly and on different occasions, that his intentions to succeed in uniting the Greek population of Asia-Minor - a total population in 1900 of approximately two and a half million people, the final remains of the Greco-Roman Empire which was once there - but they never substantiated their promises in a treaty or in any other official written statement or in any substantial form, apart from personal letters. Despite all this the Great Powers, who were then at war, with the double-dealing, treacherous diplomacy by which big nations conduct their foreign policy, did not hesitate - their one aim being to win the war - to give the same promises or signatures to others, in the knowledge that it would be impossible for them to keep them all. In the Treaty of Sevres (a market town in the South of France) in 1919, Britain and France of the great allies with the agreement of the USA, ceded Smyrna and its surrounding area to Greece and invited Venizelos to land there, renouncing and reneging on their signatures to the Treaty of St Jean de Mauriene. This decision was taken without the knowledge of Italy who had already been embittered and infuriated by a previous defaulting on a promise made by her allies in the Peace Treaty to cede to her the town of Fiume on the Adriatic Sea, a majority of the population of which was Italian. The ceding of Smyrna to Greece impelled Italy, who had at the time and for this reason withdrawn from the Allied Congress which made the decision, to plot against the three other allies and to plan a coup to take over Smyrna before the Greeks could, putting into effect unilaterally the Treaty on which her other allies had reneged. She counted Greece as a pawn in the game and subject to British interests in the Middle East and a device of British policy to obstruct Italian expansion and influence there. The obvious favouritism shown towards the Greek Prime Minister, Eleftherios Venizelos, by the British Prime Minister, Lloyd George, reinforced Italy in this point of view.

22 January 1918

Records of C.F.R. = Council of Foreign Relations, «School for Statesmen», Joseph Kraft, pp 64-67.

A strong Economic Organisation was founded which, with its dynamic influence, managed to convert the previously isolationist foreign policy of the USA into an active profit-seeking foreign policy of business exploitation. The nucleus of this Organisation contained the USA Chamber of Commerce, important economic interests, industrial and trade tycoons, eminent economists, professors of Yale University, members of American society with great political influence such as the brothers Allen and John Foster Dulles - who promoted the pro-Turkish policy of America with their domination over both the State Department and the US Congress - the imposing personality of Elihu Root, Colonel Edward House, Herbert Hoover who later became President of the USA and many other officially active members. This very dynamic organisation was called «the Council of Foreign Relations». The change brought about by the Organisation became clear gradually and in the 50 years after 1917, when American foreign economic policy was reduced to being identical with the profit-seeking motives and adopted aims of this Organisation. The historians of Standard Oil Co note: *The Americans finally realised - as the Europeans had realised for some time - the principle which governs economic dogma; that «personal interest cannot always make compromises with or go hand in hand with the concepts and views of philanthropy».*

30 October 1918

British Records: «The Ottoman Empire Surrenders to the Allies».

The defeated Ottoman Empire signed the document of surrender to the victorious allies. This very humiliating Treaty was signed by the Turkish Naval Minister, Rauf Bey, and by the British commander of the naval fleet in the Mediterrean, Gough-Calthrope, on behalf of the united allies (as has already been mentioned). The allies had previously decided to partition the territories of the Ottoman Empire and to seize its land unchecked. As far as Great Britain was concerned, the most important areas which it had already occupied with its army, were the oil-producing areas of Mesopotamia, and those geographical points, key posts for her naval supremacy, which offered her strategic and trading advantages.

1918   *Historical Records.* Emin. A., *Turkey in the World War, 1930, p 262*

At the end of the First World War (1914-1918) and according to statistical information and the tables provided by the Ottoman Empire, the then Ottoman armed forces numbered around 570,000 men. Under the term of the Treaty concerning immediate demobilisation, this mass of men had to be discharged. With the submission of the Ottoman Empire to the victorious Powers and its full unconditional surrender, there was wholesale desertion. Of this total number of men - this military mass, defeated, brutal, dejected, insubordinate by nature, underfed and with weakened morale in the situation which prevailed during this chaotic period, and with almost non-existent discipline - around half a million (according to official statistics) had deserted, taking with them their arms and their ammunitions. These deserters, now with no income or means of nutrition, formed illegal bands of irregulars known by the nickname of Chette in the countryside. *The Chette are opportunists, lawless bands of men, who rove throughout the interior of the country, robbing and tyrannising the residents of the country and even having whole villages and towns under their control.* (Tournefort p 349. Herve pp 133-134).

This type of robbery by the Chette was nothing new for the Turks who were unconsciously driven to the primitive instinct of nomadic predatory tradition, which had been somewhat dormant under the influence of modern civilisation. However, never had such a huge number of groups of combatants been seen scattered all over the country, of roving groups of irregular troops who lived by blackmail and plunder. It would have been easy, as human history has shown, to unite all this armed but disorganised rabble into a homogeneous whole, the men of which would have been willing to obey and to come under the leadership of an inspired and dynamic commander if such a person had suddenly appeared among them - a commander who would have had the personal dominance and the magnetic attraction of a symbol which draws and excites the crowds. Kemal personified such a charismatic type. He was gifted by nature with strategic brilliance, he was of an imposing stature, he had piercing blue eyes and, being aware of the intense influence which his presence had, he was always flamboyantly dressed in the uniform of a field-marshal laden with German medals awarded to him in Germany for the brilliance he had shown while studying at the German Imperial Military School. Wherever he went, his appearance made an impression.

The terrible three-year period
A chronological account of the drama of
the infamous betrayal of Greece

1
January
1919

Churchill, W., *The World Crisis, 1924. Memoirs* (ibid)

In his Memoirs, Churchill makes a very important statistical discovery which explains and makes clear why the victorious allies, while able to achieve a brilliant victory and to crush the dictatorships of the time with their united armies, could not however after this splendid achievement bring the justice they had promised to aggrieved peoples nor the peace for which mankind thirsted. He reveals the following statistical data: «*The rapid demobilisation of Great Britain* (after the end of the four-year war from 1914-1918 and the unconditional surrender of the conquered enemy nations) *began in January 1919. At this time the country (with its possessions) had under arms, on all war fronts, around three million fighting troops. By 1 July 1919 - apart from the military units on the River Rhine in Germany - there was hardly anyone still bearing arms*».The other war-weary victorious Powers, and especially the USA, joined in the race for rapid demobilisation. The fateful and grotesque irony was that the positive outcome which appeared on the horizon with this deescalation (i.e. of, according to Churchill's statements, this rapid demobilisation) was followed by the simultaneous appearance of a completely opposite escalation with the following phenomenon: while Great Britain and all her other great allies were proceeding with «a rapid demobilisation», Kemal (by clever nationalistic propanganda) was making a «rapid mobilisation».

3 February 1919

Treaty's War Records. Smyrna Affair, p 47.

On 3 February 1919 the Prime Minister of Greece, Eleftherios Venizelos, gave an account of the Greek affair to the Peace Conference in Paris. Expounding just Greek ambitions in Asia-Minor with very persuasive reasoning (making use of an exceptionally strong argument which predisposed the delegates favourably), put forward the basic and essential humanitarian argument of Greece's moral claim to be given the right to make a landing and to take Smyrna.

19 February 1919

Standard Oil Company Archives. History of Standard Oil Company by Davenport and Cooke.

Walter Teagle, the president of the biggest American oil company, at the same time as the participants at the Paris Peace Conference were struggling to bypass the difficulties which were appearing in the conflicting aims of the allies in order to succeed in coming to a common agreement, and being unaware that the British had already forestalled him in this aim, sent an urgent memorandum to the directors of his company in Paris (who were the Standard Oil Co lobby and who were working in the background so that the terms of the Treaty would contain provisions which were favourable to the company's oil interests); and another memorandum to the State Department with the following momentous proposals: *«When the Council of the Peace Conference is ready to proceed to take a decision on the division of Turkish land between the Allies into zones of influence, great care must be taken to boost the probability that we, America, can enter the game being played around the acquisition of rights to the oil-fields of Mesopotamia. I consider that our participation in the drilling and exploitation of petroleum products is vital to the nation».*

28 February 1919

Records of S.O.C. History of the Development of the S.O.C. 1911-1927 by Davenport and Cooke.

Standard Oil Company representatives, sent to Paris to carry out adroit manipulation behind the scenes at the Congress in favour of the company's aims, dispatched from the lobby of the Congress a telegram dated 28.2.1919 to Walter Teagle, executive director and president of S.O.C. in New York, which read as follows:

«The Conference of the Allies is now drawing up the details of the general terms of the Peace Treaty as far as Turkey is concerned. Great Britain, based on the rights she has had since 1914 because of her long-standing participation in the Anglo-Persian Oil Co, seeks to control all the oil-producing regions of the defeated Ottoman Empire. The prevailing opinion is that it is very probable that her ambitions will be fulfilled and that she will control the Arab-Persian basin. This will result in a monopolistic exploitation of oil in the Middle East and will mean that we will be completely excluded from drilling rights in Mesopotamia. All the directors of S.O.C. throughout the world consider the consequence of this outcome to be a disaster for this company, a much greater one than if Germany had won the world war».

7 March 1919

Italy at the Peace Conference, p 464, by Rene Albrecht-Carrie.

The Italians, convinced that the British would support Greek demands in Turkey, although at the Peace Conference they hypocritically pretended to maintain a common front with the other allies, decided in striking contrast and acting first themselves immediately and in secret from the other allies, to win the game with a daring coup, thus presenting a «fait accompli». Having such a prospect in mind and acting out their national interests in absolute confidentiality, they put their plan into action by taking sudden and effective action in order to take over the promised by Treaty territories.

12 March 1919

Authorized Italian Manoeuvres, volume II pp 61-62, A.F. Frangulis in *La Grece et la Crise Mondial*

The Italian battleship «Regina Elena», carrying out orders from the Italian government, put into the southern Asia-Minor port of Antalya and asked the Turkish commander there to allow an Italian landing-party to disembark in the town. On the refusal of the Turkish Prefect to agree to the request of the commander of the war vessel, the Italians created an artificial episode which was advantageous to their aims. Within the next twenty-four hours, they caused a bomb to explode next to the wall of the Italian Consulate. The explosion caused only slight damage but it gave the Italian captain the pretext he sought to land a well-armed naval detachment of 300 marines and to capture the town, with the excuse that the Italian Consul at Antalya had asked for Italian military protection because it seemed that both he and the Italian community there were in danger - the captain maintained that this community was troubled by Turkish threats. Five days later this naval landing-party was replaced by a detachment from the (then) well-known military task force unit of the «Bersaglieri».

24 March 1919

Smyrna Affair, p 46

This Italian coup and Italy's provocative manoeuvring agitated the other allies. Of the three great allies, the British Prime Minister Lloyd George and the American President Wilson in particular voiced great concern and anger. These arbitrary landings of Italy in Antalya Asia-Minor on 12 March and also a little later (on 28 March) at the towns of Makri and Marmari and which had not been authorised by the Peace Conference, betrayed Italy's intentions. The news that Italian troops were marching northwards and that they were near to Bodrum (ancient Halicarnassus) and going in the direction of Smyrna made Italy's final target clear. They aimed to preempt by means of a coup their claim to Turkish land which they (the Italians) would have taken control of. The contained anger of the other allies was reinforced by the news which later arrived by telegram that seven Italian warships had sailed to and anchored at the port of Smyrna completely without warning, a fact which portended that the invasion of Smyrna by the Italians was imminent. President Wilson reacted more angrily and heatedly than his other two colleagues i.e. the national leaders of Britain and France.

Churchill, W., *Memoirs, p 387*

At this turn of events, Lloyd George proposed to the other two great allies that they should send joint military units and land at Smyrna in order to prevent an Italian coup and occupation being realised. But this was the period when the allies were demobilising at great speed after a very exhausting four-year war so that the taking of such a decision which would require any new military adventure by their countries by sending an army and which would be bound to decelerate the process of demobilisation would be an action totally undesired by their peoples. The French Prime Minister, Clemenceau, was not willing, as he disclosed, to send in French troops.

Albrecht-Carrie, Rene, *Italy at the Peace Conference, p 664.*

President Wilson also politely declined to send an army with the excuse that his country had not declared war on Turkey, a fact which excluded sending an army there because his country was not in a state of war with her (an all-too-obvious prevarication because the action was not spearheaded against Turkey). (Churchill, *Memoirs,* p. 387). At this point, Lloyd George expressed the opinion that the only solution which he could see would get them out of this worrying deadlock was for the Congress to authorise the Prime Minister of Greece, Venizelos, to send an army on the allies' behalf, but this should be confined inside troopships and ready to land when given the signal if needed. President Wilson formulated a weighty question to this proposal of Lloyd George's: «Why shouldn't the soldiers land immediately since everyone knows that a landing party cannot be kept inside ships for a long time in good physical and mental condition?» Lloyd George agreed without any objection with President Wilson's hint and the proposal was submitted to the High Congress of the Allies for the relevant decision to be issued. The Italian representative had already withdrawn from the Congress on 26 April in a show of strong protest and angered by President Wilson's refusal to submit to their claim that the Slav geographical area which had the town of Fiume at its centre - it was only here that the Italian population was in the majority (and who were previously under the domination of the defeated Austro-Hungarian Empire) - should be ceded to Italy by the Peace Treaty. Following the violation of the terms of the Treaty of St Jean de Mauriene, Italy suffered a second blow at the hands of her allies, who refused to support and who obstructed her long-term national ambitions for the liberation of the Italians of Fiume.

28 March 1919

The army task force unit of the Bersaglieri made a sally from the Italian bases on the island of Rhodes towards the nearby opposite shore of Asia-Minor for a flying planned advance. This military transfer from Rhodes continued ceaselessly.

12 April 1919

Smyrna Affair, pp 46-47.

During the meeting on 12 April 1919, the Council of the Allies at the Peace Conference received from the Greek delegation a memorandum from the Greeks of Smyrna, which Eleftherios Venizelos submitted to the members. Along with this, Venizelos also submitted a file with a plethora of bitter written protests from the Greek residents of Smyrna. These were validated documents which disclosed and made known to the Council the abuse suffered by the Greek residents at the hands of the Turks. This enlightening proclamation of the Greek Prime Minister, with the assistance of these statements, officially stamped as to their authenticity, came at a very opportune time for the Council which was embarrassed by the unwillingness of the three Great Allies to agree to send an allied military unit to Smyrna. It was an appropriate action under the circumstances as it was a very urgent affair at the time. The Council suddenly found itself facing a difficult double dilemma which however had to be settled. On the one hand, an unpleasant pending item remained open on a question which had unexpectedly arisen and which demanded a quick settlement; but at the same time, on the other hand, it faced the decisive unwillingness of the three Great Allies to promote the necessary settlement by deploying an allied military unit at the critical place. The pressure of the need to find a way out and to get out of this difficulty made the Allies agree to the proposed Wilson-Lloyd George solution and they decided to allow the Greek government to go ahead with the military landing at Smyrna, so necessary in the circumstances. The taking of this decision was much helped by the long and persuasive analysis made by Venizelos when he set out the reasons for supporting an urgent Greek landing. But the decision of the Council of the Peace Conference was taken in the great heat of the moment and under the urgent force of circumstance, and this later contributed to its validity being undermined and to fertile ground being created for a school of thought which supported the treacherous betrayal towards Greece of this moral obligation undertaken by the allies. In addition, the French and the British - who during the war had sought to attract allies in order to reinforce their fighting strength against the then fully-armed Germany and Austro-Hungary and who had scattered rich promises right and left in order to achieve their aim - had made a previous agreement with Italy in which, with their official signatures, they had promised to cede Smyrna to Italy and this created a controversial question of honour. Italy had a legitimate and justifiable inclination to react and to feel betrayed when her other allies ignored the signed agreements which they had contracted and gave their promises to someone else. (But political diplomacy is in reality an adroitly conducted and cunning process of hypocritical duplicity. This policy, under the cloak of studied tact and politeness, misleads and beguiles everyone and everything until it achieves the aim it seeks).

16 April 1919

The Resurgent Years 1911-1927, Knowlton, volume II. N.Y.

After the beginning of 1919 there was an end to the indifference shown up to that point by the US government and the US Congress to the vital interests of American business in

Turkey. The State Department finally adopted the views and opinions of the national «Chamber of Trade and Industry of the United States of America on the business interests of every American in the Middle East and on the opportunities which existed there for unlimited speculative expansion». «The Government and the US Congress - as the above-mentioned documents state in their revelations - are now giving active diplomatic support to the modern business endeavour of every American industrial venture with the aim of being awarded exploitation concessions by Turkey and to the private sector American capitalist interests».

25 April 1919

Report to the Conference. *Smyrna Affair, pp 46-47.*

Telegram report to the Conference: *Seven warships of the Italian armoured fleet have sailed into the port of Smyrna in an obviously organised sequence and have anchored in opportune strategical positions. It is obvious that they are awaiting the body of the convoy of the Bersaglieri to arrive from the south of Smyrna for a combined action».* The commanders of the war fleets of the three other Allied Powers, whose ships were also anchored inside the harbour of Smyrna, with the obligation which was imposed on them by the naval code of war, had notified their governments of the fact and of their strong impression that the Italians were planning to seize Smyrna.

6 May 1919

Churchill, W., *Memoirs, p 387.*

The preliminary decision of the Allied Council to approve the Greek landing at Smyrna was notified in an official announcement to the Greek Prime Minister, Eleftherios Venizelos. (The basic terms of the Peace Treaty had been signed in the town of Sevres in France on the original of the rough draft on 23 April 1919. The definite and final draft, which said nothing about Smyrna, was signed in Sevres in August 1919). In the Council Lloyd George asked Venizelos «if Greece accepts the spoken order of the Peace Conference and if the Greek army can carry out this decision with the speed dictated by the circumstances». Venizelos, pleasantly surprised by this unexpected proposal, answered that «he accepts and that the Greek army can and will carry out the order of this decision with speed and accuracy». On the same day Venizelos sent a telegram to the administrative representative of Greece in Constantinople which contained the following: *«Please inform in confidentiality the French High Command that I have today been advised by the Prime Ministers of France and Britain and by the President of the USA to proceed with the Greek army to the immediate seizure of Smyrna».* The leaders of these three nations had indeed agreed among themselves that the Greek landing should take place with speed, to preempt the Italian coup. The loss of precious time and their fear that Italy, on learning the decision of the three Great Powers, would hasten the coup and forestall the Greeks in their landing at Smyrna, made them disregard the necessary opinions of their special advisors on the probable consequences which would follow from a serious enterprise like the Greek landing.

Evans, Lawrence, *US Policy and Partition of Turkey 1914-1924,* Baltimore, 1965, p 173.

Most of the diplomatic world and almost all military experts on the French, British and American allied sides expressed unanimous scepticism regarding the outcome of this Greek military landing expedition.

N. A. 763/72/13197.

The American commander of the battleship «Arizona», anchored in the Gulf of Smyrna, confessed in his report to the US Naval Ministry that he was possessed by a nervous agitation regarding the consequences which obviously awaited a Greek landing. Most of his naval colleagues, the commanders of the other warships in the harbour of Smyrna, had the same reservations. In his report he adds: «More than once, in meetings with the other naval officials of our allies, I have shown the need for a landing by naval landing-parties of all the warships there, in order to keep order before allowing the Greeks to make a landing».

Horton, *Blight of Asia, p 73.*

«But the British were of the opinion that they should allow the Greeks to execute the landing on their own». And Horton concludes: «This was, from a historical viewpoint, a pointless political development in the dramatic and potentially unpleasant event that Smyrna should be seized by the Greeks (without any allied assistance). However, the only real explanation of these events - and as Churchill notes with ironic humour in his *Memoirs* - is that «the Greeks were willing to proceed with the necessary military action for the execution of a landing occupation, which was urgent under the circumstances, while none of the three other Great Powers (the US, Britain and France) were willing to be caught up in this military action.

6 May 1919

Smyrna Affair, pp 46-48.

The Prime Minister of Greece, Eleftherios Venizelos, in order to please the worn-out population and to boost their morale, which had fallen very low after the country's continual wars, bypassed the diplomatic confidentiality which international protocol imposed on the handling of delicate matters on affairs which brought about international repercussions, and announced the decision of the three Great Powers to allow Greece to make a military landing in Smyrna.

At the same time he sent a telegram to the Greek government to proceed immediately with intensive preparations for an impeccable military landing. *«The troopships and their escort convoy will be officially assisted by a vanguard of British raiding vessels»* he concluded.

8 May 1919

Italy's boycott of and abstention from the meetings of the Peace Conference came to an end; these had begun on 25 April with the angry withdrawal of her delegates and the cutting off of all cooperation by her with the allies in a show of intense protest about their reaction in agreeing to a clause in the Peace Treaty which would incorporate the large seaport and city of Fiume in the N.E. Adriatic Sea and its Italian population into Italian territory; a show of strong protest because, by reneging on their promise and their signatures, they had violated the secret agreement which they had signed in

London in 1915 with Britain, France and Russia. But when the Fiume affair came before the Peace Conference in Paris for settlement, Lloyd George - according to the work of the historian Harold Nicolson - «was able in a clever dodge to lay the blame for the clearing up of the passionately intense objections of the Italians at the door of President Wilson». But the American President did not mean to make «secret agreements» which were opposed to his basic principles which involved the notorious fourteen points for world peace. *«There is disgust in America for this old-fashioned method of determining the fortunes of the world»,* he stated on 19 April 1919. The acuteness of the deadlock which had been created impelled Orlando, the Prime Minister of Italy, and his Foreign Minister Sonnino (who were beside themselves with anger at Wilson's stance on 24 April 1919), to rush out of the conference hall in a frenzy at the Peace Conference and to leave the next day, cutting off every contact with the allies from then on.

But Italy had other interests and claims and did not want with her absence from the Conference to leave the exclusive privilege to the three other Powers to decide on their own on all the questions and to settle the terms of the peace without an Italian presence and opinion. For this important reason and after they had noticed that the indirect blackmail of their dramatic withdrawal from the Conference did not bring about any positive result and armed now with a cool-headed view of future developments, they returned to the Conference coincidentally at the same time that the Council was sanctioning its initial approval i.e. that Greece should make a landing at Smyrna. Despite their fury, restrained with difficulty, and repugnance in agreeing to such a decision which overturned their planned coup for a «fait accompli», just on the eve of its execution however they could not avoid this undesirable fact which was the result of their own culpability (mea culpa). They fell into the same trap that they themselves had set. They justified their landing at the town of Antalya by maintaining that there was an urgent need to protect their fellow countrymen in the Italian community there from Turkish abuse, and that they had had an urgent invitation from them. But they could not deny the same right of protection (which they themselves had recently put forward as a explanatory argument in the case of their fellow countrymen) to the Greeks in Smyrna who were also asking to be saved from Turkish abuse, a case similar to their own precedent - which was however completely arbitrary. This event strengthened their hatred and their latent internal enmity towards the other three allies, who were stronger than them, but with an inner will to react drastically in every way and secretly in order to frustrate every diplomatic action which turned against their advantage.

12 May 1919

Evans, Lawrence, *U.S. Policy and the Partition of Turkey 1914-1924,* Baltimore 1965, p 173. «*N.A. 763.72/13197*» *Experts Sceptical of Greek Landing*

The commander of the colossal battleship «U.S. Arizona», Captain Dayton, together with the commanders of the British «H.M.S. Adventure» and of the French battleships of the allied battle fleet which were anchored inside the harbour of Smyrna, foreseeing bloodshed «opposed» the imminent Greek landing. In a common declaration, they recommended to their governments that there should be a mixed landing by allied landing-parties, which would be better received by the Turkish population, so as to take over key sites and to keep order, as a reassuring means which would help to calm the minds and to prepare for the Greek landing which the Peace Conference had decided on.

14 May 1919

G. Horton, *Report,* telegram to the State Department. Also Peter Bruzanski, *Article p 337.*

The Turks in Smyrna today, 14th May 1919, opened the doors of all the town's prisons, setting free with obviously bad intentions all the long-term convicts and the criminal element; they had been imprisoned precisely for the very criminal acts which they had committed and for which they needed to be isolated from the community as being very dangerous. This action on the eve of the Greek landing warns me of probable

46

eventualities of anomaly and unrest which may be caused by
these criminal elements.

15 May
1919

Captain Drayton, the commander of the super-battleship
«U.S. Arizona» reports: *At eight o'clock in the morning (20*
hours Standard Time) I noticed a convoy entering the harbour
of Smyrna led by a British cruiser followed by two Greek
cruisers, six Greek troopships and the battleship «Kilkis»
bringing up the rear of the convoy. The troopships, which we-
re transporting soldiers, sailed straight into the trade docks at
the end of the harbour for disembarkation.

15
May
1919

N.A. Records.

The Greek soldiers disembarked immediately onto dry
land. The crowd which had gathered there received them with
resounding applause and loud hails.

Toynbee, *The Western Question, p 271.*

The Greek soldiers, stepping onto dry land, considered it
as their primary duty on that momentous occasion to perform
a village folk dance. This untimely and unbecoming dancing
display in a hostile country, with the completely unknown
factor of the enemy's sudden reaction hanging over them, has
been described by many official foreigners and local people as
a totally unthinking act, untimely and uncompromising for the
seriousness of the moment.

N.R.C. in the *N.A.*

The first section of the disembarked Greek army headed
triumphantly along the paved jetty towards the Turkish military headquarters, which it approached with enthusiasm.
Without any previous diplomatic communication, which was
necessary under the circumstances, of the Greeks with the
Turks for a smooth succession, the leaders responsible for
them anticipated - quite thoughtlessly - only a formal handing-
over ceremony, in the standard international way, after having
completely crushed the enemy. They overlooked the fact that
they had landed in the country of their cruel and age-old enemy. But this was with the consent of the Great Powers and
not because they had played their own trump-card. Suddenly,
as they were proceeding, a single gunshot was heard (from a

nearby boat, it is believed). This gunshot provoked unjustified panic in the landing unit, which began to fire wantonly and indiscriminately. In their great panic, their shots had no specific target, although most of them were directed towards the barracks and inside their fenced-off enclosure, where the Turkish soldiers had gathered on the previous suggestion of the allies. The majority of them were unarmed and numbed by this unexpected change in their position. But many stray bullets found the dense crowd of people on the parade-ground of the barracks. The motley rabble, which had accompanied this Greek military unit along its route from the moment it had landed, found a suitable opportunity for rioting and criminal action. It started to abuse every person it met on the road in the worst possible way and without any obvious reason (on the assumption that they were Turks) and after inflicting terrible abuse, robbed them. In the Turkish districts in particular, robberies and abuse of the inhabitants were reported on a bigger scale, including the sporadic raping of women. Both Greeks and Armenians thought that they had found the opportunity to retaliate for the torture they had suffered at the hands of the Turks and they let the anger and wrath they had felt for a long time spill over at the expense of people who had done nothing to them.

(This unjustified bloodshed and the acts of abuse which followed gained the Greeks a bad reputation as an undeveloped race, stigmatised Greece with the smear of barbarism and gave the pretext to all the Greeks' enemies to exploit these criminal events and to use them as the means and fertile ground for a continuous defamatory and virulent propaganda against Greek occupation of the area).

Smyrna Affair, p 51

15 May 1919

The same day that the Greeks landed in Smyrna, the Chief Doctor at the American Hospital reported: *I was riding on horseback along the jetty by coincidence at the same time that the military vanguard of Greeks was approaching Konak (the headquarters) after landing. They took me for an officer and they applauded me, which embarrassed and worried me. I had already neared Konak when that single gunshot was heard (by some fanatical Turk in a boat which was moored nearby) - as Captain Dayton reports -, when the Greek soldiers panicked and began to fire indiscriminately. Immediately after one of them, overcome by the madness of his fear, pulled the trigger of his gun and fired; the others then began to shoot, carried away by the report and with no other pretext. The officers in charge of this vanguard were either incapable of imposing the necessary discipline or were inexperienced and unsuitable on this critical occasion. Twice I rode my horse across their lines, ordering them to «hold your fire», which they finally did.*

16 March 1919

Smyrna Affair, p 50 *(Report)*

The commander of the Turkish Army who was confined to barracks (General Ali Nadi Pasha) stated at the inquest which took place later by the Greek authorities: *40 dead of my unarmed soldiers were dead and a larger number were wounded. I am absolutely furious about this unspeakable assault and the obscene humiliations which they subjected us to. We marched along the jetty and they spat at us, they kicked us and forced us to shout «Up with Greece», and «Up with Venizelos». In particular regarding their behaviour towards myself, I protest to international opinion for my unjust imprisonment in an iron cell inside a Greek ship, to which they violently dragged me.* In the official enquiry which followed the riots, the number of human victims were estimated to be as follows: Greeks (out of the population): one hundred dead. Turks: approximately two hundred to three hundred dead and wounded; Turkish soldiers and civilians: many stray bullets wounded the spectators; murders and woundings which took place in the Turkish districts are also counted. The number of those who were injured and abused remains indeterminable.

18 May 1919

N.R.C. to N.A.

Eye-witnesses: Captain Dayton, commander of the USA battleship «Arizona» and the British naval commander of H.M.S. «Adventure», and the commanders of other battleships. Also the historians Toynbee, pp 392-395 and Horton, *Blight, pp 72-78.*

Within three days of the Greek landing at Smyrna, the Greek army command had arrested those chiefly responsible for the bloody events and the criminal acts. It obliged them to return all stolen property, whether taken from Turks or from others; it offered the Turkish military chief of staff, General Ali Nadi Pasha, one thousand gold Turkish sovereigns in compensation for his unjustified imprisonment and the abusive behaviour of the Greeks towards him (it later became known that he rejected the offer angrily); and it set up a Court Martial to try the accused parties. The Court Martial convicted 54 of those chiefly responsible for creating the criminal disturbances. Of these, three were sentenced to death, four to hard labour for life and the rest to between 4 and 20 years of hard labour. These punishments were hard and the executions took place in public and there was wide publicity to make an example of them and to warn the people that such behaviour would not be tolerated in the future. (The Inter-Allied Committee of Enquiry into the episodes later interpreted the strict imposition of these punishments as meaning that the Greek nation in this way accepted the blame for the criminal acts on 15 May 1919).

18 May 1919

Bristol *Documents. N.A. Report of Operations from 18 May ending May 25, 1919* in his *Diary.*

In his letter dated as above to Admiral W.S. Sims, a naval officer of equal rank and his colleague, Bristol speaks of the Greeks with incredible acrimony. The message is as follows, word for word: *I believe the rebellion of the Turkish people to be completely justified. Anyone who knows well the barbarous character of the Greek will agree with my informed opinion of the Greeks. For me it was very unfortunate that the Greeks should have been allowed to interfere in this part of the world. The Greeks are almost the worst race of all those in this part of the Middle East.*

19 May 1919

Lord Kinross, *Kemal's Biography. British Foreign Policy Records,* No.176, p 175.

The Italian representative, the Supreme Civil Commander in Constantinople, Count Sforza, while pretending in his official dealings with the commanders of the other allies to agree to a joint action, silently and secretly negotiated with the nationalist Turkish rebels whom he encouraged and supported in every way on behalf and for the benefit of the Italian nation. The hidden and secret Italian aim was that Turkey's newly recruited nationalist army should predominate, with the secret support of Italy in the matter of supplies of ammunition and crafty diplomatic manoeuvring, with the ulterior aim of making sure that the game should be «lost» by Britain, who was able to succeed at the Peace Conference in granting Smyrna to the Greeks. Apart from the moral encouragement which he gave to Kemal (who was contemptuously alleged at that time to be a terrorist and who aimed to assume the leadership of the rebel Turkish army, which Italian secret agents had already supplied with guns and ammunition), Sforza's scheming personal action spread its tentacles much further, as Lord Kinross reveals in *Kemal's Biography,* p. 167. In a secret meeting which Sforza sought with Kemal, he offered him his personal protection, among other things, in this official statement: *You can be sure that if you ever find yourself in a difficult position, the asylum of this Embassy will be at your disposal.* Later, when this secret meeting and Sforza's promise to the arch-gangster Kemal reached the ears of British secret agents of the «Intelligence Service» via an indiscretion, the Italians tried to deny the fact heatedly and insistently but without being believed, as is made clear by the statement made by Lord Curzon, the British Foreign Secretary:

Lord Curzon, *Documents on British Foreign Policy,* No. 176, pp 297-298. «The Italians have been intriguing everywhere».

Smyrna Affair, pp 43-45.

20 May 1919

The victorious Allied Powers recognised the official Ottoman government in Constantinople which had signed the peace and contemptuously described the groups of Turkish nationalists who had appeared at various points as insignificant gangs of terrorists and rebels against the legitimate Ottoman regime. Kemal, previously a high-ranking officer in the army who had been cashiered, had been declared as «persona guarda» (in custody) for his revolutionary beliefs. And indeed, he was under strict supervision and was forbidden to leave Constantinople, which was essentially under allied occupation. This however did not stop him from making ostentatious appearances at the biggest night-clubs and especially at the aristocratic Pera-Pallas Hotel which was frequented by high-ranking military personnel and diplomatic representatives of the Allies, and also by eminent Turkish personalities of the Sultan's Court and of the then officially recognised Ottoman government. In such places he came into contact with idealistic nationalists and with his powerful friends such as Ismet Pasha (who later became his Foreign Minister), Hussein Rauf Bey (who, as commander of the Marines and Naval Minister had signed the Peace Treaty on behalf of Turkey), Ali Fethi, another dynamic personality in the government, and many others who encouraged him and urged him to take up the initiative for a national uprising. These warm proposals made to him by his friends reinforced his personal ambitions, incited him to action and made him watchful to find a suitable opportunity.

The Sultan who was on the throne of the then Ottoman Empire was still the vapid and inept brother of the dethroned Abdul Hamid, who ruled over the still remaining shadowy state «Authority» together with the old and obviously crumbling Sultanic leadership. Of the original Ottoman army, which had numbered - according to statistics which were given to the Allies - 570,000 men, a limited number of approximately 60,000 men still remained under the command of Sultanic Turkey; these had been isolated in the Caucasus since Turkey's catastrophic campaign and defeat in 1916-1917, when they had been led by the then Minister of the Armed Forces of the Ottoman Imperial Army, Emver Pasha, on the front where he was fighting against Russia and where he himself was killed. This branch of the army was now under the leadership of a Turkish general who was named Kiazim Karabekir, who had orders from the victorious British, who had captured that region, to disarm the Turkish soldiers and to pile up this ammunition in a certain storehouse near the northern border where it was intended to render them useless. The British appointed a Colonel Rowlisson as executive supervisor to be responsible for the faithful execution of their orders, whose advice Kiazim was obliged to carry out immediately. Although there had been many desertions from these remains of the Turkish army (60,000 men), there was still however a residue of around 10,000 - 15,000 men who were supposed to be keeping the peace in this region but who were actually being prepared by Kiazim, a secret nationalist and friend of Kemal, with crafty and clandestine actions for a nationalist uprising under the dynamic inspiration of his friend, who hoped that he could manage to elude the supervision and the confines of the local perimeter within which he had been obliged to remain. But in the intervening period which followed after the total withdrawal of the British troops from that region, Kiazim grabbed the unhoped for opportunity given to him and, defying the orders of Rowlisson (whose Turkophile predilections caused him to show a classic indifference), opened the munitions arsenals «storehaouse» and distributed all the guns and ammunition amongst all the male Turkish partisan population who could carry and use a gun. On the other side of the picture which showed the mirror image of this military situation, and under the orders of the Sultanic government and of the Minister for the Armed Forces of the Ottoman Empire of Turkey, there remained a small residue of between 9,000 and 11,000 soldiers (of doubtful battle strength and discipline) in this now shadowy government regime. The official Sultanic circles in Constantinople continued to denounce the armed nationalist groups who were rising up against the Sultan and his Treaty with the Allies as insurrectionists and guerrillas who were apparently being officially pursued by the government.

Lord Kinross *Kemal's Biography,* p. 167.

Unexpected events brought about rapid developments. The situation was helped indirectly by the incessant machinations of the allies, who were all aiming at the interests of their own countries (which were vital and extensive in Turkey). Although the allies seemingly cooperated in an apparently joint harmonious consensus, they secretly contravened their agreements with devices of intrigue and machinations if the result of their joint actions was harmful or not beneficial to one of them. The Turks, informed of the secret infighting between the allies, began to take courage and to react with every crafty and insidious trick which came into their eastern and cunningly elusive minds.

At the beginning of April 1919, a mass slaughter of Christians took place by means of systematic attacks which resulted in the extermination of whole towns and villages. Where, by whom and why? In the Pontos and Caucasus regions, by the Turks who were provoked and incited by the furious Turkish propaganda against the Greeks.

Kiazim Karabekir, the former general who was responsible for the Caucasus regions, and who was now a nationalist guerrilla, had great military confidence in Kemal whom he had had the opportunity of meeting earlier when in Constantinople on military business. In a secret meeting then, they had agreed on all the prerequisites and fundamental bases which were necessary for a successful national action. On leaving, he promised Kemal that he would try in every way to prepare people's minds for a nationalist uprising. The High Commands of the Allies in Constantinople, obviously alarmed by the horrific mass slaughter of the Greeks, asked the Sultan to send a trusted government officer with military orders to arrest the rebel general Kiazim Karabekir and to put a stop to the widespread anarchy and bloodshed. The nationalists then in the Sultanic government who were friends of Kemal, assisted by the beneficial diplomatic intervention and support of the High Italian Governor in Constantinople, Count Sforza, managed, by manipulating the officers in charge at the bureaucratic service, to print papers bearing the details of Kemal's identity and to give the leadership of this military mission to Kemal. But it was obvious in all diplomatic circles that the military leader who should be sent by the legitimate Sultanic government on this special mission (to restore order and peace by neutralising the guerrillas) would have to be someone very trusted by the regime because he would have a wide region of ten provinces under his control. When the allies learned that there was a plot to choose their arch-gangster enemy Kemal, they objected strongly to the underhand and scheming choice of the arch-terrorist (who was undermining the foundations of the legitimate government) as the most dangerous and unsuitable person for this job. But having had the foresight to equip himself with blank official passes and managing to pass through the guarded and supposedly strictly controlled exits, Kemal had already slipped out of their hands and was out of the reach of the nets of their wakeful observation.

20 May 1919

Symrna Affair, p 45

«The passes which Kemal had in his pocket had been issued on the orders of Count Sforza, the Italian high commander in Constantinople». The Italian diplomats, who had reacted from the beginning against the aspirations of the allies (Britain and France), helped greatly on this occasion to ensure Kemal's speedy escape. (Count Sforza, the cleverest intruiger of all the allied high commissioners in Constantinople, with great adroitness created opposition between the French and the British concerning their territorial claims and economic interests, falsely betraying them by fiendishing allowing French secret agents to learn the aim of every scheming manoeuvre of the British and thus bringing about direct competition by means of French counteractions and causing the aspired-for aim to be finally aborted. At the same time he cooperated secretly with the guerrillas, strengthening them and pointing out to them where, when and how they could oppose the allies» decisions and also how they could avoid the partition of Turkey as laid down by the terms of the Peace, as well as how to throw the Greeks out of Symrna).

20 May 1919

Kinross, *Biography,* p. 167.

On 20 May 1919, four days after the Greek landing at Smyrna, Kemal reached Samsun and his friend Kiazim - who at the same time received an urgent order from the Sultan to arrest Kemal! Kiazim was the one who had provoked the uprising of the Turks against the Greeks and he was to blame for the bloodshed and the mass destruction. But he acted with underhand secrecy and hypocritical adroitness in order to be able to fool the Sultanic regime. Kemal (as his biographer Lord Kinross writes in *Attaturk*, p. 177), full of happy excitement that he had managed to get away, pinched himself in disbelief at his indescribable and unhoped-for luck in escaping from the collar of strangulation which had guarded him. He found the situation there much riper than he had dreamed and, more importantly, well prepared for a full-bodied Turkish uprising. Printed Turkish propaganda aroused people's spirit and the anger of the Islamists by «increasing» the number of Turks murdered in Smyrna by the Greeks to tens of thousands, thus giving rise to blind rage and mania among the masses. The propaganda did not hesitate to increase finally the number of Turks killed in Smyrna to the fantastic total of 40,000. The Greek occupation of Smyrna was a gift to Kemal, offering him the final pretext for an uprising. (The fact that the allies showed deliberate tolerance and that their strict checks allowed this explosive propaganda material in favour of the Turks to be transported and circulated throughout Asia-Minor, is one of the many signs which reveal the duplicity and the double-crossing game played by the victorious Powers in Turkey, tricking the Greeks and their Prime Minister).

20 May 1919

N.R.C. to *N.A.* Horton, *Blight,* pp 78, 82-92. Toynbee, *History*, p 165.

Just one week after the Greek landing in Smyrna, the Greek Prime Minister, Eleftherios Venizelos, appointed Aristides Stergiades, a fellow-Cretan, as High Civil Commander of Smyrna and the occupied territory and gave him the impressive title of Consular Resident Commissioner. Stergiades was a dour man who was well-known for his uncontrollable temper and his often frantic outbursts in moments of annoyance and anger, and on certain occasions this influenced him and made him take hurried, ill-considered and erroneous decisions which were ill-balanced and which had grievous consequences. He had an obvious predisposition to give judgement in favour of the Turks whenever they came to him with frictions which they had in their dealings with the Greeks, for fear of being accused of taking the side of the Greeks. This feature, along with the other disadvantages which could be discerned in his character, made him very disliked by the Greek population there.

20
May
1919
N.R.C. to *N.A.* De Novo *Dissertation,* p 103. *Smyrna Affar* pp 63-66.

On 20 May 1919, an emergency Council of State was convened in the United States of America. The Secretary of State, John Payne, disclosed to this extremely serious government committee that the oil reserves being drilled at US oilfields had fallen to a very low level due to huge consumer demand, and he warned the other members of the government that there was a very great danger of there soon being a shortage. He proposed to the Council of State how this very serious problem should be dealt with; research and the estimates of the special service at his ministry had concluded that the only solution - which was considered to be an urgent one - which could be quickly put into effect was the «conversion of the oil-powered engines of our modern ships back to the old system of propulsion by steam with coal». This proposal of Secretary Payne was obviously and heatedly opposed and was, as the Naval Secretary Joseph Daniel put it in an unanswerable phrase, «an impossible step backwards». He continued by challenging Payne's recommendation with exceptional vehemence, emphatically stressing the following argument: «Oil gives a 70% greater thermal propulsion unit than does coal. An ocean-going ship can sail for 57 days continuously without stopping to take on supplies of oil, while a coal-powered ship has to stop to take on the necessary coal supplies every 14 days. The «speed» factor in naval warfare is one of the most important factors in victory. The United States battle fleet would immediately lose its prestige and the imposing presence of its dynamic value together with the loss of the valuable factor of «speed», which is reduced by 45%-60% by using coal». The Council of State agreed with the opinion of the Naval Secretary, Joseph Daniel, by an overwhelming majority. In order to economise on the use of oil in the interests of the adequacy of its battle fleet, the USA resorted to other measures, regulating the problem by means of necessary limitations on domestic consumption and of urgent imports of oil from other countries.

25 May 1919

N.A. (Bristol *Documents*), report by Bristol to the State Department: *I believe that the Greek occupation of Smyrna was a British political trick to extend its influence in the Middle East, with the willing cooperation of the subservient Greeks.*

29 May 1919

N.A.

At the end of the First World War of 1914-1918 and following the surrender of the Ottoman Empire, which war had reduced to ruins, the victorious Allies had established in Turkey the authorities which would run the de facto occupation of the country and which were based in Constantinople, the then capital. The Treaty provided for the partition of the territories of the Ottoman Empire into occupation zones divided between the Allies and for their unlimited exploitation. Each of the representatives of the four great victorious nations had been given the magnificent title of «High Governor». The USA, whose armed assistance had helped to bring about the final allied victory, was held at that time in international respect and honour. The High Governor of the USA in Constantinople had been given wide powers by his government with the added privilege of being able to act freely and unfettered in the interests of his country. The High Governor for the USA was that fanatical Turkophile Admiral Mark L Bristol, who was responsible for carrying out the then internationally known Turkophile American foreign policy; he was a fitting person for this job because his mentality coincided with the direction and the programme of the then government, and he was appointed with a view to carrying out the political line and the proposals of the State Department.

Constantinople at that time was not only the military and

diplomatic base of the victors of the Great War but also the centre of international intrigue and intense but hidden competition between the Allies for their conflicting national and plutocratic aims. It was also a place which was awash with secret agents (with orders to trace the aims and the plans of their competitors), with informers and mercenary agents sent by large companies, with cunning nefarious propagandists and with a plethora of previously titled people who were now vanquished in war and pitifully impoverished both officially and unoffically. The course planned by the State Department for the diplomatic actions of the USA representative, Bristol, was for his department to create, with shrewd actions, a climate in Turkey favourable to the Americans. He was to attract the interest and the love of the Turkish people for America and especially to achieve his favours with those Turks holding dynamic influence and maintaining the sceptre of power, the symbol of the ruling political class. The ulterior motive of this political course was the hidden purpose of obtaining from Turkey facilities for every American business, but chiefly to make them grant to America certain concessions in the Turkish oil-fields, land where she had ambitions and which would satisfy the vital oil needs of the USA.

4 June 1919

N.A. 763.72/1320 (*Report telegraphed by* Horton to the State Department).

All American businessmen and all their European counterparts are, following the occupation of Smyrna by the Greeks, gloomy and have a mournful air because they will now have the Greeks to control the legality and to give permission for the methods they are using to make their businesses succeed. They believe that this fact will have unpleasant repercussions on the productive sector of American business.

7 June 1919

N.A. 763.72/13197 (*Report by* Horton to the State Department). *Blight of Asia.*

Horton refers to the bloodshed, the violence, the thieving and the abuse suffered by Turks at the hands of the Greeks on 15 May 1919, the day of the Greek landing, crimes against which the Greek leadership took immediate measures of atonement with the arrest of the guilty parties and with cruel and exemplary punishments. The Greek government suffered for these criminal wrongdoings in having to defend itself before international public opinion which had risen up against these bloody outrages, and in having to offer compensation to the victims. Horton adds the following critical comment: «*I find it incredible that the Allies in this case considered it preferable to send Greek soldiers to capture the town and to keep law and order in a place with such a large enemy population*». All American specialists had expressed this opinion at the time, as had foreign observers and experts. Horton continues: «*What is clear to me and to all who understand human mentality is that the wild and violent deeds which were perpetrated by the Greeks immediately after the landing were spontaneous and natural and could have been foreseen by anyone with any basic knowledge of human nature. These people had been displaced, they had lost their homes, they had seen their relations being murdered and their wives being raped. It is very probable that there were many among the army of occupation who had either dwelt in Asia-Minor or had relations and friends there who were martyred by the Turks*». And he continues: «*These are acts of violence carried out against Turks in distant regions by Greeks who had been flogged by them and whose daughters had been raped by them and who had suffered every evil but who until that day had no refuge and were forced to endure the death threat*».

8 June 1919

Toynbee, *History,* pp 401-402. Horton, *Blight,* p 78.

Rightful praises were conferred upon all those Greek leaders (chairmen of local councils, mayors etc) who immediately began to walk among the crowds and to urge restraint and calm and to advise the Greeks to stay in their villages. Horton notes with emphasis: "*That order and calm were restored in this way is nothing short of a miracle if you consider the persecutions these people had suffered so recently*».

9 June 1919

N.A. (Bristol *Documents*).

Telegram from Bristol to the State Department:

«*The opaque but remorseless struggle which is taking*

place over oil is keeping me in a state of disquiet and vexa-
tion. It is an infernal and acute competition between the Allies
which is conducted with crafty diplomatic manoeuves and in-
cessant intrigue. The agents of their secret services do not
hesitate to resort to the most underhand and inhuman methods
to prevail over and push aside their rivals. They are all trying
to gain priority from the Turkish Authorities in the acquisition
of exploitation concessions, with exclusive drilling rights in
those areas of Turkey which have oil-fields. The whole situa-
tion appears to be a cold-blooded if hidden oil war. I think we
should act more drastically while there is still time so that we
will be given preference in the granting of an oil-drilling con-
cession with certain percentages of production».

14
June
1919

(Council Records)

Venizelos resorted to the Supreme Council of the Peace
Conference with an appeal to the Allies to allow the extension
of the Greek occupation zone, maintaining that only in that
way could the continual bloody attacks made by Turkish terrorists on those areas beyond the Greek demarcation line be
effectively repulsed. These attacks, he announced, are committed by Turks suddenly and with a total lack of restraint, as
they know that the Greek army does not have the freedom to
go beyond the set boundaries of the occupation zone. Venizelos requested that a resolution should be issued which would
give the Greeks freedom of military movement, protesting
that, after the signing of the agreement between Greece and Italy, an agreement which determined the boundaries of the two
zones (Greek and Italian), the Turkish attacks originated from
the Italian zone with full moral and material support from the
Italians.

The Peace Conference was indifferent to Venizelos' appeal and unwilling to satisfy his request.

June
1919

Horton, *Blight*. Marjory Housepian, *Smyrna Affair*, p 30.

Written depositions made by witnesses who had survived,
kept in international historical archives and libraries.

The campaign of Turkish propaganda against the Greeks,
often frantic with hate, broke out in a very wild and violent

outburst in 1915; this was the continuation of a persecution and destruction which had begun at the time of the Balkan wars when Greece, Serbia and Bulgaria, in a joint alliance, defeated the Turkish troops and ruled over the Balkan area which had up to that time been occupied by Turkey. The exterminatory pogrom against the Greeks had now broken out again with the Greek landing in Smyrna in raw violence and inhuman bestiality similar to the destructive slaughters which had been carried out by Mohammed the Conqueror. Turkish propaganda had unleashed a vitriolic press campaign against the Greeks, exhorting the Islamic Muslim faithful to kill the heathen «giaour» wherever they could find them. By means of frantic propaganda - as eye witnesses report - they stuck proclamations everywhere: in the Turkish schools, in their coffee-shops, at their mosques and religious centres, on all government buildings, even at street corners, urging the Turks with explosive slogans to destroy the Greeks and to cleanse Turkey from these faithless dogs. The fanatic virulence reached the incredible point where the «Muezzin» (the special officials who call the faithful to prayer by chanting from the minarets) encouraged the faithful in the name of «Allah» to rid the land of Turkey from the «giaour» (faithless i.e. non-Muslims). The number killed by this explosive propaganda came, according to contemporary statistics of the International Organisation N.E.R., to many hundreds of thousands of innocent Greeks. The inhuman atrocity of the murders accompanied a maniacal mass paroxysm whose aim was to destroy completely everything belonging to the faithless. They set fire to the houses (having first robbed them of all valuables), to the villages, the townships, to the wine-growing areas and even to the vineyards which had been well-kept by the luckless Greeks.

Horton, *Blight,* p 30.

Horton gives a vivid descriptive picture of the ghastliness of the Turk, such as the following: To the north of Smyrna, the old and prosperous town of Phocaia (in ancient times, the Aeolic colony of the Phocaeans) no longer exists. Its inhabitants, having first suffered inhuman tortures at the hands of the

Turks, who were mastered by an unbalanced fanaticism, were exterminated. Their savage executioners obtained grotesque delight in seeing the wounded writhing in their death agonies. Many girls underwent bestial rape. *Many Greeks from the sea-side towns who could escape to the nearby islands testify to the events as eye-witnesses, and their desire for revenge was fostered from that time.*

15 June 1919

FRUS Records (Bristol Documents)

At the Peace Conference, Turkey, with the strong support of Italy, registered intense protests and the sizeable - as her delegate maintained - indignation of the Turkish people concerning the bloody slaughter carried out by the Greeks and the abuse of the Turks during the Greek landing at Smyrna, and demanded that an investigation should take place, that sanctions should be imposed and that the Greeks should withdraw from Smyrna. The Allied Council, in contrast to the indifference it had previously shown to Venizelos' appeal and its unwillingness to examine the Greek accusations, now paid attention to the Turkish protest and indignation. It examined the documents which were brought forward and showed a lively interest, issuing a resolution in accordance with which a four-member inter-allied Committee was to be convened to carry out investigations into the outrages which had occurred. The change in the political climate at the Conference - according to the far-sighted judgement of Venizelos - was obvious.

It is historically well-known from the experience of long observation that there is in the politics of nations an unwritten but indestructible law: «The will of the strong always prevails». And in this case the unforeseen and capricious motives of international politics brought it about that it was the Greeks who sat on the accused bench and the Turks who were the official court prosecutors; the jury was made up of the members of this Committee (who were sympathetic to the Turkish side) and the Judge of the court (of this international enquiry which actually took place) was the fanatical Turkophile Admiral Bristol - the official representative of the USA and of her great interests in Turkey - who had a pre-judged opinion concerning the Greeks!

Buzanski's dissertation (which refers to the findings of the Committee): *«The bias is obvious»*. (Also in the work by the same person: *Admiral Mark L Bristol and Turkish-American Relations, 1919-1922*, University of California, 1960, pp 71-75, (ibid) *Bristol and his Intelligence Officer Lt R Dunn etc.*, p 74, 1960).

So it was not strange that the findings of this Committee had a one-sided view and were an acrimonious indictment against the Greeks. Bristol, with the assistance of the fertile imagination of Intelligence Officer Lt Robert Dunn (from the confidential Special Espionage Service) who was commissioned by the USA to the High Command at Constantinople, expressed the decision of the Committee in the most crushing phrases as far as the Greeks were concerned, putting with his mastery over words the Turkish accusations against the Greeks in the most pungent and damagingly colourful expressions.

The findings of this report, so derogative to the Greeks (but beneficial to the Turks as a useful means of aggressive and effective propaganda against the Greeks) were repressed (annulled) and removed from the Minutes of the Peace Conference by the strong personal pressure exerted by the British Prime Minister Lloyd George, a pressure based on the justified fact that the Greeks «had not even been allowed to participate in the Peace Committee, nor even to put forward their own witnesses in order to counter the indictments of their accusers». However and despite all this, Bristol, totally arbitrarily and illegally, secretly leaked a copy of this report to the Turkish newspapers which from that point on began to publish it continuously for propagandist purposes, each time printing a version which was more exaggerated and inflammatory to the patriotism of the Turks. The unimaginable distortion of the truth by the Turkish newspapers (with the unavoidable republication in many European and American newspapers) had a bad effect on public opinion in many countries. The false contentions of the Turkish press concerning everyday Greek crimes helped greatly in converting what had recently been liking for the Greeks into sympathy for the Turks for their victimisation and their oppression by the Greeks. The pro-Turkish propaganda in the European Press was handled with exceptional mastery by specialist advertisers, engaged by the various Italian, French and American interests in Turkey. In contrast, the poor foreign campaign by the Greek government paled into insignificance at this point. The unfavourable swing in public opinion against Greece in many European countries and in America was the primary factor, together with other important causes, which led to the accumulation of difficulties which the Greek nation later faced.

However, the diplomatic uproar which was caused by the enquiry and the «decision» of the inter-allied Committee - even though it had now been cancelled and was invalid - added an indirect but very damaging factor for Greece. Because, although the «findings of the Committee» had been officially repressed by the Conference and had faded away, the impression made and left on the delegates at the Conference and on diplomatic circles by the widely-circulated copy which was arbitrarily made public by Bristol, acted like a seed on the then fertile ground of widely international anti-Hellenism and helped to develop vindictive thoughts concerning the Greek landing in the minds of many advisors. The documents which, with the official file, were submitted to the Peace Conference by Venizelos on 12 April 1919, which contained a plethora of persuasive allegations «that the Greeks in Asia-Minor are being abused by the Turks» - and the argument which he put forward to the Conference as a basis for his claim to take Smyrna with the aim of liberating the oppressed Greek populations - «were «proved» by the enquiry carried out by the inter-allied Committee to be supposedly completely inaccurate and to be unfounded allegations».

Buzanski, pp 71-75, CA. 1960.

This rescinded decision, although it was invalidated as false and inaccurate, however created a vivid and unforgettable impression which remained in the Allies' memory. It was the blossoming of an idea which had been cultivated for a long time in their minds and which finally ended up as a well-

developed conclusion favourable to them. They banked on this
in order to get out of an imbroglio which was undesirable for
their interests and out of the obvious moral obligation, which
they had undertaken with their order which they had unanimously given to Greece to make a landing in Turkey. An order
which was the source of their obligation to subscribe and give
support. Their conclusion, which they reached in an ignoble
pettifogging piece of sophistry, took the following train of
thought: «Since the decision which was issued by the Peace
Conference concerning the Greek landing at Smyrna was
based on evidence which has been officially proved as misleading; on facts which have been proved by the enquiries of
the inter-allied Committee to be imprecise and completely
unfounded. The formal order for the Greek landing was thus
invalid since it was based on fraud and deceit. It follows that
this «Order» of the Conference was legally invalid and conse-
quently revocable as non-valid!» By means of this reasoning
they reached the conclusion that Venizelos, with workmanlike deception, had extracted this decision concerning the
landing at Smyrna from the Peace Conference; but this however, for this reason - i.e. because of the fraud - had no legal
validity nor true justification to be executed. As a result, the
landing which took place at Smyrna was an arbitrary Greek
action for which Greece was now answerable and fully responsible for the consequences. She should not therefore expect any help from the Allies for this war adventure in which
she had become embroiled with the basically arbitrary landing
which she made in Turkey. With this hypocritical and artificial
pettifogging, the Allies thought they had got off the hook of
the moral, legal and diplomatic obligations which they had
undertaken and of their responsibility for the terrible consequences of this deadly polemic and economic maelstrom into
which the Greeks had been sucked with the promotion, encouragement, diplomatic promises and order of the Allies.
(They plotted without even issuing an «Invalidating Decision»,
shamelessly breaking the law).

15 June 1919

Horton, George (in his Report to the State Department), *N.A. 376.72/13152. Smyrna Affair,* Marjory Housepian, p 53, New York, 1966.

Strong, well-organised Turkish forces attacked the Greek military guard of approximately 11,000 men at Pergamo (a holy place for the Muslims, where the grave of Mohammed the Conqueror is situated) - a town which is approximately 80 kilometres from Smyrna - and drove them back. While marching in retreat, this Greek military guard suffered such great losses from continual Turkish attacks sideways and frontal on the way that only six hundred (600) of the 11,000 soldiers reached Mainemeni alive. It is obvious - concludes Horton in his report - that the Turks have total freedom of action (with foreign encouragement and support).

19 June 1919

N.A. Collection in National Archives of the USA. Files of the Department of State # 763.72, 767.68, 867.00, 8868.48.

The news of the Greek landing at Smyrna and of the bloodshed which followed was allowed (with the strange consent or forebearing of the so-called Allies of Greece) to circulate in the Turkish newspapers in inflammatory articles, totally unobstructed and with wide circulation all over Turkey. The number of Turks slaughtered by the Greeks in Smyrna and the surrounding area was swollen by Turkish propaganda to tens of thousands. The front pages of all the daily Turkish newspapers which were in circulation at that time were bordered with a deep black band of mourning.

And the Turkish flag, wherever it was flying - officially or unofficially - was also hung with black mourning crepe, the symbol of national mourning.

23, 24 June 1919

Kinross, Lord, Kemal's *Biography,* p 174, London, England. Horton, George, «Report to the State Department». *N.A. 736.72/13199.*

9 July 1919

«The surprise attacks by the Turks against Greek army units in advanced positions and outposts took place with Italian provocation and ammunition».

23 June 1919

Bristol *Documents, National Archives of USA.* Also, Library of Congress.

Famous American reporters and contracted correspondents of those US daily newspapers with the widest circulation «have asked me» reports Bristol «to facilitate them in being granted a press pass» (a licence to enter and freely circulate inside a foreign country at war). «I warned them with the cruel frankness which a pre-decided political policy of this country involves that I shall mediate in their gaining a pass and facilitate their attempts only under the condition that they agree to support in their reports my intentional proposals for a nationally beneficial line in government policies». These three reporters (John Clayton, Constantine Brown and Mark Prentiss) since they had no other option in order to gain the necessary passes, submitted to the coercive condition which Bristol had placed on them as a precondition of his necessary mediation in this case. «I indicated to them» continues Bristol in his report «and I insisted on this point, that they should go preferably to places where, following the Greek-Turkish slaughters, the Greek army had caused bloodshed, killings and damage to the Turkish population, and that they should not hesitate to describe the inhuman Greek actions in their news reports».

30 June 1919

Horton, George, *Blight of Asia,* New York, 1926.

«The feeling of irresistable indignation was spontaneous just as the uprising of the Turkish people on the Greek invasion of their territory was natural. To the Turks it was unbelievable to think that they had lost so suddenly and unexpectedly the ruling authority which they had had for centuries over the Greeks, who had up to that time been their slaves. It was a great shock to them to realise this upset in the long traditional habit of exploiting the work and the hard labour of this enslaved and - to them - mean population of faithless helots. It was for them the greatest offence against their Islamic faith that they should be ruled by those of another religion who had until recently been subject to them and enslaved to them». But the responsibility for this uprising and the bloodshed which followed was thrown by the Allies onto the Greeks because, fully conscious of this unavoidable harm, they landed as masters without any allied backing among an enemy population!

«The Turks» continues Horton «felt this grabbing of their land by the Greeks and the enforcement of their mastery to be a much greater insult and offence than the white inhabitants of Mobil (Alabama, USA) would have felt if the order had been given to an army of their previously enslaved black subordinates to rule and have power over them from then on».

Earle, Edward Mead, *The Great Powers etc.,* New York, 1923. Gibbons, Herbert Adams, *Europe Since 1918,* New York, 1923.

«Large French banking institutions and the ruling economic lobbies and unions which controlled the French economy claimed the repayment of 60% of the debt owing by Turkey from her pre-war loans».

The payment of the instalments on this debt had been suspended during World War I. But now, with the terms of the Peace Treaty for the dissolution of the Ottoman Empire, Turkey's creditors were faced with the terrible threat of losing all the money which they had lent; this was due to the break-up of the nation and the unavoidable upset as far as the consequences for all the debts were concerned of a state entity which, via the International Treaty, had ceased to exist. This eventuality would have been a very terrible blow, totally unacceptable to them. With the sharp insight of the experienced economist, they realised that only a viable Turkey could pay off this debt. This economic reality weighed heavily on the scale of their decisions and strongly promoted their intensive attempts for a turnaround in France's external economic policy. This aim became feasible with the political changeover of 1920, which they achieved with liberal amounts of money which bought off the political conscience of the majority of voters, with the result that the electoral course of post-war France was influenced positively in their direction. The new President of the French Republic, Alexandre Millerand, strongly influenced by the financial circles to whom he owed his election, replaced Clemenceau, who had been the great French Prime Minister during the war and who had inaugurated the new foreign policy, with another who was recommended by the conservatives, who accepted and believed in the old French economic dogma of bleeding white the inert wealth of underdeveloped peoples.

With the removal of Clemenceau and the changeover in the French political line, a vigorous and effective reaction was noted at the Peace Conference to the term of the Peace Treaty of Sevres concerning the dissolution of the Turkish state with the hacking up of its territories which it provided for. They succeeded in their aim with the assistance of Italy and indirectly with that of Britain. The survival of Kemal's revolution and of the new Turkish state were the creation of the coordinated efforts of all the European and American economic forces. It was these forces which, with their diplomatic and military reinforcements, contributed to the speedy strengthening of the previously weak and non-viable Turkish nationalist movement which, in this way, managed conclusively not only to defeat and to overwhelm the Greek army but also, by using the most bestial and inhuman methods ever recorded by history, to massacre ruthlessly and to rid New Turkey completely of Christianity.

The disgraceful deception carried out by the strong against the weak with the making of devious promises, something which had been repeated over and over again down the centuries, was chronicled yet again and figures irrefutably in the annals of human history. The deceitful, capricious and inhuman behaviour of the big, strong so-called allies of new Greece, which was small and insignificant as far as its strength was concerned, contributed to the carrying out in the years that followed of the most horrible «genocides» of two old and historic races: the Greeks and the Armenians; this was due to the allies' materialistic national interests with their conscious (so much the worse) awareness of the atrocities which would certainly follow. They encouraged and revitalised in these peoples their national yearning to liberate their enslaved and oppressed compatriots. They drove them in a workmanlike way to pay the price of a big war adventure, which was disproportionate to their small military and economic strength, with the spoken and even more so with the more official written decisions of the Treaty of the Sevres, formulated in the text of a worldwide declaration of the terms of global peace which bore the signatures and the moral responsibility of their nations. They promised and proclaimed the granting of political and material support. To the Greeks they also gave the order of the High Allied Peace Conference to make a landing in Smyrna. But this favour was at the time, and that time only, when this venture coincided with their own interests (i.e. that official order was based on and sprang from their ever mercenary secretiveness). When however the international economic whirlwind changed the direction of their interests to the other side, they did not hesitate to made an immediate U-turn - political, economic and moral - and, unmoved, to perpetrate a disgraceful betrayal of honour which resulted in the mass, hardhearted and complete extermination of two races with millions of unprotected and betrayed souls, and Christianity from the entire Continental Asia.

Kinross, Lord, *Attaturk,* New York, 1926.

**3
July
1919**

The Turkish nationalist terrorist Kiazim Karabekir convened a nationalist assembly, on behalf of his friend Kemal, at Erzerum (Theodosioupoli in the old Eastern Roman-Grek Empire days and later Erzen). The electoral representatives agreed in a majority vote to a resolution of nationalistic content entitled «the Charter of Principles», which quickly became the title of the national revolutionary movement renamed as «the Turkish National Pact». The assembly also elected as President Mustafa Kemal, who was wanted by the Sultanic government. On the same day a telegram arrived from the government at Constantinople from the Sultan to General Kiazim with the order to arrest Kemal for military insubordination to strategic government orders (he was strictly forbidden to leave Constantinople, being held under harsh limits and supervision, but he had escaped secretly). The unpropitious moment at which the telegram arrived provoked loud cackles and sarcastic laughter among the delegates to the assembly.

Marjory Housepian, *Smyrna Affair,* p. 71. Kinross, Lord, *Attaturk,* 1965.

At around this time in Erzerum, the Turkish nationalist guerrillas received with wonder but also with obvious pleasure several famous visitors, who had been sent by the allied nations on whose behalf - so they all thought - the Greeks were fighting against them. The British Colonel Rawlinson, representative of the British Armed Forces Ministry, was in Erzerum enjoying the lavishness of the Turks. According to the official programme of his mission, Rawlinson had undertaken to take care, under his own supervision, of the destruction of the war weapons of the defeated Ottoman Empire. This varied and plentiful weaponry was piled up at storehouses in the Caucasus with the expectation that it would be brought by rail to a nearby area of Georgia near to the border and there to be destroyed by being blown up. But Rawlinson, an ardent Turkophile, instead of carrying out the programme of his mission with his personal supervision of the total destruction of the accumulated materials of war, tacitly turned a blind eye to their supposed «theft»; but in reality all these deadly materials were shared out among the Turkish population and whatever was left over was transported to secret nationalist hideouts. In contrast to the aim for which he had been sent there, he became united in a close friendship with the higher officers of the nationalist revolution and in particular with Kemal, to whom he promised that on his return to Britain he would try to convert the policy of the British government to be in favour of nationalist Turkey, a promise which he tried to keep but without success. The others similarly failed on this point, like Calthrope, the admiral in the Mediterranean who, on behalf of all the Allies, had signed the initial official Peace Treaty with the ruined Ottoman Empire. In a memorandum Calthrope reported that «he tried without success to make those in charge in the British government wake up to the future potential which he foresaw in the nationalist movement in Turkey». Other official visitors to Kemal's lair were British Major General James G. Harbord, the American Louis Browne and many others.

31 July 1919

Churchill, Winston, *Memoirs*, p. 388.

«The friendly preference shown to Turkey had always

been the distinguishing feature of the British military mentality».

It is useful to note that for some centuries, Great Britain had used the military strength of the Ottoman Empire as the bulwark against and safe obstacle to the ambitions of world domination and daring aims of the Russian Empire. The long-standing British Turkophile tradition made her military and naval forces lean obviously in favour of Turkey and express bluntly their opposition to Greek occupation and military enterprise.

23 August 1919

Horton, George (in his Report to the State Department). *N.A. 867.00/925*

«I received a visit from the officially appointed representative of big business there ie of American companies based in Smyrna which are carrying out obviously intense if economically risky profiteering activities. On behalf of all the American businesses he expressed complaints and added that he was conveying to me the decision taken by the businesses after joint consultation to protest to their government, demanding that they take protective measures for their businesses. Emphasising this protest, the representative of the businesses ended with this relative juxtaposition: *You see very few foreign businesses in Greece because the economic climate there does not leave room for profit. Our joint proposal is for you, as representative of the USA, to unite your presence together with other consular representatives of the Allies, in a joint action towards all the allied governments with the objective aim of taking and issuing inter-allied decisions to remove the Greeks from here. And leave us alone to exploit the Turks as before».* From this report of Horton we can see clearly the anti-Greek reaction of all European businesses which had interests in Turkey. This reaction had begun to have repercussions in all European governments.

23 September 1919

Smyrna Affair, Marjory Housepian, p. 71, 1960.

Kemal, the President of the «National Pact» convened the Turkish Assembly at the town of «Sivas» (ancient Sevasteia) and there unanimously founded the «de facto» National Turkish Republic. This assembly - which now took the name

«The National Congress of Sivas» - declared Kemal as President for life of the new National Turkish Republic.

23 September, 1919

Edib, Halide, Turkey's Head of its nationalistic propaganda «*The Turkish Ordeal*», *N.T. 1928.*

«*And the Americans also set about trying to win the favour of Kemal*». Louis Browne turned up at the Assembly of the Congress of Sivas; he was a recognised American journalist and had been sent by a committee of enquiry which had been formed by special order of the President of the United States. Browne was brought into contact with Kemal by the leader of the Turkish propaganda machine, Halide Edib, a very clever woman who had been educated in America, with the aim of smoothing and of warming relations between America and the nationalist Turkish government, but with the real ulterior purpose of having this government recognised by the United States. Browne's intervention had beneficial results for Turkey, as is made clear in the classified reports in the archives of the State Department in the *N.A. (National Archives).*

24 September 1919

Delaisi, Francis, «*Oil, its Influence on Politics, 1900-1939*, p. 69».

London, England, 1922. Reprint Minneapolis, *N.N.* 1963.

STRANGULATION OF THE FREEDOM OF THE PRESS IN THE UNITED STATES OF AMERICA

29 September 1919

Roskill, S.W., *Naval Policy between the Wars, 1968.* Reveals the hurried attempt and the zeal of the naval powers to modernise the propulsion power of their ships, by converting the system of steam power of their navy from coal-powered to oil-powered.

Cummins, Henry Harford, *Franco-British Rivalry in the Post-War Near East,* p. 132, Oxford, England, 1938. Reveals the competition between France and Britain in the Near East after the end of the Great War 1914-1918.

Van Eaten Documents, Quoting Charles E Vickery - Executive Director of the Near East Relief Organisation.

The general director of the N.E.R. protested to Bristol about the arbitrary confiscation of the organisation's assets, of money which was destined for the relief of misery in the Near East. But this was money which Bristol despotically grabbed and earmarked for other purposes.

C. E. Vickery threatened Bristol that when he returned to America he would publish this illegal high-handed act in all the press. For answer, C.E. Vickery, a respected scientist and distinguished personality who was very well-known throughout America, received the following sarcastic laugh from Bristol, who was clad in the armour of authoritarian power: «You will not find in the whole of America a single newspaper, not even a pamphlet in circulation, which will agree to publish your accusations!» This answer, given by Bristol with an imperious sneer, *reveals the terror* which the (U.S.A.) State Department had then unleashed on all American newspapers and magazines.

The US Congress, with its statute law «Concerning the Press» which had been passed during the war, gave the government the right of control and the power to censor the publication of every publisher (whether a business or an individual) and also the right to exercise a «veto» and to reject those papers which contained opinions which were opposite to the official line of American foreign policy, as publicly voiced by the State Department. The ambitions of the U.S.A. at that time and the tactics which they followed in their foreign policy were of a clearly profiteering nature, and they aimed to apply them enthusiastically by carrying them out in New Turkey. They used all the diplomatic and other means at their disposal and all their business mastery to extract from the nationalist government of New Turkey the oil-drilling concession in her Mesopotamia region, and the favourable protection of every trading and industrial American activity on her territories.

The government orders which had been given to Bristol were to try in every way to create warm friendly relations with powerful people in Turkey by in some way showing political generosity beneficial to them - a handout whose motives were opaque due to their adroit and fine handling but which were

seductively captivating enough to make the Turks love and respect America more than any other foreign power.

This mentality aimed to make the Turks show preference
through liking and to support every US trading and industrial
enterprise in Turkey. (In the end they succeeded in this).

Kinross, Lord, *Attaturk,* p. 219. Major Harbord James,
G., *Mustafa Kemal Pasha and his Party,* World's Work, pp
176-192, June 1920.

One week after the declaration of the «de facto» Turkish
Republic by the Congress of Sivas, US Major General James
G Harbord arrived at Mustafa Kemal's fortress, having been
sent by the State Department to examine the possibilities of
carrying out the proposal of the Allies which had been submitted to the Peace Conference and so that the US could undertake the order for the viable administration and protection
of the newly-founded state of Armenia. Harbord, expounding
to Kemal the recent history of the exterminatory persecutions
which the Armenians had suffered at the hands of the Turks,
demanded territorial rights of occupation for America. Kemal
rejected the US demand, saying to Harbord: «It is better for us
to die in battle for the freedom of our nation rather than be
subjugated to foreign peoples». Kemal's answer impressed
Harbord who, making a mental parallel with the stand of
George Washington who freed America from the tyranny of
the English, answered Kemal: «And we (the Americans)
would do the same if we happened to be in your position!» (in
other words we would organise a patriotic revolution just as
you are now doing). Harbord adopted Kemal's views and made
a proposal to this effect to the State Department which had
calculated (in order to avoid expense, responsibility and the
outcome of an imbroglio of unknown duration) on accepting
Harbord's recommendations and rejected the proposal of the
Peace Conference to undertake the commission in favour of
the state of Armenia. The wretched result of Harbord's very
clumsy and short-sighted handling of this very critical matter,
which concerned the undertaking by America of the «Armenian Order» and the subsequent rejection of the proposal at the

State Department were the ensuing exterminatory slaughters of the Armenians and the abolition and disappearance of their newly-founded state.

Bristol Documents, N.A. 867.00/1939.

Report by Bristol to the State Department: «The information service of the Ottoman Empire is deluging the USA High Commission with telegrams, asking that the Foreign Ministry (State Dept.) of the USA and the Peace Conference be informed. These messages describe the atrocities being perpetrated by the Greek army against the Turks; they say that victims among the Turkish population now (stated imaginatively and for propaganda's shocking impression) come to 30,000 dead with a much greater number of wounded and they maintain that the damage which has been caused to Turkish property by the Greek army to date is more than 50 million pounds».

Kinross, Lord, *Attaturk*, p 244.

Kemal unexpectedly received at his refuge a very official visitor, George Picot, the High French Governor of Syria. The area of Syria (at that time a very large administrative region which included the Syria of today, Palestine and the Lebanon) was under French occupation. Picot, on the pretext of the ostensible protection given to him by the immunity of an apparently personal initiative of this instruction given by high French administrative power, proposed to Kemal on behalf of the French government (although it had deliberately been rumoured that he was acting on his own apparent initiative so that any failure on his part would not harm French prestige) negotiations concerning the planned French occupation of Cilicia (a large south-eastern Turkish province), and set out the French conditions for this planned action. Kemal discussed this with Picot but he did not yield to French demands, setting out in exchange his own conditions. Picot, following the political orders he had been given by his government, sidestepped the terms which Kemal had set before him and, leaving the topic of the discussion indeterminate and pending, left with demonstrations of warm friendship on the part of Kemal.

After this - i.e. following Picot's visit - leading articles in the French press swung in favour of Kemal's nationalist movement, and France officially and openly began to supply it with arms and ammunition.

4 December 1919

Bristol Documents, in the *N.R.*, incorporated in the *National Archives*.

Letter from Bristol to the US French Ambassador, Frank Polk, at the American Embassy in Paris (a letter which voices Bristol's characteristic inhumanity) «......*as you know, it is my remorseless philosophical principle to use the most drastic measures which will contribute to the success of the purpose which I seek. Success and compassion are two ideas which are not compatible. I have found that the line I am following pays back in abundance*».

13 December 1919

G.S. Gibb and E.H. Knowlton, *History of the Standard Oil Co.*, volume II, pp 272-277.

A work which gives a representative description of the quest for «liquid gold», as oil was then called (of the many causal factors perhaps the most important if secret underlying motive for the human bloodshed in the first two decades of the 20th century). It gives an account of the huge growth of this company within a relatively short period of time. *«In the headlong rush, it trampled like a steamroller over human rights, made Rockefeller into a billionaire and helped to steer American foreign policy in a purely profiteering direction. An economic U-turn with the clear aim of America to expand its exploitation rights all over the world».*

13 December 1919

Earle, Edward Mead, «*Two Faces of the American Position, pp 346-347*», «*Navy Records*», in N.A. «*Smyrna Affair*, p 63».

«On a government order, battle-cruisers of the USA fleet, thanks to the advantage of their great speed, which shortened distances by sea in terms of time, were used for this exceptionally fast crossing with the aim of transporting speculative businessmen and industrialists with samples of their products to various parts of Turkey, reinforcing with this government promotion and in this totally improper way the transportation of original industrial products with the aim of demonstrating, attracting and expanding American businesses in new markets. On the orders of the Naval Secretary, they sailed regularly between Constantinople and Batum, carrying agents of the Secret Intelligence Service, certain journalists, specialist oil explorers and businessmen».

The American Navy had never before been used to promote trading enterprises, nor to carry industrialists and the variety of attractive samples of their industrial production which they brought with them. An American battle-cruiser was ordered, for an exceptionally urgent oil company mission, to sail the given distance to the destination reaching 30 knots, i.e. full speed, to take oil explorers to a newly-opened well near to the region of Batum on oil-producing subsoil. The radio officers on these battleships - following the highest orders - sent and received messages concerning US trading and industrial enterprises in Turkey.

13 December 1919

Bristol Documents in the *National Archives.*

Copy of Bristol's letter to F. Gates, Principal of the then internationally famous educational Academy «Robert College» in Constantinople: «The taking of Smyrna and the surrounding area by the Greeks is yet another crafty move by Britain in order to spread her influence and interests in the Middle East using the Greeks who are subservient to her». «We fought for four years to crush Prussian imperialism and its aims of achieving world domination, but it still remains for us - as I believe - to fight for another similar period of time to crush British imperialism and its ambitions and acts aimed at world domination».

18 December 1919

N.A. 867.00/1085.

Report of the Intelligence Service at the US High Commission in Constantinople to the State Department: *«The Greek occupation of Smyrna and the continuing war damage and killing of Turks are being used to their utmost by Turkish propaganda to arouse and excite the patriotism of the Turks. A tantamount lagendary to THE CLARION CALL HAS BEEN*

SOUNDED for an uprising of all the people of the Turkish Race».

19 December 1919 Earle, Edward Mead, *U.S.A. Chamber of Commerce for the Levant*, p 339. Marjory Housepian, *Smyrna Affair.* G.S. Gibb and E.H. Knowlton, *History of Standard Oil Co.*, volume II p 272.

«The fact that the State Department began to give its active support to American businessmen abroad was not only of great importance for the historic leap in the rise of the Standard Oil Co of New Jersey, but was also a fundamental fact which made it possible to understand the enigma of the global expansion which this New Jersey company suddenly achieved. The anticipated profits of the company are - according to its estimates - astronomical. The spirit which now predominates on the company's Board for the future is that «the opportunities for speculative expansion are recognised as being limitless». This stimulating encouragement to the US business world in the East originated in the spirit which then predominated in the State Department.

December 1919 «*Petroleum Diplomacy in the Near East from 1908 to 1928, pp 159 and 277»*, quoted in *Davenport and Cooke,* p 29. Also in *Mohre,* p 156: The role played by international diplomacy in this war for the acquisition of oil in the Middle East.

British Documents

Lord Curzon, the British Foreign Secretary, made the following characteristic statement at the end of the First World War: «The Allies floated to victory upon waves of oil», quoted in Davenport and Cooke, p 29. Also Mohr in *Oil War*, p 156. (This amazing statement makes obvious the persistent attempts of Britain to dominate in oil).

«*The Oil War*, pp 37, 156, 166», Anton Mohr, New York, 1925.

In this scholarly work, the famous researcher Anton Mohr reveals in detail and with documentary evidence the deeper but hidden internal pretext for which the Great Powers were willing to sacrifice millions of lives in order to acquire secure rights to «liquid gold» as oil was then known. The idea of a permanent flow of oil to the great nations dominated the thoughts of their leaders and was a part of their vision for the predominance of these nations at the beginning of the twentieth century, influencing to a great degree the decisions and actions of the then leaders in power so that they had to acquire it by any means. The nightmarish pursuit of this idea is voiced better than any other statement could by the confidential advisory exhortation of the Prime Minister of France, George Clemenceau, by his illustrious and intimate friend, Henri Meringer, with the crude injunction which he gave him on 12 December 1919 in a memorable letter to him (a long time before atomic weapons of annihilation were discovered):

12 December 1919

Meringer, Henri, to George Clemenceau, President of the Council of Ministers, Paris: *«Whoever dominates oil dominates the world»*. France, Ministry of Foreign Affairs, Paris, National Printing Office.

Beginning of 1920

Smyrna Affair, Marjory Housepian, 1966, p 73.

With the entry of the New Year, French foreign policy became even more obfuscated. The powerful economic lobby in France, with its great pre-electoral economic support, won the elections and appointed as President the Turkophile Millerand, who replaced Prime Minister Clemenceau. With Clemenceau out of the way, anti-Turkish French policy took a large and obvious turn in the opposite direction i.e. in favour of Turkey. French interests in Turkey appeared clearly on the French economic horizon and were given priority in the foreign policy of the new government. The important help given to Kemal was now manifest. France, with its new government which had been installed by President Millerand, had now abandoned diplomatic pretexts. The French mask of equivocal diplomacy was off for ever. And France made clear her true intentions in favour of Turkey.

Beginning of 1920

N.E.R.., «Report to the Organisation Council»
(From the official Minutes of the meetings).

Slaughter, displacement and destruction of whole villages and Greek towns have continued ceaselessly and with intensification since the time of the Greek landing at Smyrna and the extension of the Greek occupation, which has revived Turkish hatred for the Greeks of Asia-Minor.

25 January 1920

«The Marash Affair», Dr Kerr in *The Lion of Marash,* (the extermination of Armenians) Houghton Library, Harvard University.

Fanatical groups of Turkish guerrillas burst upon the large Armenian town of Marash, the capital of the Armenian state of Cilicia. They started by systematically setting fire to the town which they inhumanely contrived to carry out after midnight, while the inhabitants were sleeping deeply, by encircling them with fire - creating a precedent for setting fire to towns and villages - with the diabolic intention of burning the population therein. Around the burning town, groups of Turks were shooting and killing all the terrified inhabitants who were trying to avoid the flames and the hell of the fire. After exterminating the town's inhabitants, they turned towards the other towns and villages of the Armenian State of Cilicia, sowing devastation as they went. In the fury of their crime, they did not hesitate to kill even the French soldiers who happened to be contracted to guard certain French philanthropic institutions. The number of victims killed was estimated by the international service of Near East Relief and by the International Red Cross to come to hundreds of thousands. Those Armenians who were captured alive, who had escaped the fire or who were from the far-off districts were forced to march to their deaths to the barren icy wastes in the depths of the East - these were either killed during the inhuman journey which lasted many days or they were left to die of cold, fatigue or hunger.

28 January 1920

Bristol Documents, N.A. 867.00/1096. M. H. *Smyrna Affair,* p 82.

Report by Bristol to the Secretary of State: «The foreign press is publishing information and news which are opposed to the foreign ambitions and interests of the USA. I believe that it is necessary to take strict limiting measures to put a stop to the reprinting of English translations of these foreign news reports which are avoiding the controls and are being reported by the press in the USA; and to stop the transmission of information which militates against the line of foreign policy being followed by the national government. We must ensure that the American public are given correct information which will go hand in hand with the government line which has been marked out and which is taking pains to cultivate a favourable atmosphere for our affairs in Turkey. I consider that control of press publications must continue and that the supervision of the provisions of the relevant law should be increased». This proposal of Bristol to muzzle the press - which however was immediately accepted by the State Department - originated in the clamour of certain newspapers against Turkey for the killings and the continuing extermination of Christians. Again, strangulation of the press not to reveal the truth.

4 February 1920

G.S. Gibb. E.H. Knowlton, *History of the S.O.C.,* volume 11, pp 272-288. Marjory Housepian, *The Smyrna Affair,* p 67.

The director of the Standard Oil Company, E. J. Sadler, made a hurried journey to Constantinople with the special aim of informing Admiral Mark L Bristol, the High Commissioner and representative of the USA, of the special importance which Mesopotamian oil had for the US. He informed him that with the intensive drilling of American oilfields due to the great demand which had been brought about by the general use of the motorcar and by the new oil-powered engines which had replaced coal-powered ones, American oil reserves were beginning to be exhausted and this was causing anxiety to the government. He emphasised the national need to ensure oil sufficiency for all the country's needs by means of new foreign sources and intimated that the participation of the USA in the drilling and exploitation of the oilfields of Mesopotamia was a vital matter for the country. He said that the question had been well studied and calculated by S.O.C's technical researchers. Bristol, who as American representative tried to implement the aspirations of the State Department in Turkey, completely agreed with Sadler's views and, in an urgent report to the Secretary of State, proposed that America's foreign policy at the Peace Conference should aim to exert strong pressure for the internationalisation of the oil products of Mesopotamia. This diplomatic aspiration for internationalisation was adopted by the government and its official foreign policy was orientated in this direction by doing a sudden U-turn. The representatives of the USA at the conference received an order from the State Department to intensify their diplomatic actions, the aim being the participation of America in a fractional sharing-out of oil.

16 March 1920

Marjory Housepian, *The Smyrna Affair*, p 74.

The recent elections which had been called by the shadowy Sultanic regime, produced members of parliament who unexpectedly came out into the open in favour of the ideology of Kemal and the now manifest nationalist movement. This sudden outbreak of nationalism was accompanied by inflammatory anarchistic slogans and this worried the Allies for their safety in occupied Constantinople and their «de facto» domination within the boundaries of the special area i.e. within that representative centre of the Ottoman government. In order to pre-empt a coup, the Allies empowered the British Chief of Armed Forces, General Milns, to proceed to immediate action. The same day, General Milns, with his small army of a few platoons, entered Constantinople before daybreak and occupied all the public buildings, the telegraph offices, the telephone building etc and imposed immediate censorship on the press - a very delayed action. At the same time he arrested a large number of active nationalists whom he exiled on the island of Malta. In revenge, Kemal imprisoned some British officers who had remained on supervisory duty within Turkey; one of these was Colonel Rawlinson who in the meantime had returned to Erzerum.

April 1920

Kinross, Lord, *Attaturk,* p 225. Marjory Housepian, *The Smyrna Affair*, p 72.

The then Sultanic Grand Vizier, Damad Farid, official representative of the Ottoman Empire at the Peace Conference in Paris, humbly representing his country and appealing for the lenient judgement of the victorious Allies, expressed Turkey's deep national regret for the crimes which had been perpetrated during the last war. And, confessing that «*it was so terrible that it makes the human conscience tremble for ever in hor-*

ror», he made an appeal to the French and the British to help him with their military strength to crush the guerrilla movement of Kemal. But the Allies - who, in their own interests had begun to show, with their obvious forbearance towards the crimes perpetrated, their favour towards Kemal and his nationalist movement, the predominance of which they were already helping by supplying ammunitions - took no notice of the appeal of the Vizier Damad Farid. By turning a deaf ear to the urgent pleading of the then official representative of a Turkey which was recognised by them, they basically refused, tacitly and with criminal indifference, to help him to crush the Kemal movement at its birth, resulting in all the tragic consequences which followed and culminating in the bloody extermination of Christianity in Turkey.

Du Veou, Paul, *La Passion de la Cilicie, 1919 - 1922*, Paris, 1954.

In the meantime and while the Peace Conference was still discussing the appeal of the Turkish Prime Minister for allied help to crush the Kemal movement, French agents had accelerated the secret communications being conducted with Kemal, achieving the favourable (for them) sought-for aim in exchange for the granting of assistance; for they were already supplying Kemal with guns and ammunition and this was something which the Italians had done since the beginning of the Greek landing, even transporting the weaponry which they provided in their own military lorries which could pass undisturbed through the inter-allied check-points which searched every cargo being transported.

Kinross, Lord, *Attaturk*, p 225.

Britain, with the selfish British priority of its ever profiteering foreign policy, in a similar way to the French method, instead of accepting the request of the Prime Minister of the official Ottoman government and of reinforcing his attempt to crush Kemal's terrorism completely, on the contrary not only turned a deaf ear to his request but also withdrew the remaining military units which it still maintained in the regions of Samsun, Eskishehir and all of Western Anatolia, fundamentally leaving all this area under the jurisdiction of Kemal.

9
May
1920

Harold Nicolson, *Curzon, the Last Phase, 1919-1925*, p 164, Boston, Ma, 1934.

The eminent British historian, Nicolson, referring to this critical historical period which coincides with the death rattle of that unbridled dominating exploiting institution known as «imperialism», makes a noteworthy revelation: «After 1919, Great Britain, influenced by the change brought about by the twentieth century in economic and social beliefs, wanted to alter that dissonant term «imperialism» (a term which had begun to make a bad impression) by converting it (only superficially) into a softer sound, making it somewhat gentler on the ear - by projecting the dogmatically harsh meaning of domination which this word contains via a technically misinterpreted version of the popular liberal institution of «democracy», expressing the true meaning contained in the word «democracy» by means of a verbal terminology diplomatically dressed up to sound humane with the expression «Benevolent Autocracy»). In conclusion Nicolson notes with derisive disapproval: «Once we substituted the term imperialism with the phrase Benevolent Autocracy, we provoked a verbal (if not ideological) confusion. It was an ill-fated inspiration to want to substitute a spurious verbal term for the imperialism which we carried out in the interests of our economic needs, and to adopt as a camouflage for this harsh reality an outlandish counterfeit phrase, borrowed from the terminology which encompasses the verbal content of the liberal institution of democracy».

24
May
1920

Marjory Housepian, *The Smyrna Affair*, p 75.

The political leaders of the four-member alliance of the Great War proceeded to make an announcement, revealing the terms of the agreement of the Peace Treaty (as this had been previously drawn up by the delegates to the Peace Conference) to the political leaders of those states not participating in the decisions and to Venizelos, the Prime Minister of Greece. The attempt of the representatives of the Allies to conclude the terms of the Peace had begun in November 1918, just after the end of the war. The ever-pending document, with its continual amendments, was finally signed in August 1920 in Sevres, France (known as the Treaty of Sevres).

Venizelos revealed to his countrymen the terms of the Treaty of Sevres, which were beneficial to Greece. The Peace Treaty almost doubled the land area of Greece with fertile land which would make the country self-sufficient and a centre for the exporting of products; its population strength would be increased with the millions of Greeks in Asia-Minor and it would elevate her to a respected and appreciable nation on the Mediterranean Sea.

Although the document setting out the terms of the Peace Treaty was still in the pending stage however, since the final agreement was imminent, the Allies were forced to submit to the pressure from both the victorious and the defeated peoples who demanded to know the final terms of the Treaty but which the Allies - after almost two years - were still not in a position to announce due to their conflicting interests and to the unending dragging on of the meetings of the Conference. Beleaguered humanity was impatient to learn the results of the conclusive opinion of the Allies on the inhuman crime of the war which cost millions of dead and wounded victims, which brought unspeakable misery and privations to almost all the world and which dislocated the rhythm of life for countless families. The Treaty of Sevres (as it was called after the name of the town where it was signed) «Ceded Smyrna with three kilometres of hinterland to the Greeks»; «Founded a free Armenia»; «Created a free Kurdistan»; «Divided up the eastern part of Asia-Minor into French, Italian and British occupation zones and dominions»; «Ceded to Britain Mesopotamia and «the Straits» to the sea i.e. the passage of Chanac (the Dardanelles)»; «Ceded Syria to France»; «Maintained Constantinople as an international city»; «Reduced the Turkish army to the level of a token force - and this under the continuous supervision and control of the Allies - and left Turkey with a shadowy area for a state»; and there were some other terms of secondary significance, but terms which were also burdensome for the defeated.

Marjory Housepian, *Smyrna Affair*, p 75.

The very harsh terms for the partition of the Ottoman Empire and the distribution of her segregated national territorial areas between the Allies shook into action all the nationalists in Turkey, who had begun to react and to reinforce their nationalist guerrilla movements, which were still in their infancy and which up to now had appeared in some scattered and still incoherent armed units but who now joined the Kemal nationalist movement in large numbers.

THE PEACE TREATY

The text containing the terms of the Treaty was widely publicised by the world's press and was announced in detail by all the media of the time. The repercussions and the impression which it created were controversial and divided world opinion. The Treaty was well received by those who believed that its terms and resolutions were favourable to them and it created joy. It brought bitterness, anger and indignation to the defeated peoples and to those whom it harmed. There was however a third category of people who did not believe that the contents of the Treaty was capable of being put into practice and this third group showed either disenchantment or mocking derision.

Far-sighted and clever observers of this period could foresee the element in the terms of the Treaty which would not be feasible. Analysing with an objective strictness the terms of the Treaty of Sevres in relation to whether they could be put into practice, they could see clearly the negative fact that it was not possible to execute them. This Treaty, as drawn up, failed to take into account the very different reality which had taken shape since the time of the truce and since the time when its original resolutions had been formulated, almost two years before, with the international political situation as it was at the time and with the completely different political form which it had assumed during the intervening period. The adaptation of the terms of the Treaty to the change in the general shape of conditions on the world stage was a factor which made it completely impossible for these terms to be put into effect.

The observers in this third category «concluded with their far-sighted vision» that those who drew up the terms of the Treaty of Sevres were either people who were mentally obtuse and could not see what was happened around them or were people for whom time had stopped as if they were hermetically sealed away from society and far-away from everyday life. The turnaround which had occurred in the complex mix-up in the political direction of the Allies, with their conflicting interests, was all too obvious. The slogans which they had used during the war about their ostensibly moral and honest struggle which aimed to secure human rights and to liberate enslaved peoples had been virtually forgotten. Their multiple national and private interests in Turkey had once again dominated their thoughts and guided them into actions which aimed at preserving the integrity of Turkey so that they could - or so they thought - feed off its wealth as they had done before the war. The conflicting economic interests of all the Allies pushed them into interacting secretly so that the ambitions and interests of no other power should prevail except their own. They thus ended up at the point where they preferred Kemal's New Turkey to prevail and every one of the allied powers began to help Kemal with ammunitions, in the strengthened hope that in exchange for this important help they would extract exploitation concessions in Turkey. This turnabout in the countries who were now allies in name only, was seen and understood by everybody.

Only the Greeks, Armenians and Kurds were the most credulous and naïve. They took it seriously and believed in the terms and the favourable and really democratic contents of the Treaty of Sevres. Their yearning for the liberation of their enslaved peoples made them delude themselves and stopped them from discerning the naked and disgusting reality. By declaring attractive principles while fighting hard for an uncertain military outcome, the Allies could win the sympathy of all the liberal peoples on earth, achieve the undivided assistance of the small nations in their struggle and win the war. Believing in these misleading sweet words, it was chiefly the Greeks and the Armenians who fell victim to an inhuman deception and became the hopeless victims of their own credulity.

29 May 1920

Howard, Henry, *The Partition of Turkey*, p 248, 1931, Oklahoma City

The terms of the Treaty of Sevres, which completely ignored the territorial concessions to Russia, which had been agreed by the signatures of the Allies in their joint allied Treaty with the then Tsarist Russia, incensed the Soviets and prompted them to seek revenge in the arms of Kemal whom they began to supply with military weapons.

7 June 1920

Kinross, Lord, *Attaturk, Kemal's Chanak Venture*. Housepian, Marjory, *Smyrna Affair*, 1966, pp 75-76. Walder, David, *The Chanak Affair*, New York, 1969.

The anger and indignation about the harshness of the terms which the Treaty of Sevres imposed upon Turkey, was manifested in a desperate military reaction. It was the guerrilla movement (as far as the official government of the Ottoman and still Sultanic Empire was concerned) of a well-organised number of newly-conscripted revolutionary soldiers under the leadership of Mustafa Kemal (a former officer in the Sultanic army), who managed to unite some nationalist groups and to attack the British in the Straits of Chanak (the Dardanelles) which Britain had governed since the Allied victory. Kemal was well informed by his spies that the garrison of the British defenders of that area was insignificant. As Churchill confessed, the rapid Allied withdrawal had debilitated their military strength in the occupied lands to a serious degree, although the requisite skeleton of a scanty military defence force still remained at the important points.

13 June 1920

Walder, David, *The Chanak Affair,* p 160.

Kemal chose the zone of «Ismit» in Chanak, opposite which he activated a sudden and intense attack. He drove back the British vanguard and encircled the remaining military garrison force inside the fortress of Chanak. The position of the defending fortress under siege conditions - with the attenuation which had befallen the army ranks - was critical since they had to face the enemy on two sides: on the east, with reinforcements on the Asia-Minor side, and on the west with reinforcements of fighters from the side of Eastern Thrace. The British Prime Minister, Lloyd George, perplexed as to how to ensure immediate assistance to the besieged fortress with military reinforcements, which it was not easy to do immediately from another part of the country, again resorted (as Churchill reveals in his *Memoirs*) to the amicably disposed Greek Prime Minister Venizelos. Venizelos, very conveniently for this situation, had already got a budding Greek army near there. In the telephone call which he received, the Greek Prime Minister showed himself to be favourably disposed if the Council would release him from the prohibition from proceeding further than the three kilometres and would leave him free in all his military actions. Lloyd George immediately transmitted this proposed solution to an urgent problem to the Supreme Council of the Allies at Paris.

The Council found itself equally perplexed at how to face the immediate danger which was happening to the garrison at Chanak - because if the Dardanelles fell into the hands of the rebels, then Constantinople was in danger and this was the seat of the Allied governmental representatives and of the officially recognised Ottoman government which had signed the truce. With their territorial sovereign power over the capital of their defeated enemy, the Allies manifested the absolute jurisdiction of the conqueror over the subdued Turkish regime.

Churchill, Winston, *Memoirs*, p 387, London. Nicolson, Harold, *Curzon, The Last Phase, 1919-1925*, p 250, Boston, 1934.

The Council unanimously agreed with Lloyd George's proposal and proceeded to issue an resolution of approval which released the Greek army and which allowed it to proceed beyond the three kilometres, i.e. beyond the boundary of the zone which had been previously defined, so as to be able to help the Allies by crushing the nationalist Turkish rebels and by removing the threatened danger. *«Immediately follow-ing the resolution of release, Lloyd George asked Venizelos, who had been invited to the Council, if he accepted the pro-posal and if he believed that the Greek army was in a position to go it alone and if he could remove the danger of an attack by Kemal which the Allies were facing».* In other words, the danger of predominance by the enemy with this military action and of the capture by the rebel army of that large geographical area, with Constantinople as the most critical and disputed point. And Lloyd George persisted in asking if the Greek army could break the stranglehold of the encircled garrison and free the besieged British army unit at Chanak.

24 June 1920

Venizelos, aiming at a corresponding reciprocation and support from the Allies in the Greek matter, agreed to the pro-posal saying in the following words: *«If I am allowed to carry out this action, I can guarantee to the honourable Councillors that the Greek army is capable of crushing Kemal's attack within a few weeks and of removing the danger that the Allies are facing from both the Eastern and the Western sides».* De-spite the strong objection and reaction of all the Allies' spe-cialist military advisors concerning this Greek interference - since they believed that a campaign of this size was far beyond Greek military powers - the Greek armed forces mobilised and proceeded immediately northwards. Marching northwards and liberating one town after another, including the most impor-tant and, for the Turks, holy town of Prousa, they reached the critical point. In a remarkable strategy by their High Com-mand, they lost no time in clashing with Kemal's nationalist rebel troops and in overpowering them. Within a few weeks - as Venizelos had promised - the Greek army had defeated Kemal's newly-conscripted nationalist army and drove back the remnants towards the East; this swift Greek success made a great impression on the Allied military officers as they had not expected it.

July 1920

Kinross, Lord, *Kemal's Biography*, p 268.
«Kemal's Turkish guerrillas were defeated by the Greeks

and, disorganised, took flight». This Greek military achievement had a three-fold consequence: 1. The British garrison at Chanak was saved from total disaster. 2. It captured Eastern Thrace and thus relieved the Allies from the threat posed by the Turkish nationalist army units in the West. It also averted the danger of the immediate capture by Kemal of Constantinople and the surrounding area and his domination there. 3. It increased the respect of foreign military officers for the Greek army and the Greek factor.

Nicolson, Harold, *History*, p 251.

The British historian, Nicolson, gives in his elegant and expressive account of the events a lively description of developments: «The Greeks saved the Allied positions from the threat facing them on both sides, both from Asiatic and from European Turkey, at a time when these positions were in danger of being destroyed by Kemal's rebel forces, which on the run took refuge in the internal depths of Asia Minor. It remained for the Greeks to crush Kemal himself».

Housepian, Marjory, *Smyrna Affair,* p 76, New York, 1966.

Kemal, after being routed at Chanak, retreated hastily and attempted to reach Ankara as a safe refuge. On reaching Ankara, his first task was to ensure his personal defence and safety from those around him, as there had been sporadic hostile demonstrations against him. After this, he used the time necessary to calm down and to mollify the general mood after the upset and confusion which his crushing withdrawal had caused him. He also used the intervening pause in enemy action while the Greek army was carrying out the necessary military reorganisation and refitting, and got down to the many problems which he was facing to which he had to find an urgent solution. Kemal had to face the difficult job of rebuilding his wounded personal prestige and his mastery which he had lost in the humiliating military defeat; he had to clear the ranks of the mass of new conscripts of those rebels who were against him, who came to the surface after his defeat at Chanak; he had to reorganise the decimated volunteer force in the army, to repel and annihilate the sickly military attacks which the Sultanic army, sent there from Constantinople, was trying to mount against him, with the order to arrest him and to dissolve his small army; he also had to take care of his military replenishments and to lick his wounds.

Nicolson, Harold, *History 1919-1925*, p 250, 1934. Housepian, Marjory, *Smyrna Affair*, p 76, 1936.

In the autumn Kemal, with the military replenishments which had been supplied to him by firstly the Italians, then the Soviets (who also granted him the southern regions of the Caucasus) and following this the French, together with the continuing military assistance of the Italians, felt himself to be strong and ready to face and to crush the Greeks. And, selecting a suitable point on his front, he activated a sudden and virulent attack against the Greeks.

But the Greeks met his attack stoutly and, neutralising his sudden strike, put to flight the panic-stricken army of new conscripts. Not stopping their pursuit and chasing Kemal's panic-stricken army unit of nationalists deep into the East, they arrived at a point near to the strategic railway junction which connects Constantinople with Konia. It was at that point in 1920 that Lloyd George boastfully announced to the Cabinet: «The Turks are beaten back and fleeing with their forces to Mecca».

However, this unhoped for change meant that this very bad turn of events for the Turks was an even bigger disaster for the French and the Italians than they could tolerate, as far as their interests were concerned,. The continuation of the pursuit of the broken enemy and the ceaseless advance of the Greek army to the East came into radical opposition and conflict with the great interests which all the western Allies had in Turkey and which were at a critical stage. But this unexpected military development was even more critical for French capitalists, to whom the potential capture of the country by the Greeks would have as a consequence the cancellation of the anticipated repayments by Turkey on the debts owing on the large national loans which the Ottoman Empire already owed to them. They felt that the complete destruction of the Turkish nationalist army and the domination of the Greeks was for them a severely undesirable future contingency, an irreparable economic blow and basically against their interests, which would in this event suffer inestimable damage. They wanted to avert this disastrous eventuality and set themselves in every way to do so.

Gibb, George S. and Knowlton, E.H., *In the Settlement of the Division of Turkey*, pp 277-285.

All the Allies had ambitions in Turkish territories and in their wealth-producing wells whose land areas, in accordance with the terms of the Peace Treaty of Sevres concerning the partition of the Ottoman Empire and its special detailed provisions, were to be shared out among their nations. France and Italy, literally upset by the emerging predominance of Greece, demanded that the Greek advance should stop at once, ordering their government representatives at the Supreme Allied Council that the Council should immediately issue a resolution ordering Greece to stop the advance of its army. The ever-Turkophile policy of Britain, because of the oil and of her other vital interests in Turkey, agreed with the Allied Council which voted by a majority for the resolution despite the somewhat faltering hesitation of Lloyd George. The three Allies, however, as absolute judges, did not wait on this very urgent occasion to waste time on diplomatic formalities. Token military forces from the three Allies, France, Italy and Britain, were transferred at great speed and were interposed in between the pursued and their pursuers with their guns trained against their supposed allies, the Greeks. It was an active and very drastic message to the Greek military authorities immediately to stop their advance and their pursuit of Kemal's newly-conscripted army which was fleeing in panic. With this self-evident betrayal by Greece's Great supposed Allies, the foreseen final ruin of Kemal was prevented. The worst result, however, for the Greek army was the fact that the positions in which they were checked by the three supposed allied powers were, from a military point of view, much less safe than those which they had originally abandoned in June in order to save the Allies from the apparent destruction at the hands of Kemal.

Nicolson, Harold, *History 1919-1925*, p 250, 1934.

Nicolson notes in conclusion, with stinging and genuinely British derisive sarcasm: *By turning their guns against the Greeks - their own allies - the Great Powers saved Kemal's panic-stricken newly-conscripted army at the eleventh hour from final destruction»*. And he continues with obvious mockery: *«During the months which followed, the Great Powers began one after the other to abandon belligerent Ally Greece»* and openly to help Kemal's nationalist movement.

Evans, Lawrence, *The San Remo Conference*, pp 297-298, 1965.

During July and while the three American Secretaries of State for Foreign Affairs, the Navy, and Home Affairs, were having discussions in urgent meetings with their advisors and were planning how they could manage to extract from Turkey the concession for the drilling and exploitation of the oil-producing areas of Mesopotamia, a piece of news exploded like a bomb; it was a stunning revelation for them: France and Italy had already in April of that same year contracted secretly and with the total ignorance of America an agreement at San Remo - a town in Italy - in accordance with which they shared out between them the oil-rich areas of Turkey which contained the subsoil of Mesopotamia.

Davenport, E.H. and Cooke, S.R. in *Current History* p 24, «American Oil Claims in Turkey».

Earle, Edward Mead, «*Two Faces of the American Position* pp 346-348». American policy and its true aims in Turkey.

August 1920 Housepian, Marjory, *Smyrna Affair,* p 77.

The long protraction of the war in Asia Minor and the almost two-year long continual absence of Venizelos abroad, occupied in an unending struggle whose aim was to neutralise the emerging reactions and opposition to the swift development of the Greek campaign - opposition which was subversive and skilful which was brought forward from time to time by the Allies in their own interests - helped to throw Greece into internal turmoil.

At the end of the summer, there were popular uprisings with terrorist riots during which the Vice-President of the government, Repoulis, was assassinated by the supporters of Venizelos themselves, as it was reported; Repoulis, as deputy to the Prime Minister, ruled the country in his absence. These worrying messages made the Greek Prime Minister Venizelos to decide to return to Greece to bring back law and order to the country, with his popular political personality.

Venizelos setting out on his return journey, two days after the signing of the Treaty of Sevres, and while he was walking across the platform to get into the train which was waiting for him at the railway station in Paris, two royalist young Greeks shot at him fourteen times, aiming their shots in the direction in which he was walking (from a considerable distance owing to the police guard). Venizelos was only slightly grazed thanks to the bullet-proof vest which he was wearing, but he arrived in Athens disconsolate and ill. Full of anxiety and justifiably downcast, he found the national situation much more turbulent than he had feared and expected. The people's patience had been exhausted by the long period of time during which it had been suffering hardships; their mental exhaustion and fatigue had disenchanted the hypnotic ecstasy into which they had fallen two years before after the stirring eloquence and the attractive promises of Venizelos. These people were not in a position to examine in depth the huge problems which their Prime Minister had been facing abroad. This unthinking loss of patience on the part of the Greeks now eclipsed the national successes and the heightened respect which the country had gained in comparison with its previous undervalued insignificance, a respect which lent some glory to the name of Greece. Many of the men under arms were far away from their families and their homes, still serving in the army under a national order and enforced duty since the time of the Balkan Wars (1912-1914). Despite the terms of the Treaty of Sevres, which were favourable to Greece, the end of the war did not seem to be near, neither did the hope that the weary population of the country could soon draw breath.

On top of all these intolerable and terrible things, great indignation and grumbling had broken out among the population against the Venizelos regime, caused by the unreasonable abuse and oppression which the tormented people had been suffering since the beginning of the acting government which ruled the country in Venizelos's absence *with its very strict administrative measures.* This situation suddenly went from bad to worse, at an even more serious point for Venizelos, by the anomaly of a bad escalation of the complex national situation which was brought to the country by the unexpected death of the then Greek king, Alexandros, with the problematic dilemma of his successor.

25 October 1920

ALEXANDROS, KING OF GREECE, DIES

His death was, according to the official medical bulletin, the terrible result of a gangrenous infection which originated in a bite by a small tame and pampered monkey with which the king played in his spare time. (It is very strange that three experienced doctors who were famous in Greece and who were royalists, although not the palace doctors, who had undertaken the responsibility of his therapy, could not treat a small infection from the bite of a playful tame animal, when it is well-known that most children who play with domestic animals - dogs and cats - often suffer such bites but without dying from infections arising from them). The tragic illness of the young king, which lasted for several weeks, and the medical bulletins which were reported widely to the people by the newspapers, had the effect of turning the attention and the temporary interest of the people to the human struggle of the king and to allay political unrest for a while. With the king's death however, the people's attention turned again to the interminable bloody war and, in a political uproar, they demanded their politicians to bring their boys home. The political situation became even more blurred when Prince Pavlos, (Paul) the third son of the enthroned Constantine, refused to accept the Greek invitation to take the throne, stating that his father had never abdicated from his constitutional rights to the throne and so he still continued to be the legitimate king of the land.

This royal impasse embarrassed the leaders of the political parties who decided, in order to get out of the difficult situation in which they found themselves, to hold a national plebiscite to ask the people which they preferred out of the two: the invitation to and return of the exiled king Constantine, or the search for a new king from the Crowned Heads of Europe, without however weighing up, with the deliberation which the situation demanded, the serious consequences which could follow from an untimely and hurried popular verdict at this critical turn for the nation. A verdict whose unconsidered and frivolous character was foreseen with certainty in experienced political circles. Greek politicians proceeded to hold the plebiscite, urged on by a short-sighted fanaticism and by the party political benefits which they foolishly expected to gain from the desirable and certain (for them) victorious and triumphant (for the Venizelos party) outcome of the popular verdict, after the terms of the Treaty of Sevres which were favourable for Greece and which doubled the size of the nation.

Housepian, M. *Smyrna Affair,* p 77. Frangulis, A.F., *La Grece et la Crise Mondiale,*(Greece and the World Crisis) volume II, Paris, 1926.

As was expected by forward-looking observers, the electors in this plebiscite decided, with an overwhelming majority, in favour of the return of the exiled King Constantine who, returning to Greece in a cloud of triumphant enthusiasm, festivities and celebrations, again took up the sceptre of royal power. These unexpected political shifts, imponderable for the terrific speed with which they took place, had very bad consequences for Greece. Venizelos, the only Greek political observer recognised on the world stage who was also versatile and sharp-sighted, who had the adroitness to penetrate inside the disingenuous horizon of diplomacy and thus to blunt the point of the machinating European political environment which was turned against Greece, had gone far away. He was frustrated and his soul was bitter because the capricious and ungrateful Greek people unexpectedly voted against him with a surprisingly overwhelming majority in the elections which took place for the appointment of a new constitutional Parliament (elections which those directing the internal electoral policy of his Party, with blind fanaticism and in a completely ill-considered way had persuaded him to proclaim, maintaining that they had seemingly diagnosed the enthusiasm of the Greek people for his great national success and the terms of the Treaty of Sevres which were favourable to Greece). But worse than any other more dramatic consequence for Greece was the fact that, with the return of the German King Constantine Glucksburg, the former Allies of little Greece now became pointedly the enemies of the Greeks and this soon became obvious in a series of enemy actions.

16 November 1920

Nicolson, Harold, *History,* in *The Last Phase, 1919-1925,* Boston, 1934.

«For the Allies, the return of Constantine to the throne of Greece was a «godsend» - a pretext and excuse to be released from the irritating and annoying moral obligation for them to support - even if only seemingly - the Greek question. Constantine was «anathema» to the Allies because of his German sympathies, his warm feelings for his father-in-law Kaiser William II and especially for the help which he gave him during the Great War».

23 November 1920

Churchill, Winston, *Memoirs,* p 388.

«For Venizelos's sake, great tolerance was shown by Great Britain on many matters which were not desirable, but there was no tolerance for Constantine». And Churchill continues: «In Great Britain, the general feeling of the British people for Greece (following the return of Constantine) was now not simply resentment, but a total extinction of sympathy or even interest for that country».

24 November 1920

Frangulis, A.F., *La Grèce et la Crise Mondiale*, volume II, Paris, 1926. Housepian, M., *Smyrna Affair*, p 78. Mears, Eliot Grinnell, *Modern Turkey*, 1924, p 60.

Lloyd George was the only one of all the Prime Ministers who seemed to show stability in his policy of British support for Greece, stating that «the return of Constantine to the Greek throne does not change British policy». But this statement had been unanswerably refuted in the announcement of the Foreign Office to the Greek government via the French Ambassador to Greece just two weeks earlier on 8th November 1920, which contained the following «verbal note»: *«The Governments of Great Britain, France and Italy do not want to intervene in the internal affairs of Greece but they find themselves constrained to declare publicly that the reinstallation on the throne of Greece of a potentate whose position and behaviour to the Allies during the war was the source of great danger and difficulties for them.....now creates an even more unfavourable situation in the relations between Greece and the Allies.....Great Britain, France and Italy jointly with the United States of America have unanimously agreed in the Supreme Council to the following decision: Greece will no longer receive any economic support for whatsoever reason. This decision has as an immediate result an abrogating cancellation of the allied loans to Greece which were granted during the government of Venizelos. This decision concerns the balances due on the loans which have not yet been paid».* (Unedited translation by Frangulis from his French, in the official edition, text, page 175).

November 1920   Churchill, Winston, *Memoirs*, p 416. Gibbons, Herbert, Adams, *Europe Since 1918*, pp 430-432, New York, 1923. Frangulis, A.F., *La Grèce et la Crise Mondiale,* volume II, p 180, Paris, 1926. Pallis, A.A., *Greece's Anatolian Venture - and After*, p 67, London, 1937.

Information concerning the differences in opinion of Venizelos and Constantine, differences on foreign policy which split the Greek people sharply and fanatically.

December 1920   Housepian, Marjory, *Smyrna Affair*, pp 76-77, New York, 1966.

At the beginning of December 1920 and following two months of obstinate attempts, Kemal's Turkish nationalist forces managed to overwhelm the Armenian army and to dissolve the newly set up state of the Armenian Republic in the

Caucasus, a state to which the Allies had given the promise of protection and had guaranteed its territory in the terms of the Treaty of Sevres. Unfortunately however, when this tragic disaster and destruction actually happened, they gave no real help! The Armenians - those who survived after their desperate battles with the Turks - having no other way out of the Turks' barbaric and destructive domination, sought refuge, with the approval of the Soviets, in the small province which remained to them in the Soviet region on what was later the border between Turkey and the Soviet Union called Yerevan. The Soviets, who felt hostile towards the Allies because of their violation of their signatures and their national honour in the terms of the joint treaty of alliance with Russia which they had drawn up in 1914, and for their grabbing of the oil-producing areas in the region of Batum, saw this as a suitable moment to make peace with Kemal's nationalist Turkey, signing with him an agreement of friendship. The Soviets, in a show of friendship, granted Kemal sovereignty over two previously Armenian provinces in the Caucasus, which bordered onto Turkey, and began from that time to reinforce him openly in his war against the Allies and the subservient Greece.

24 December 1920

Edib, Halide, *The Turkish Ordeal*, p 6, New York, 1928.

«We are the only obstacle to the spread of Bolshevism».

The agreement of peace and friendship with the Soviets gave Kemal's nationalistic propaganda an important and intimidating weapon against allied capitalism, a weapon which he used to the utmost and with great skill to achieve a favourable outcome for himself in the game he was playing against the victorious allied West. It was an intimidating threat which he hurled against the Allies at every opportunity. The motif of the propaganda was as follows: We could have become a strong «Islamic Barrier», the sole obstacle to the spread of Bolshevism, stopping its infectious miasma from proceeding westwards, if you had behaved to us with tolerance and goodwill. But since you have shown us ill-will and cruelty, we shall have our revenge by now allowing the miasma of communism to infect Turkey - via our now free communication with our friends the Bolsheviks - and to spread from us to attack the West».

Halide Edib (Minister of Propaganda in Kemal's government and a very clever woman with an exceptionally good western education) points out in her book: «The Turkish Ordeal» «But we should never forget, not even for one second, that Kemal's movement was a deeply nationalistic and not a communist movement». «We all (the nationalists) know this very well». But the bluff of this intimidating propaganda for the Europeans, and chiefly for Great Britain, was like a danger signal. The British government was so afraid that it sent agents from its Intelligence Service to Anatolia to sound out the nationalist government of Kemal for peace terms.

Beginning of 1921

Bristol Documents, N.A., 867.00/1455.

Report by Bristol to the Secretary of State at the State Department. «In order for the British government to have diplomatic cover in the event of an adverse situation, the British secret agents sent as envoys to Ankara were deliberately not supplied with official credentials so that if they happened to fail in their mission and their identity was revealed, they could easily pass themselves off as ordinary citizens acting on their own initiative without any official responsibility».

January 1921

Churchill, Winston, *The World Crisis,* p 419, volume V, New York, 1929. Woodward, W.L. and Rohan, Butler (eds), *Documents on British Foreign Policy 1919-1939*, First Series, volume XIII, Her Majesty's Stationery Office, London, 1963.

Churchill (who held the all-powerful office in the government of «Lord of the Admiralty») sent an urgent and angry proposal to the Prime Minister Lloyd George with the following awful warning: «The Turks are being pushed into the arms of the Bolsheviks. It is clear that with the spread of Bolshevism into Turkey, it will be impossible for us to hold on for long to Baghdad and the oil in Mosoul without sending a very strong army of occupation there, with the commensurate consequence of a very expensive stay of unknown duration».

16 February 1921

Housepian, Marjory, *Smyrna Affair,* p 79, 1966.

The Supreme Council of the Allies took a (favorable)

step towards the Kemalist government in Ankara which was equivalent to a «de facto» real recognition of it. It invited Kemal and also the Sultan of the official Turkey to send representatives to London to a conference which was being convened with the aim of agreeing with the Greeks on concluding a peace. This futile conference did not put a stop to the hostilities but it expedited matters for the French and the Italian envoys to promote their negotiations with Kemal's people on concluding a peace between nationalist Turkey and their nations.

21 March 1921

The Peace Agreement between Italy and Kemalist nationalist Turkey was signed and endorsed on this date.

10 August 1921

Mears, Eliot Grinnell, *Modern Turkey,* p 601, New York., 1924. Gibbons Herbert Adams, *Europe Since 1918,* p 432, New York, 1923. Horton, George, *Blight of Asia*, p 190, New York, 1926. Housepian, Marjory, *Smyrna Affair,* p 79-80, New York, 1966.

At its conference, the Supreme Council for Peace proceeded to make the following declaration: *«Greece is in a situation of war with Turkey exclusively on her own; the states of Britain, France, Italy and Japan will remain as non-participants and strictly neutral».* But neutrality on this occasion meant that French and Italian ships could with impunity supply Kemal with guns and ammunition while actually forbidding the Greeks to apply the international military law which allows one belligerent to blockade the ports and coastline of the country of the other belligerent which is being supplied illegally with guns and ammunition by other «neutral» states. In such a case, the international law of the sea in wartime allows the first belligerent party to obstruct this illegal transgression by means of a naval blockade of those coasts through which this illegal supply of war materials is being sent by the transgressors i.e. the supposedly neutral and non-participating countries. But with the arbitrary high-handedness of the Great Powers, this international right was taken away from Greece. However, despite the reaction and the events which were hostile to Greece, the Greeks won a very hard and frenzied battle which was started by the Turks at Afion-Karachisar in the middle of August 1921, and drove the Turks out from that area. Both sides suffered severe losses in dead and wounded.

15 August 1921

Housepian, Marjory, *Smyrna Affair,* p 80, New York, 1966.

After his defeat in the battle of Afion-Karachisar, Kemal withdrew with his beaten army to the north of Turkey and to the front which he held at Eskishehir. His army spent all the winter there in comfort, supplied by the Allies with everything necessary for passing a relaxing winter, at the same time making intense preparations for the coming summer. In striking contrast, the two hundred thousand men of the Greek army lived in misery during that very severe, icy winter deep in the interior of Turkey, lacking many necessary supplies. Greece was actually bankrupt after the rescinding of the loans agreed by the Venizelos government. And, to cap it all, the winter that year was very severe without the soldiers having the necessary winter clothing. The soldiers' mess allowances in food was inadequate in both quality and quantity. The soldiers' equipment was old and worn-out by use and disproportionate to the army's urgent needs. Its leadership was discouraged by this unhappy situation. The men in the army, isolated in the depths of the East and almost forgotten and abandoned in an enemy country with the festivities and celebrations back home for the king's return, felt resentful and frustrated.

16 October 1921

Churchill, Winston, *The World Crisis,* volume V., New York, 1929. Ibid: *Memoirs,* p 456, London, England.

«For more than nine months the Turks waited, comfortably supplied, while the Greeks suffered» from the severe winter, the inadequacy of their provisions and deficiencies of all kinds.

20 October 1921

Churchill, Winston, *Memoir.* Ibid: *The World Crisis,* p 434, volume V., New York, 1929. Housepian, Marjory, *Smyrna Affair,* p 79, New York, 1966.

In Ankara Kemal's Foreign Minister signed a Peace Treaty on behalf of nationalist Turkey with the representative of the French government and former French Minister of Propaganda Franklin Bouillon. Bouillon - as British political officials discovered - had been in Ankara since the spring, carrying out confidential consultations with the Ankara government; these acts of intrigue on the part of France, and totally secret negotiations carried out behind the back of the British government provoked reactions. But the French government tried to disguise the truth stating that «what people are saying to each other is all rumour and village gossip» and that it was not having secret consultations. The raw truth however revealed that France, with the negotiations conducted with Kemal, had ensured for herself and had been given the concession of exclusive exploitation in all the mineral areas of Turkey and also the sole right to priority in its dealings with Turkish banks; also full trade preference would be given to here at Turkish ports, on the railways and on the country's riverboats. In exchange - and as was proven by the undeniable development of events - France promised in this treaty to grant Kemal active aid so as to repel the invading Greek army and drive it into the sea. Although France had been supplying arms to Kemal for a long time and had been reinforcing his nationalist movement, on 20 October 1921, they began to supply him openly with all kinds of military materials without any pretext. Heavy artillery and long-range mortars began to arrive from the French army in Syria in abundant quantities while for the first time bombs from French aeroplanes, piloted by Frenchmen, were dropped and hit Greek fortified positions (which had been pointed out by spies) on the war front, at a time when Greece was on the point of bankruptcy and its army was poor and was lacking even the essentials.

20 October 1921

Nicolson, Harold, *History*, p 260. Kinross, Lord, *Attaturk*, p 235. Gibbons, Herbert Adams, *Europe Since 1918*, New York, 1923. Ibid: *History*, p 452.

«From this date, France obviously and without any false excuses or diplomatic pretexts, began actively to support Kemal and his nationalist troops, with the undisguised aim and sole purpose the victory of the Turkish nationalist army and the throwing out both of the Greek army and more generally of the Greek population from Asia Minor. Aeroplanes piloted by the French with the national symbol of the French Air Force easily distinguishable, now openly bombed critical Greek targets, while at the same time the French secret service channelled information to Kemal's staff on every vulnerable military point on the Greek army front».

20 October 1921

Kinross, Lord, *Attaturk,* p 384, New York, 1932. Housepian, Marjory, *Smyrna Affair,* p 79, New York, 1966.

The machinations and secret French negotiations carried on with Kemal for many months by Bouillon, the empowered envoy in Ankara, and the beneficial advantages gained by France at the expense and behind the back of the British government, inflamed the British and all the ruling politicians in Britain to such a degree that, with a sardonic sneer, they gave the French ringleader and intriguer Bouillon (the former Minister of Propaganda in France) who had contrived all this plot the nickname of «the Boiling Bouillon» (a well known food sipped).

November 1921

Churchill, Winston, *The World Crisis*, volume V, New York, 1929. Ibid: *Memoirs*, London England. Nicolson, Harold, *History,* p 263. Ibid: *The Last Phase, 1919-1925*, Boston, Ma., 1934. Fisher, Louis, *Oil Imperialism*, p 81, New York, 1926.

A sensational drama was being played out at that time in Paris, the capital of France. Two disconsolate supplicants were nervously pacing up and down in the VIP waiting-room at the French Foreign Ministry; these were the Prime Minister and the Foreign Minister of Greece. They were waiting to hear the final decision which the High Allied Council had reached after Greece's impassioned appeal for urgent assistance from the Allies in its struggle in Asia Minor, which was at a critical point. But the warm pleas of their desperate entreaties left the Councillors unmoved and proved to be disappointingly unavailing. The decision of the Supreme Council which was announced to them was very hard for Greece and continued to remain unalterable and hostile. The ballot of the councillors and the unanimous resolution on the verdict which was issued as a final and unalterable decision and announced to the Greek officials who were waiting full of suspense read as follows: *«No more guns from now on, no more mortars, not one soldier from the Great Allies, not one shilling (the twentieth part of a pound) will be given for the Greek campaign in Asia Minor».*

Housepian, Marjory, *Smyrna Affair*, p 78, New York, 1966.

However it is an enigmatic fact which remains for historians as a unanswered question but which eludes every intelligent explanation. A question which teases the curiosity of every intelligent person and excites the interest for an explanation, it is the incomprehensible insistence of King Constantine and of the government which brought him back, in continuing a military struggle which was now obviously doomed to failure by the manifest reaction and hostile behaviour now so clearly shown by the Great Powers. A hopeless struggle and one which was manifestly opposite to the will of the Greek people who, by voting against Venizelos for this very reason, brought them to power on a programme and a mandate to stop the war and to bring the boys back to their country. Historians, in the dilemma set before them by this enigmatic question, resort to the «assumption» that it is easier to start than to finish a war.

The terrible economic impasse in which the country found itself and the weakness of the government of the time to secure foreign loans for Greece, brought the rulers to a dramatic dilemma of true desperation concerning the very difficult position in which the nation found itself. In order to find the urgently needed money in these circumstances, the government was forced to adopt the only way out which could be thought up by the quick-witted mind of the Minister for Economic Affairs, (Protopapadakis from the island of Naxos) who devised a plan which he set for approval before the Greek Council of Ministers, which was at a real impasse. His invention was a compulsory internal loan (a hypocritical title). The naked truth was that it was a seizure of money (embezzlement), an arbitrary act with a sudden and high-handed halving of the paper money in drachmas which was in circulation throughout the land. In other words, exactly half of the drachma money supply in banknotes belonging to all Greeks was removed suddenly and without any warning. This very sharp economic «bite» caused terrible upset and uproar among the people, who from then on began to organise rallies to demand the end of the Asia Minor campaign which they called with deep hatred the «guzzler» and a «financial cesspit».

The money which entered the government's coffers from this compulsory loan relieved the government somewhat and gave it a temporary breathing space, but only for its internal needs. The necessary foreign exchange for supplying the army with ammunitions continued to remain pitifully inexistant, a portent of ominous developments.

December 1921; January 1922

Churchill, Winston, *Memoirs*, p 434, London, England.

«For approximately nine months, the Turks waited comfortably in the warmth while the Greeks suffered throughout the icy-cold of the severe winter».

Spring 1922

Housepian, Marjory, *Smyrna Affair,* pp 81-82, 84-85.
Edib Halide, *The Turkish Ordeal*, p 383.

In the spring of 1922, the British newspapers began to reveal the atrocities of the exterminations and the bloody brutality of Kemal's nationalist supporters and soldiers, which they had managed to hide for more than a year from the world outside the Turkish borders, thanks to the friendly and willing cooperation of American and French official diplomatic circles. The diplomatic circles of these countries had instructions from their governments to cooperate with the nationalist government of Turkey and to try at the same time to promote their national interests there by exciting the gratitude of the Turks at their suppression of everything which would provoke and arouse worldwide anger and clamour against the nationalist Turkish government.

However, certain European functionaries, in responsible high positions, revealed what had happened during the winter: Another mass march to their deaths of local Greeks and Armenians into the uninhabited interior of Turkey. They collected them up in groups from their towns and villages and forced them by pushing them inhumanely at the points of their bayonets and with rifle-shots into an endless march towards the deserted mountains and the ravines of far-off Anatolia and beyond the uplands of Diarbakir. Men, women and children, lightly clothed and totally hungry, were pushed inhumanely in this unceasing march, falling on the road from their exhaustion of many days, from starvation, from the narcotic somnolence brought on by the chill from the severe cold and from the rifle-shots if they did not proceed. It was another very plain mass genocide of these two christian ethnic races, the most hated by Turks. When the spring melted the snow, then the bare reality became obvious in all its horror. All along this death-bearing route among dry, rocky and cliff-filled areas, left and right and in a continuous line of gorges and ditches, it could be seen that all the earth's cavities were full of piles of bodies. These facts were kept secret for one and a half years by the skilful success of their international concealment.

May 1922
Suddenly however, in May 1922, a detailed account by Yowell, the former director of the philanthropic organisation «Near East Relief in Harput», made the revelation; this appeared in the headlines of the English newspaper *The Times* and provoked passionate anger and indignation both in Britain and in America. Mark Bristol, with his partner-in-lies Florence Billings, an agent of Near East Relief in Constantinople, made a joint denial which was published by the Turkish press which, spreading propaganda as a routine matter, denied the *Times* article acrimoniously, branding it a shameless lie. However the bloody and heartrending account which was revealed by Yowell's publication was confirmed by other witnesses, one of whom was the eminent and famous Dr Mark H. Ward, whose diary was published in England after American newspapers had refused to publish it. The State Department, frightened by Yowell's revelation and the great excitement and mass reaction which this article would cause among the American people, tried desperately to deny it in American daily newspapers and journals. Hard reality prevailed over this prompted lie however, despite the attempts of the American government to

deny it however and despite the pressure exerted by the State Department through Allen Dulles, director of the Intelligence Service (thus counterfeiting and representing the opposite of the truth to the American people), despite the coordinated attempt of the diplomatic agents in the Intelligence Service, whose ringleader was that unrivalled distorter of the truth Admiral Mark L. Bristol (who assured the Foreign Minister of Kemal's government that he would deliver Turkey from this terrible accusation with an official denial). It became widely known and was recorded in revealing historical writings of irrefutable authority, and in reputable newspapers and journals throughout the world.

The seemingly inexplicable willingness of the British press to reveal the extermination atrocities of the Turks is explained by the spirit of revenge which dominated the British press at that time for the vitriolic and coordinated attack by the Turkish press against fickle Britain.

10 May 1922

On 10 May 1922 a news article in the Turkish newspaper *Yeni-Ghun* revealed to the Turkish people the active participation of Kemal in the extermination of the Christians in Asia-Minor. At the beginning of the summer of 1922, another nationalistic campaign of annihilation of Hellenism was launched and this time exterminated (according to the cumulative totals of those inhabitants of Greek towns and villages who were wiped out) approximately 100,000 Greeks in the Pontos region - along almost the whole of the coastline of the region of Asia Minor towards the Black Sea, which was inhabited by Greeks - where the Greek population was thriving and proportionately outnumbered the Turks. This mass execution of the Greek inhabitants was again disclosed in an impressive coverage in the British press of a macabre piece of news which caused uproar and anger in public opinion.

Summer 1922

In the middle of the summer of 1922, the Turks were fully armed with ammunition and were ready to charge and their fanaticism, inflamed by skilful handling, was at fever pitch against the Greek army. During this same period, the military leaders of the Greek General Staff, realised that the

Greek army in Asia-Minor could not tolerate another such winter. The terrible impasse to which they were brought forced them to contrive a cunning plan to find a smooth and uneventful way out of that impasse for the army by drastic extortionary means. This plan was to coordinate the Greek military forces and to make a violent attack to seize Constantinople, the then temporary Staff Headquarters of all the Great Powers who had emerged victorious from the First World War of 1914-1918. It was an action which would blackmail the Allies, who were obviously Turkophile because of their many interests there, and would force them to rid themselves of Greek occupation by mediation, pressurising Kemal to agree to allow the Greek army to make a smooth and undisturbed withdrawal, without battles and bloodshed, without retaliation and without causing tragedy among the local Christian population of Greeks and Armenians.

As Winston Churchill writes in his *Memoirs* (p 442) and as Marjory Housepian writes in *Smyrna Affair* (pp 84-85), this crafty Greek trick would have succeeded and the Allies, by exerting strong pressure in Ankara, would have allowed the Greeks to make a safe withdrawal but for the totally arbitrary act, taken on his own initiative, of that Turkophile English general, Sir Charles Harington, who was totally against the Greek campaign. Without any instructions or orders from his superiors, he bluffed and his bluff made the undecided Greek military leaders shrink from proceeding to carry out this drastic action which however had been decided beforehand jointly by the Greek political and military leadership. The Greek military leaders of this campaign made a very great mistake which had bloody consequences and for which the nation did not forgive them neither will it ever forget. With complete gullibility and self-delusion they asked for approval for this enterprise - it was carefully thought out and was clearly aimed at blackmailing the Great Powers - from the British General Harington who was in theory the shadowy leader of the negligible number of allied units there - as if blackmail needed to be approved first! The obviously Turkophile General Harington (with a predilection which was to be expected from the now clearly reactionary stance taken by the Allies against the Greek campaign) put forward strong opposition to the request of the Greek leader to carry out this act of blackmail against the Allies and sent a message threatening that, if the Greeks dared to proceed towards Constantinople, he would confront them with all the allied forces there (a rhetorical intimidation and clearly a bluff, since the Allies maintained no forces there except for small garrisons).

After Harington's message, the Greek military leaders responsible for the rapid success of this enterprise of blackmail which would save them, being too paranoid and cowardly to advance because of a gullible and unforgivable piece of stupidity, stopped and in their cowardice called off the putting into action of the only way-out that had remained to save «the Greek army as well as the Christian population of Asia Minor».

Another bad result caused by the programme of this campaign was that it caused upheaval in the order and harmony which had previously prevailed in the army's units. The two regiments which were to complete the capture of Constantinople had gathered in Moudania, where Greek ships were waiting to take them home to Greece via the Marmara Sea after they had achieved the success they were anticipating - this was to be the beginning of the army's repatriation.

But in their abundant stupidity their dream of going home came true too early. The small French garrison there, having been notified by Harington, tried to block their route on the ridiculous pretext that this was supposed to be a neutral zone. This was not true and two leaders of Greek battalions, ignoring the false prohibition, managed to lead their men into the Bandirma Hills (Panormo). The others, behaving with uncharacteristic servility, instead of ignoring the handful of French or of turning back as the other two majors had done, surrendered to a small and insignificant French garrison which gave them up in turn to Kemal's forces as prisoners of war! In his correspondence to a friend - which can be found in the U.S.A. National Archives - Admiral Mark Bristol wrote on 31 August 1922: «I think that the Greeks would have won their game but they lost, thanks to the initiative of General Harington who, acting spontaneously without asking for instructions from his government or from anyone else, deployed the few British soldiers in his garrison on the Tsataltzas line with Turkish gendarmes behind them on the pretext of blocking the Greeks' route». The Greeks hesitated because of Harington's trick and did not proceed to carry out the planned manoeuvre which would have saved them. Churchill in his *Memoirs* puts it cynically: «It was a ridiculous situation. Harington turned the guns of the Turkish detachment of gendarmes against our own allies!»

July 1922

Kemal, having been informed of all this, judged it a suitable moment to take advantage of the opportunity given to him by the circumstances. Since the beginning of July he had begun to redistribute the strength of his army with strategic mastery, giving special attention to the various crucial points of the enemy front from which the Greeks had withdrawn units in their desperate attempt to capture Constantinople - an attempt which they finally aborted.

13 August 1922

On 13 August 1922, Kemal left Ankara secretly and nobody knew why or where he had gone. But his secret disappearance had a strategic motive (he trusted no one and it was kept from the many traitors with which he was surrounded). In the middle of August Kemal finally coordinated his plan of action with his staff generals. As a part of their coordinated general action, they marked their ordinance survey maps, with precision and analytical detail, with all the known Greek positions (learned from underhand betrayals) battalion by battalion, regiment by regiment, division by division. Kemal was going to follow the old strategic tactic, so divisive to the enemy's strength (and which had been used by Mohammed the Conqueror) of further attenuating the Greek fighting forces by feigning attacks at far-off points of the front and thus breaking down the main central nerve line of the Greek front, which was his aim. But he prepared his army to attack along the length of the front which extended for 15 miles (24 kilometres).

114

26 August 1922

Churchill, Winston, *Memoirs*, p 444. Kinroll, Lord, *Kemal's Biography*, p 349. Edip Halide, *Ordeal, p 383.* Lt Perry, *Report*, 24-10-1922 in «*Bristol Papers*». Housepian, Marjory, *Smyrna Affair*, p 86.

On 26 August 1922, Kemal gave the command for a general attack and the final decisive great battle with his order to his army and with his personal command to everyone from now on: «Men, the end of your road is the Mediterranean!» It was the only strong and terse declaration of this historic order of the day and it roused the nationalistic impulses of his soldiers. At daybreak on that day, Kemal's soldiers made a sudden and violent attack on the lines of the central section of the front and, finding the Greeks unsuspecting and unprepared, they created a notorious breach. There was no counter-attack to contain the Turks who broke through the Greek lines with such impetus and speed that even the soldiers of the special garrison of the local Staff Headquarters of the Greek army corps who were on continual standby, unexpectedly found themselves surrounded between the first and second Turkish armies without being given time to react as they were too surprised, unsuspecting and criminally unprepared to confront this attack. Most of the unit officers on the northern front were overwhelmed with discouragement and a fatalistic inertia. Instead of circulating among the soldiers on the front, trying to encourage them and to boost their morale and thus keeping them on continual standby for any sudden attack by the enemy (an eventuality which seemed certain) they were, on the contrary, fatalistically banking on a quick salvation from this hopeless situation by drawing up the military manoeuvre of the capture of Constantinople by blackmail in order to coerce the Allies to intervene for peace - a hope which was simply hypothetical and there was no certainty as to the successful outcome of their campaign. However their burning desire to return to their country made them dream and believe in this doubtful and desperate campaign as if it were something tangible and certain which would have a favourable and quick result. An additional factor in their pitiful failure was yet another unforgivable omission. Both those who contrived the plot of this desperate military manoeuvre and those government and army leaders who were responsible for its success, instead of covering the planned campaign with the veil of a strict secrecy, with criminal folly allowed it to circulate widely. It was known to enemies and friends alike, to the military and to civilians in both large and small urban centres.

However, this plan (as has already been described above) was not put into practice due to a second Greek blunder and lack of judgement: to the weak-spirited and cowardly mind (which lacked the ability to think cleverly and quickly when the occasion demanded) of the leader of this rescue mission to whom the last hope of the nation had been entrusted. The nation had an ardent desire to get off this terrible hook peacefully with an escape from the desperate impasse to which the army had reached and reduced to, as had the many millions of local Greeks and Armenians of Asia Minor. The Greek leader who had been selected for this critical campaign, apart from his pusillanimity, was so obtuse that he did not understand the all-too-obvious bluff played on him by Harington, whom he humbly asked to give him permission !!! for the Greek army to abolish by means of blackmail the then entrenched allied regime in Constantinople - another colossal folly to ask this from a man universally known to be a Turkophile who had a manifestly hostile approach to the Greek question).

Nota Bene.: The unimaginably terrible disaster which followed this calamitous blunder can be analysed into two basic causes, each cause having three sub-divisions:

A' SERIOUS ERRORS: Political errors, military errors and diplomatic errors.

B' CRITICAL SHORTCOMINGS: The lack of the necessary secrecy, the lack of nationalistic zeal and the lack of creative inspiration with the necessary accompanying creative daring.

17 August 1922

On the north-western front (in the region of Eski Sehir), the Greek army and its deeply discouraged leaders collapsed at its first clash with the Turks. It had already begun to withdraw after the order from headquarters and the soldiers turned with-drawal into flight towards Moudania (on the Marmara Sea) where Greek ships had gathered to meet the troops - a prepa-ration which had taken place with the badly calculated pros-pect of the hoped-for disengagement and the anticipated suc-cess of the Greek plan. Most of these Greek army units were encircled by the advancing Turkish army and were taken pris-oner. The Greek army lost a unique opportunity on the central Anatolian part of the front, which was Kemal's main target and the place where he made his great strike and broke through the line. Because of the strategic clumsiness and in-ability of the leading officers of the Greek army - who were overwhelmed by the general discouragement and who could not put into immediate practice the strategic tactic laid down by the Code of Practice of carrying out a vehement and obsti-nate counter-attack - the Greeks lost their only opportunity of achieving an outflanking manoeuvre and, by converging, to unite with the military body to the south - a staff section led by the able General Trikoupis - so as to complete the encir-clement and to take the Turkish invasion column prisoner (a strategy recommended by German generals at a much later date). On the contrary, the breach caused confusion which helped in the outbreak of local anarchy and mutiny in the heart of the division with the result that the Greeks, instead of encir-cling the enemy, were themselves encircled. From this point on, their disorganised retreat and flight began.

The flight was begun first by those officers who lost their nerve, thus setting the example of escape to the soldiers on the line who, influenced by the stampede of their officers and following this example, did the same. This incontinent flight lost no time in becoming general and finally in turning into uncontrolled panic. (These details have already been certified by historical documents and are beyond refutation. There have been confirmed and recognised descriptions, corroborated by well-known international historical writers).

September 1922

In the southern section of the front and to the south-east of Afion-Karahisar, General Trikoupis carried out an obstinate counter-attack against the sudden and virulent attack of the Turks. But the complete absence of a coordinated and analogous strategic counter-attack and cooperation from the generals on the northern front led to the terrible consequence of the failure of Trikoupi's counter-attack. The tragic result was that the southern section of the army was also encircled by the swift units of the Turkish cavalry and Trikoupis himself was captured; he was a general who had military flair and nerve but who lost the battle because of the absence of coordinated and analogous battle action by the generals of the next front to his in the central section of the army. The Turks destroyed - as was later confirmed - five whole Greek battalions on that lamentable day and took thousands of prisoners. It went down as a true debacle and as a black day for the Greeks.

September 1922

Kinross, Lord, *Kemal*, p 198.

Kemal had in the past declared the following to his supporters: «If it is Allah's will for us to be defeated, then we should set fire to all our houses, to all our belongings and to leave behind us only ruins and a wide and valueless burned desert». Now, in their ruin and their panic-stricken flight, the Greeks did the same; they set fire to the towns and villages through which they passed, they killed and mutilated many of the Turkish inhabitants whom they found in their houses, they stole jewellery and gold rings from the women and any other valuables which took their rapacious fancy and then took to their heels. For approximately one hundred miles (160 kilometres) the Turkish soldiers, obeying Kemal's nationalistic and burning instigation, pursued the Greeks closely without respite and passed through the burned and still smoking ruins of one village after another, one town after another, until they reached their enemy on the threshold of Smyrna.

FALL OF AND FLIGHT FROM OUSAK

1 September 1922

The Greek army in this section, after giving an apathetic and hurried battle with the advancing Turks, abandoned the strong fortification of Ousak, 140 miles (224 kilometres) from Smyrna. It is worth noting that the General Staff of the Greek

Army considered the fortress of Ousak to be an impregnable stronghold. But a stronghold without any strong-willed defending fighters is of no strategic value. It was there that the Greek army gave, without any relish and with great difficulty, their final weak and only semi-organised battle. There were no other significant or particularly fortified positions for resistance between here and the sea. But even if there had been, they would have been unavailing by this time as the psychology of panic reigned everywhere. It was now an admitted fact that in this sad and sorry state there was no organised or disciplined army capable of resistance. The spirit of panic had now conquered both the soldiers and almost all their officers who, obviously now and without keeping up any pretence of their personal dignity, tried to save themselves in swift flight.

4 September 1922

Housepian, Marjory, *Smyrna Affair*, pp 93-98, New York, USA.

The British Consul at Smyrna made an official proposal to the British civilians who had businesses or land there or who were prosperous and had private means in the best suburbs of Smyrna, to leave the area of Smyrna completely for the time being as disturbances were predicted. The Consuls of the other nations sharply criticised this act of the British Consul on the excuse that an exodus of British from Smyrna would cause strong fear amongst the inhabitants and would strengthen the spirit of panic. Only George Horton, US General Consul, who in thirty years of diplomatic service had acquired great experience in the barbarity of the Turks, refused to criticise this prudent and timely advice and what turned out to be a correct prediction.

Housepian, Marjory, *Smyrna Affair,* p 99, New York, USA.

The exceptionally worried and undefended Christian population of Smyrna, terrified by the news that the Turkish army was approaching, desperately requested means of escape by sea, which however did not exist. The Greeks and the Armenians in particular, when they learned that the Greek administration there was getting ready to abandon the town, gathered in their churches and asked their priests to act immediately to ensure their timely protection by the Allies. The priests made a joint appeal to the Archbishop of Canterbury in Britain, begging him to seek to mediate with the British government to achieve even a temporary truce with Kemal in order to stop the Turkish army outside the town, or at least to receive a confirmation that the Christians would have British protection. This heartrending appeal ended with the following passionate words: «*In the name of Christ, hurry up and prevent an imminent catastrophe*». The English cleric, the Reverend Charles Dobson, went and personally handed in this very urgent appeal to Sir Osmond de Beauvoir Brock, the Admiral of the British squadron who was in the port of Smyrna on a big battleship «the Iron Duke», so that the appeal could be sent quickly to Britain. But, as written in the ship's calendar, this arrogant and egocentric British officer did not consider that the appeal of the religious leaders, whose letter the Anglican priest Dobson had given him, was an urgent question or a hurried matter which should immediately concern him and take him away from his other obligations, and he placed it among the other papers in his naval file and did nothing.

September 1922

Horton, George, General US Consul in Smyrna, *Blight of Asia*, dated 3 September 1922

Horton overturned the false assertions in the announcements of the Consuls of the three other Allied Powers concerning the local population, and their joint official statements to the worried inhabitants of Smyrna that the retreating Greek army which was arriving would protect them. Enraged at the concealment of the very serious situation and at the distortion of the truth contained in these announcements, which was so dangerous for the uninformed people, he ended his silence with plain and unanswerable proofs to the visitors at the American Consulate and with trenchant phrases indicated the following facts: «The greek soldiers, exhausted by their long and tormenting trudge, having thrown down their arms and having retreated in panic and in great disarray, could only just stagger to the coast. They were dusty and ragged; their muddy uniforms were torn to pieces by the brambles and thorns of their unguided march through unknown areas. They advanced towards the sea in a hurry to be saved, to leave on the ships like thrashed dogs; they were in a condition of extreme exhaustion». There was no Greek army to save the local population!

4 September 1922

Housepian, Marjory, *Smyrna Affair,* p 98. George Horton, *Diary.*

The American Consul, Horton, tactfully suggested to all the Greek-Americans who would like to leave Smyrna that they should gather at the Smyrna Theatre on the great quay. About one hundred Greeks who were US naturalised subjects asked to leave immediately at their own expense. Consul Horton willingly, out of lively and friendly interest, organised the hiring of a small ship and they left for Mytilini (the island of Lesvos). A.S. Merrill, a Lieutenant in the US Navy, reports the following in his diary with obvious hostility: «These damned Greeks without a doubt will now be swearing *terrible curses at the Turks* (in the Greek language) but their salvation is now ensured behind the protection of the American flag instead of these ruffians staying behind to take their proper place in the great fracas which awaits the others!» Merrill, an officer in the Secret Service at the office of the Turkophile Admiral Mark L Bristol in Constantinople, showed (as did his boss) pointed antipathy towards and contempt for the luckless Greeks and he was willing to believe the worst lies put about by Turkish propaganda concerning them.

4 September 1922

Housepian, Marjory, *Smyrna Affair*, p 96. Horton, George, *Report* in the *USA National Archives, N.A. 763.72/13120.*

Telegram from George Horton on 3 September 1922 to Admiral Mark L Bristol in Constantinople: «I beg you in the name of humanity to ask the State Department for American intervention in Ankara and to give a long-term cessation to the pursuit being made by the Turkish army to allow the Greek army units to leave and to avert the eventuality of a catastrophe at Smyrna». A «No», a categorical refusal, to Horton's telegram of appeal, arrived from the State Department. Bristol had sent this telegram by radiogram the same day but Horton received the negative response on 6 September 1922 i.e. three days later, by which time the Greek authorities there had already packed their bags and left Smyrna. The danger was obvious but the appeal made subsequently by Horton to his co-Consuls of Britain, France and Italy and also to the governments of the Allied fleets based there to intervene did not provoke the hoped-for Christian sympathy of humanity and a positive reply. The stereotyped answers which he received from all of them had more or less the same contents: they had express orders from their governments to desist from every action which could be construed by Kemal's nationalistic government as protection on their part of Turkey's enemies (and the enemies of Turkey, as it was intimated, were in this case the Greek and Armenian populations of Smyrna). The French Admiral Dumesnil expressed himself with greater hostility. He announced to the Consuls that he would act against the Greeks by confiscating all the passenger and cargo ships there if there was even the slightest hostile demonstration against the town's Turkish population before the Turks could enter and capture the town. The same hostile line against the Greek and Armenian populations was observed by the American representative in Constantinople, the Turkophile Admiral Mark L Bristol who, with Lieutenant Commander Captain J.B. Rhodes, temporary deputy to the commander of the battleship «Litchfield», sent a hurried message to the US General Consul at Smyrna not to let it appear in any of his actions that America was protecting the Greek population, which was hostile to Turkey. The higher governmental authorities in Washington (the State and Navy Departments) warmly approved Bristol's orders. The most urgent government programme for Washington under these circumstances was its attempt to create, via its Turkophile diplomatic actions, a favourable climate for the USA so that it could win the sympathy of the nationalists and especially the friendship of the then conquering and all-powerful ruling classes in Turkey from whom they hoped to achieve rich considerations in the trading and industrial exploitation of

Turkey. Their most desired ambition was in particular a concession to exploit her oil-fields in the rich mineral deposits of Mesopotamia which both Britain and France coveted and for the acquisition of which a secret war of intrigue and scheming was then taking place for dominance between the victorious so-called Allies.

Smyrna Affair, p 94.

According to the mathematical calculations carried out by the American services (N.E.R., S.O.C. etc), the likely conclusion was that the numbers of Greek refugees flowing into the city exceeded thirty thousand a day; they were arriving from the interior of Asia-Minor and they had already flooded the town and its suburbs by 5 September 1922 and after. Most arrived on foot with their children, their draught animals and all the most important portable contents of their houses. Some of these unfortunate refugees were taken in by friends and relatives, some were taken in compassionately by complete strangers but their number was so great that the city's streets were full of them in suffocating crowds and the road networks which led to the city from the eastern parts of the country were jam-packed with thousands of them. Grotesque convoys of men, women and children made up the processions, numb with great despair and fatigue which, according to the testimony of reliable eye-witnesses, broke your heart.

It was a procession which cut a very dramatic figure and which Ernest Hemingway, the world famous writer who was then correspondent in Turkey for the Toronto (Canada) newspaper *The Daily Star* called «A silent procession». The Consul George Horton never forgot the spectacle of an old woman who stumbled as she walked «with a skeletal son racked with a high fever who was sitting straddled over her shoulders. The son was taller than the mother and his legs reached and almost touched the ground». She shuffled through the streets, bent with the double weight of her son and of the belongings which she was carrying. She was drenched from head to toe with sweat and dust from the innumerable miles of the dirt road of their heart-breaking trudge.

Smyrna Affair, p 96, 99.

All the Greek Political Administration of Smyrna and the General Army Staff with all their military following had already packed their bags and were ready to embark on the ships which were waiting for them in the harbour to go to Greece. The disclosure that the Greek Authorities were departing from Smyrna created turmoil among the Christian population who, together with the refugees from the interior, amounted to countless thousands of souls. All this sea of fearfully worried people was in a condition of real panic as they all understood that they were being mercilessly abandoned to their terrible fate for ever and that they would soon fall victim to the brutality of the bloodthirsty Turks. But neither the European Consuls nor the leaders of the allied battle fleet which was based there had orders or instructions from their governments as to how to face this very critical situation and, obeying express instructions, they avoided any initiative or action of their own which would displease the Turks.

Smyrna Affair, p 97.

On 6 September 1922, the American battleships «S.S. Simpson» and «S.S. Litchfield» (as flagship) sailed into the harbour of Smyrna; its Lieutenant Commander, J.B. Rhodes, was Bristol's representative, under the leadership of the Commander of the «Litchfield», Captain Arthur Japy Hepburn. Admiral Bristol in Constantinople, the day before the battlecruiser sailed, briefed J.B.Rhodes on the orders which he would give to them all on his behalf: In the harbour, he told him, there would be many allied ships. But all these Allies were at war with Turkey, whereas America was not. «Rhodes» he said to him «you must be careful. Don't agree to any cooperation with the Allies. But at the same time you must counterbalance your every action, expressly and solely, with being humane». But how Rhodes could counterbalance his actions with the Allies without the necessary cooperation with them, Bristol obliquely did not clarify. But the limits of humanity meant by Bristol were clear. They concerned only the protection of life and property «of the Americans»!

124

Smyrna Affair, p 99.

On 7 September 1922, the harbour at Smyrna had filled up with a whole armada of forty-two (42) ships ie twenty-nine (29) battleships and thirteen (13) auxiliary passenger ships, which represented almost all the great Naval Powers of the world. It was never learned why the terrific strength of this war fleet of 22 armoured battleships had gathered in the big harbour of Smyrna at that time, since their leaders remained inactive with stony hearts; they were indifferent spectators of the terrible tragedy which was unfolding there, unsympathetic so-called Christian spectators but really hypocrites as they refused protection to the non-combatant Christian population who were being butchered, despite their warm and desperate pleas.

However it is a historic fact that, with their intentional and criminal inactivity, they contributed to the completion of this terrible and unspeakable catastrophe and to the slaughtering, with bloodthirsty brutality, of the greater part of the unfortunate inhabitants of Smyrna, together with countless thousands of luckless refugees. A brutal crime aimed at the terrified, abused refugees who, with their hearts in their mouths, flooded and suffocated the city, its streets and all its suburbs and whose numbers neared two million souls, according to the final calculations which were made. European pseudo-Christians allowed the only double genocide in the annals of Christianity (an unforgivable crime) to take place so as to exterminate Christianity for ever from the once Greco-Roman Asia Minor - that Christianity, with its taming influence, whose most important and most basic dogma is love for one's neighbour. It was a real Christianity in Asia Minor, which had sallied forth and converted Europe and America which were then still in barbarian darkness.

Smyrna Affair, p 99.

Characteristic of the then American mentality was the strict order given by Admiral Bristol to J.B. Rhodes to protect the American businesses in Smyrna and especially the large oil company Standard Oil Company; Rhodes had anchored the American battleship and its marines in front of their buildings for protection.

Smyrna Affair, p 99.

On the morning of 8 September, the Greek High Civil Administrator, Stergiadis, made an official announcement that Greek jurisdiction over the area would cease to exist from ten (10) o'clock in the evening of the same day. This announcement increased the frantic fear and disquiet in the local Christian population who were already in a state of inward agitation; they surrounded the foreign Consulates, calling for their intervention for protection.

The French and Italian Consulates proceeded to make a joint announcement that the inhabitants had nothing to fear, shamelessly misleading the people with their disingenuousness. On top of this (and obviously by their own secret action), a false and counterfeit proclamation was published in the newspapers, supposedly by the Turkish Field Marshall Kemal, in which it was stated that any Turkish soldier found to have harmed a non-combatant from the population, no matter what the nationality, would be executed immediately. Those who were not naïve or credulous saw that this announcement was spurious, bogus and without foundation. The more prosperous Greeks had already left, abandoning the city and all their property. The rest, not being able to do otherwise, awaited the fateful development and the deadly enemy, overwhelmed with unspeakable suspense and disquiet.

Smyrna Affair, p 100.

Stergiades, the High Greek Civil Administrator of Smyrna, was the last official Greek to abandon the city between 7 and 8 o'clock in the evening of 8 September 1922. Having given up the keys of the Military Headquarters («Konak») to the French Consul, he walked fearfully and speedily with bent head to the coast and towards the motor-boat which was awaiting him, protected by a double line of a marine security squad but under the piercing disapproving curses and scoffs of the dense crowd of refugees who had been mercilessly betrayed and abandoned to a brutal death and the mania of the blood-thirsty Turks who were advancing behind them. He looked haggard and ten years older, bent under the weight of his guilty conscience for the tragic wretchedness of the calamitous turn of events with which he himself had cooperated with caustic zeal. He climbed with assistance into the motorboat which took him to the ship which was waiting for him and the ship set sail immediately, the last and ignominious time that Stergiades sailed out of Smyrna.

The ship soon disappeared into the thick darkness of the night, accompanied by the boos of the crowd.

Horton, George, *Blight of Asia*

«A deadly hush fell over the whole city, as if the inhabitants were holding their breath in their fear. But no crime happened. No check and no patrol in the streets to keep the peace. Despite the dark forecasts that there would be disturbances during this interim period, Smyrna remained quiet and as silent as the grave».

Lieutenant Merrill (of the US Secret Service). His report to Bristol: *Bristol Papers* in the *N.A.*

«It is 11 o'clock in the evening of 8 September. Quiet prevails everywhere».

And again he continues in his report, the next ill-starred day of 9 September in the morning: «I found no one wandering the streets except for our marine guards who are on duty at posts where American business interests are situated but which are inadequately guarded enclaves». And Merrill continues: «I thought that the sound of my footsteps on the pavements would be clearly heard in Constantinople. It was still dark, without a moon. You would have thought that even those refugees who were lying on the ground had suddenly vanished into thin air. Each was rolled into a separate ball on the ground and they were all silent, deep in deathly expectation».

Bristol Papers in the *USA National Archives*

An unexpected guest arrived at a dinner given by the British Consulate in Constantinople on 8 September 1922 and at which Bristol was on the official list of diners. It was Lord Beaverbrook, a famous English personality of the day who had a penetrating astuteness. The sudden appearance of Lord

Beaverbrook with his witty, ingenious and farsighted mind brought confusion to the train of thought of the American Admiral Bristol, who was the honorary guest at the dinner, to such a degree that his initial intention of using his diplomatic prestige to extract secrets and the indirect approval of the British to support his plans was blurred and disappeared from his thoughts. Beaverbrook, a prominent newspaper proprietor in England who was very famous at that time, was of short stature with an asymmetrical head which was disproportionately large for the size of his body. He had the habit of firing direct questions point-blank, which embarrassed other people, but at the same time he would refuse bluntly to listen to an answer full of formal diplomatic excuses.

Turning to Bristol with: «What is your opinion about Rumbold?», he disconcerted him suddenly with his first question. There happened to be latent rivalry and animosity between the American Bristol and the British Admiral Sir Horace Rumbold, the High British Commissioner in Constantinople, who represented British interests. Bristol, very noncommittal, avoided answering this caustic question but his dodge met the ironic smile of Lord Beaverbrook. Finally and with embarrassment, Bristol whispered with diplomatic hesitation: «I like Rumbold - I find him a good buddy».

«He is a good buddy but he has very little brain» was Lord Beaverbrook's answer. Second question: «What do you think of General Harington, the leader of the British forces?» Bristol's answer: «Frankly, I like him a lot» and he stumbled a little, adding: «The fact that he was promoted by the military authorities shows his capability». To this response (a diplomatic ruse), Beaverbrook said, snorting contemptuously: «War isn't won by generals nor by Prime Ministers!» Lord Beaverbrook's rough questions made Admiral Bristol angry. But with the egotism for which he was well-known by many, Bristol continued with obstinate insistence to refuse to withdraw the meaning of his initial answer, throwing the following phrase at Lord Beaverbrook: «He has a very good reputation!» «War is not won by generals nor by political leaders!» repeated Lord

Beaverbrook blisteringly, emphasising the unanswerable contradiction.

Lord Beaverbrook had come to Constantinople on a special mission from the British government and he fostered lively Turkophile sentiments which were very well-known in diplomatic circles. But now that he had seen for himself the unforeseen catastrophic developments and had weighed up matters rationally, he began to feel great sympathy for the Greek question. And he fired at Bristol the real fact which was beyond contradiction: «Our behaviour to the Greeks was rotten!» Bristol found Lord Beaverbrook's U-turn from Turkophile to Hellenophile incomprehensible! «We have behaved to them with dirty duplicity!» continued Lord Beaverbrook, talking to himself rather than to Bristol. «They were prompted and supported by us in beginning their campaign. But we abandoned them without support at their most critical moment so that the Turks could exterminate them and destroy them for ever! Lloyd George, as British Prime Minister, supported them and prompted them himself to make the landing at Smyrna. He supported them with every means except for giving them money which his Treasury did not have to give. And now we are leaving them exposed to disaster!» And turning to Bristol, he asked him suddenly: «And what are YOU (i.e. the Americans) doing in this matter?»

«America is standing on the sidelines just watching the outcome because although she had contracted a close tie with the Allies during the European War, she did not declare war on the Turks as you, the other Allies, did, neither did she cut off diplomatic relations with Turkey» answered Bristol. «Then, sir, why have you no Embassy here?» asked Beaverbrook with penetrating acerbity. «Because we do not have diplomatic relations» answered Bristol hazily; he was by now completely embarrassed and was giving confused answers as can be seen from his last contradictory and obviously unfounded response. Bristol adds in his diary that, in an indirect answer he also said the following to Lord Beaverbrook: «I have been here for three and a half years. I have seen for myself this horrible war which has been going on in Asia Minor in which people have been sacrificed for no reason, in which horrific crimes and inhuman savageries have been perpetrated, in which towns and villages have been destroyed, in which thousands and thousands of people have been forced into exile; I have seen and I believe as an incontrovertible fact that it is one of the most execrable crimes which modern civilisation has shown the world». Lord Beaverbrook jumped to his feet with pride. «I'm going to Smyrna» he said and cut off all further conversation. (If Bristol really said that, as he's claiming, by citing in his diary that the did so, then and in all likelihood he did it after Lord Beaverbrook had tearcely cut off all further conversation).

9 September 1922

    Churchill, Winston, *The Decline and Fall of Lloyd George*, p 158.

    Lord Beaverbrook went to Turkey as the special envoy of the British government to come into contact with Kemal, who was then the leader of the nationalist government, in the hope of persuading him to formulate the terms of the peace which however would satisfy the British government. But when Beaverbrook confirmed that the Turks were on the brink of total victory, he returned to London without carrying out his mission.

    Smyrna Affair, p 100.

    The American warship «S.S. Lawrence» sailed hurriedly into the harbour of Smyrna at 7 in the morning of 9 September; its commander at that time was Captain Arthur Japy Hepburn, leader of the naval squadron who had been sent from Constantinople by Admiral Mark L Bristol, who had begun to be worried about Smyrna. He had read a hysterical anxiety in the urgent telegrams of Consul Horton and his intuition, which was due to his (Bristol's) Turkophile ideology, told him that in the event of a disaster there was nobody there in whom he could have absolute trust to see that his strict orders were carried out except for the unsuitable Merrill.

    All the higher leaders representing the naval war units based there, and the competent Consuls of their nations, and in particular of the official Italian delegacy from Rome, were ready, in their dress uniforms, to give an official welcome to the higher officers of the Turkish army who would very soon enter the city and to extend to them their congratulations on Kemal's brilliant victory, but also to declare to them that their nations were willing to cooperate with the Turks. A sensation was caused by the absence of George Horton, the US General Consul, from this humiliating «show», so very unbecoming to their national prestige, «this theatrical pantomime» of the representatives of the European nations and of America. Horton, despite the obviously Turkophile line which his country was officially following in its diplomatic relations with Turkey, would not agree to sacrifice his conscious personal judgement regarding the Turks, an opinion which had crystallised from his long experience of them. Neither would he agree to circumstantial and conscienceless orders from higher functionaries that he should humiliate himself by extolling them at the expense of his own moral humiliation, to pretend by bad acting simply in order to promote on this occasion the success in the profits game which was then being played by the trade and industrial clique which was governing his country and which was directing the profiteering course of its foreign policy.

9 September 1922

Captain Arthur Japy Hepburn

As he himself expressively put it in his official log of the American battleship «S.S. Litchfield» for the day of the ninth (9) of September 1922: Calm prevailed in the city (Smyrna) before the Turks invaded».

George Horton, (US General Consul in Smyrna and eye witness to the terrible drama of the catastrophe).

In his deposition made in 1923 before the US Senate Committee of Inquiry on the questions of «Immigration and Naturalisation - a special inquiry into the tragedy of Smyrna» he said: «On Saturday the ninth of September 1922, absolute calm and order prevailed in Smyrna until the moment when the Turks rushed in with their front-line cavalry with the Chetes in the vanguard».

Smyrna Affair, p 102.

On the battle cruiser «S.S. Lawrence», which Bristol had

sent with all urgent speed to Smyrna, there were three civilian passengers, sent under the ostentatious but false cloak of the executive directorship of two very well-known philanthropic organisations called American Red Cross and Near East Relief. But the naked truth was that their mission was to act under the misleading cover of seemingly compassionate charity, in an artful but profit-seeking propaganda, not seen by the public, for the spread of American influence in Turkey and the promotion of American industrial products.

These three civilian passengers were each supposed to be some executive officer: the first, whose name was Claflin Davies, was supposed to be the American Red Cross representative; the second, whose name was H.C. Jacquith, bore the title of «Director» of the organisation Near East Relief; and the third was Mark Prentice, who was advertised by Bristol as his assistant representative. But in reality he was the official professional representative of the businessmen, sent on purpose on this occasion by the USA Chamber of Commerce for the still unexploited region of Anatolia. He was, bluntly, an experienced propagandist for the promotion and spreading abroad of the many varieties of industrial products of American business.

Prentice, in order to communicate freely with the interior of Anatolia, with the aim of achieving his real mission, entered as the supposed leading official of the NER organisation, on the apparent excuse of his sympathy for the tribulations being suffered by the minorities in Asia Minor. Within the short space of a week it was revealed that Prentice would also be acting as special correspondent of the famous newspaper "The New York Times», which published only the news which went hand in hand with American foreign policy, news which was supplied by the US government and which was the only permissible source of foreign news allowed by the then imposed censorship for all the American press, which was coerced into agreeing.

Prentice, following the Turkophile political line of the American government, sent news reports to America which were damaging to Greece. He echoed the completely warped Turkish propaganda, so full of lies, about the political events which were taking place. The truth about the Greek question in the Asia Minor campaign and about the conduct of the Greek army was indescribably abused by Prentice's pen.

But Bristol had taken care to ensure the sieving of the political and military news which was to be transmitted in America by means of two other well-known journalists, John Clayton and Constantine Brown, two people who were submissive to him and who fed the American press. In order to be able to extract permission from Admiral Mark L Bristol, the all-powerful US representative in Constantinople, to be able to circulate freely as journalists in the military zone, they agreed without objection to become Bristol's mouthpieces with servile allegiance to the false Turkophile orders which he gave them. But unknown to Bristol, who believed that he had achieved exclusivity in the transmission of censored military and political news which favoured America's clear interests, the dynamic correspondent for the London newspaper «The Daily Mail» was stationed on the British battleship «Iron Duke» anchored in the harbour of Smyrna, with the mission of promoting British interests.

9 September 1922

On Saturday 9 September 1922 at around eleven o'clock in the morning local time, the Turkish cavalry made its appearance at the northern part of the quay, as A.S. Merrill (who served in the American Secret Service) mentions in his report and who at that moment - as he says - happened to be in the American Consulate having discussions with the US General Consul, George Horton.

Suddenly (as he reports) piercing shrieks of mortal fear were heard outside the Consulate and down in the street where a crowd of refugees was crushed together. Surprised by the mass scream of danger, they jumped to their feet and hurried to the balcony to see what was happening. They saw a line of Turkish cavalry marching slowly along the coastal avenue towards the Military Headquarters. It was the vanguard of the Turkish army, which was following behind; the company was led by the slight but brave figure (as is emphasised by that Turkophile Merrill) of Captain Cerfedin-Bey who was splashed and painted red with fresh blood from top to toe, including his uniform. From the totally distraught crowd of refugees, who were seized with hysterical terror and who were pressed against the Consulate building «you couldn't make out even one calm face», Merrill notes in his report and continues «but the men of the cavalry took no more notice of the crowd of refugees than they would have done if they had been going along a deserted path in the hills of Asia Minor».

At the northernmost point of the quay, the sailors on the American battleship «S.S. Litchfield» which was anchored there were among those who were present as eye witnesses to the unexpected appearance of the Turkish Cavalry General Murcelle Pasha, who had been made famous «by Bristol's mouthpiece American journalists» as the man who had encircled the Greek units with lightning speed.

The following revelations are reported both in the log book of the battleship and in the depositions made later by the officers and men of the crew of the «Litchfield», the main features of which are reported as follows. The witnesses described vividly the human part of the formation: as the battalion of the Turkish cavalry marched along, with General Murcelle the leading horseman «They were covered in dust, they had a harsh expression on their faces, they were a group of men hardened by battle and steeped in the inhuman savagery of a long war. Many of the men in this cavalry had the clear north-eastern features of the Mongolian race, features unknown to the Mediterranean Sea human races, which brought to mind the far-off picture of the historic invasions of Ghengis Khan with his hordes of Mongols. The shape of their faces, their eyes, skin colour, hair and the shape of their bodies were of a type of human which was very rare in the Mediterranean part of Europe. They advanced on their horses, with their semi-curved shining swords held high and ready in their right hands trampling along the mass of those refugees who couldn't press themselves toward the wall's space being crowded already and could be pressed not any father. On their heads they wore small black fezzes, decorated with the Turkish emblem - the half-moon and star». At Konak (the military Headquarters and residency) the Turkish flag had been raised and was again flying.

At that same moment the Turks, seated on their horses with an imperious air, advanced slowly, making an impressive procession, while the unfortunate hordes of refugees who were amassed in the streets had been seized by a frantic fear and everyone, with a panic-stricken push, tried to avoid them; the military representatives of the great allied powers hurried to the Military Residency to convey to the Turks the congratulations of their nations on the glorious victory of the Turkish army against the Greeks and their wonderful tolerance towards the local Greeks and their provocative stance?

The foreign diplomatic officials of Smyrna, in their telegraphed reports to their capitals, voiced the same flattering Turkophile sentiments which the British Reverend Dobson summarised in his diary: «I felt real relief that a suitable authority had arrived in the city to take over its smooth and calm administration».

The US General Consul, George Horton, who violated the proposals and orders which he had received on this occasion, was a striking exception to the hateful flattery and behaviour which was humiliating to the dignity of all the foreigners who had responsible government posts. The correspondents of the European newspapers in Smyrna bombarded the foreign press with their telegraphed reports containing their descriptions given to them by Turkish propaganda, a string of monstrous lies which completely distorted the naked truth. Three days later they reported in their messages that the Greeks and Armenians in concert had started a fire to burn the Turkish army, that they had set up ambushes and killed Turks and that if there had been bloodshed as a result, they were the cause. In addition, the American journalists Brown, Clayton and Prentice, conforming their news reports in accordance with the authoritative orders given to them by Bristol on behalf of the State Department not to deviate from the political line followed by the US government, continued to send to the American newspapers (under oppressive censorship which was however unseen by the people) falsified reports, extolling Kemal's strategy, the amazing bravery which distinguished the Turkish units, the supposed exemplary order which they brought to and maintained in the city and the incredible tolerance (a dirty lie) which they showed to the provocations of the local Greek and Armenian populations. And a few days later, in their emphatic reports: «There was no slaughter as the Greeks and Armenians are saying». «Absolute calm and order prevails». (These utterly distorted articles and unpardonable lies are accessible to everyone today in the archives of the American newspapers, and future historians can see the false lies for themselves and put the falsified story straight).

10 September 1922

MELVIN JOHNSON, petty officer in the US Navy in his written deposition:

«As escort guard to American officials and while I was escorting Commander Halsey Powell of the battleship «S.S. Edsall», I saw mounted Turkish officers and soldiers rushing into the crowds of refugees and falling savagely on them, trampling on them with their horses with the obvious intention of killing them. Standing up in their stirrups so as to get greater force, they bent down and impaled the trampled refugees with their bayonets and with all their might, in their shoulders, their heads, wherever their bayonets fell». Melvin Johnson made this deposition on 21 September 1922.

10 September 1922

COUNT SENNI, Italian Consul in Smyrna, reveals:

(The US Vice-Consul Maynard Barnes notes in the Consulate Journal): «The Italian Consul, Count Senni, confided to me that Kemal is having in Baljova (a close-by suburb of Smyrna) a conference at this very hour with his assistants with the aim of taking a final decision on the premeditated destruction of the Armenians».

11 September 1922

MAJOR CLAFLIN DAVIS made the following deposition:

«As the only officially recognised representative of the Red Cross in Smyrna, I went in a motorboat to the British

Admiral Sir Osmond Brock as well as to the newly- arrived French Admiral Dumesnil and I asked them to mount a joint action to seize temporarily several empty cargo ships which were anchored in the harbour of Smyrna, meant for cargoes, and to save at least some of the unfortunate masses of refugees from the slaughter. Both admirals refused categorically, each saying that the orders of his government were not to seem as if they were helping the enemies of the Turks i.e. in this case, the Greek and Armenian refugees who were the enemies of the Turks».

11 September 1922

Witness official deposition of the British SERGEANT MAJOR FRIPP, guard at the British factory «Oriental Carpet Co» which was nearby the Armenian neighbordood.

«On the morning of Monday, 11 September, feeling anxious and afraid, I noticed that all the area around the carpet factory in the Armenian quarter had been surrounded by many Turkish military companies. After a short while, a crier made an announcement through a megaphone, asking all the Turks who happened to be in that area to remove themselves immediately. In the afternoon of the same day a second proclamation was made, again by a crier, which threatened that anyone harbouring an Armenian in his house would be arrested and taken immediately to a Court Martial and would be executed. Just after dusk and in the shadow of night, groups of Turks began to break into Armenian houses, to kill their inhabitants savagely and to loot their property».

11 September 1922

REVEREND HARTUNIAN writes the following in his diary:

«I myself saw, with my own eyes, today, Monday 11th of the month, Turks pouring petrol onto the houses in the Armenian quarter and setting fire to them at various points on the streets in the quarter».

11-12 September 1922

Turkish platoons, carrying out their orders, continued their inhuman work systematically in all the Armenian quarters, killing and looting. The Anglican vicar, the Reverend Dobson, writes the following in his diary: «On opening the door of my house to go over to the British Consulate, to which

I had been called because of some urgent problems for which they considered my presence necessary, I saw in front of my door and all along the row of houses in the street, between one and two hundred Armenian men tied hand and foot and thrown face down on the ground. As soon as I arrived at the Consulate, I communicated with the Red Cross and appealed for them to intervene to free the men. The person who received my message assured me that he would take every possible action. When I returned to my house the next day, exhausted after my arduous work at the Consulate, I believed that with the action of that philanthropic organisation, the unfortunate Armenians would have been freed. Drawing near however, I saw to my horror that the Armenians were still tied up but were now dead from savage sword and bayonet cuts and were rolled up in a slime of blood and mud».

11 September 1922

Bierstadt, Edward Hale, *The Great Betrayal,* pp 24-25 (See also the description of the assassination of Archbishop Chrysostomos in Padu, Rene, *«Les Derniers Jours de Smyrne»*, Societé General d'Imprimerie, Paris, 1923).

Just after midday on Monday, 11 September 1922, the Turkish High Commander Noureddin sent men to arrest the Greek Archbishop Chrysostomos and to bring him to his Residency Konak. The reverend priest arrived there separately from the Turkish escort, accompanied by a French naval detachment of 12 men. The old Archbishop ascended the stairs of the Residency with difficulty and, entering the General's office, held out his hand to greet him. Noureddin, instead of taking it, spat at him in uncontrolled anger and, showing the veneriable and eminent priest a file which was open on the table, said to him savagely: «Based on these sworn statements, the court in Ankara has already sentenced you to death. It only remains for the people to carry out this judicial decision». And shouting out with unsuppressed violence «Take yourself out of my sight!», he made a sign at the same time to the guards, who pushed the Archbishop out.

The reverend priest descended the stairs of the mansion slowly and at the same time Noureddin went out onto the balcony, shouting to the crowd of fanatical Turks who were gathered there (from a French translation): «Give him what he deserves». The savage brutality which followed is absolutely horrific. They fell upon him like hungry wolves. They put out his eyes, they cut out his tongue, his ears and his nose, they pulled out his hair and his beard in their frantic mania, they cut off his hands and did other unspeakable horrors. Then they put a chain around his butchered body, hung him on the back of a car and dragged him around the square and towards the Turkish quarters. The French marines who had escorted Chrysostomos to the Residency and who were waiting for his return, went crazy when they saw this brutal savagery. Some of them hurled themselves instinctively forward to give human protection to the victim, but the leader of the detachment forbade them to proceed. They were an insignificant minority under the circumstances and they would doubtless have met the same fate as the unfortunate Archbishop from the maniacal crowd had they thoughtlessly proceeded to take action. The French leader of the detachment himself had his pistol ready in his hand, but he was trembling from head to foot from the outrageous spectacle. One of the French naval detachment testified later, saying bitterly: «That's why we didn't dare to use our own arms». «They finished off Chrysostomos in front of our very eyes».

The savage slaughter of Chrysostomos was immediately notified to all the military and diplomatic leaders of the nations, but without any actual condemnation of the savage atrocity. The French Admiral Dumesnil was on board the newly-arrived battleship «Jean Bart», the flagship; on hearing the terrible news brought to him by his aide-de-camp, this fanatical Turkophile Catholic responded with malevolent relish to the horrific fate of the Orthodox priest in an answer which would have been worthy of a depraved mind: «He got what he deserved».

Smyrna Affair, p 120.

12 September 1922

The news that the Turks were carrying out mass murders and expurgations in the Armenian quarters reached all the foreign Christian ships which were anchored there and the leaders of the battleships of the battle fleet, so awesome to the eye, of the great Allies and of the supposedly Christian European and American naval Powers. But they gave no assistance, showing obvious ruthlessness and astounding inertia. But the unexpected juxtaposition of this brutality shook them because the bloodthirsty ferocity of the Turkish crowd also spread against foreigners. In Bournabat and Boudja, the loveliest and richest suburbs of Smyrna, the Turks brutally killed an elderly English doctor, D. Murphy, and a Dutch couple without reason or mercy, and also the nationals of other countries in other areas. At dusk on the same day, outside and around the wall of the Armenian cathedral, inside which more than a thousand terrified Armenians had locked themselves for safety, the Turks threw mortars to knock down the walls of the big church, which was built of strong stone, and to machine-gun all those who were shut inside. The bells of the Armenian Cathedral tolled sonorously, giving the desperate signal of immediate danger, to get urgent help from the four Great Christian Powers who were nearby in their fully-armed battleships. But no help was coming from anywhere!

13 September 1922

Lt Commander H.E. KNAUS of the battleship «S.S. Litchfield», Supervisory Commander of the American naval guard at various points of the city, officially responsible for the protection of US trading and industrial interests in Smyrna:

Knaus writes in his daily report of the two most noteworthy events of the day as follows: «The condition of the refugees is terribly pitiful and really tragic. The majority of them are slumped on the ground and stacked up like potatoes, absolutely terrified; they have not eaten for many days, and many of them are thirsty and have no water nearby. As soon as Turks approach, the expression on their faces shows unspeakable terror».

Smyrna Affair, pp 121,133. Malvin Johnson's report.

«After my return from the American Educational Institute for Girls and as I was driving from the quay, I found myself at a point near to a row of houses where a French officer with two sailors were standing with their backs to the wall and two Turks were aiming their guns at their chests. The officer was speaking quickly (in a language which the Turks did not understand) and was trying to gesture to them to desist from the murder. I suddenly noticed that one of the Turks, who had seen that I was watching from inside my car which was going slowly, had turned his gun on me and was taking aim. I just managed to escape an unprovoked shooting by putting my foot down on the accelerator and driving straight at him, which made him slip and fall; and the bullet, when he pulled the trigger, veered off and did not hit me. Today in my obligatory tour around the guarded area, I saw more than one hundred dead bodies.

13 September 1922

Bristol Papers

Major CLAFLIN DAVIS, deputy Director of the American Red Cross, sent the following telegram to Bristol: «The whole of a population of more than 700,000 is dying of hunger». But Bristol was unmoved by such appeals made by bodies subordinate to him, if it concerned not Turks but other races, especially Greeks and Armenians, and his usual response was total silence.

13 September 1922

MELVIN JOHNSON, petty officer in the US Navy, writes the following in his journal:

«On the orders of Captain Arthur Japy Hepburn, commander of the US naval powers there, I was on guard duty at the American Educational Institute for Girls, a well-known boarding-school in the Armenian quarter. During the night of Tuesday 12 September and after midnight before daybreak on Wednesday the 13th, I saw a big lorry approaching through the streets, which were completely deserted at that hour; it was full of iron barrels and large sacks and was going very slowly around the boarding-school building which I was guarding. I saw the driver making short stops, getting out and leaving sacks and barrels on the pavement outside the school. When the lorry driver saw that I had noticed him, he told me with a smile that he was leaving rice and potatoes for the school-children. Such generosity on the part of the Turks was difficult to believe and so, as soon as the lorry had gone, I went to examine the contents of the sacks and barrels. The sacks were full of bombs and gunpowder and the barrels contained petroleum. The Turkish intention was obvious but I could not - in accordance with my orders - leave the School unguarded at that time of night to notify the American authorities in time».

During the early hours of the morning, the wind changed to the opposite direction, from the Turkish quarters towards the city and the harbour. As Wednesday 13 September wore on, fires were started at various points of the Armenian quarter and the violent flames were rekindled by the intensity of the wind and the flammable materials with which they were fed by Turkish arson squads.

13 September 1922

«Report» by the Health Officer of the American School, M. KALFA

After one o'clock at night, the School Nurse, M. Kalfa, noticed three centres of fire in the neighbourhood, not far from the School. At midday on the Wednesday, Melvin Johnson, petty officer on the «Litchfield» and guard at the American School, called the Headmistress Miss Minnie Mills and the School Nurse M. Kalfa and, pointing through the dining-room window, said to them in fright: «Look, the Turks are starting fires»! They were going systematically from house to house, dousing them with oil and petrol and setting fire to them. At 3pm, all of the street which could be seen from the dining-room window had caught fire.

13 September 1922

A.S. MERRILL, of the American Secret Service in the service of Admiral Bristol at Constantinople, responsible for doing his utmost by intervening in any way to facilitate and promote American ambitions in Turkey.

His «Report» dated 13 September 1922 to Bristol: «No one can believe if he has not seen it with his own eyes what a timid lot all these Christian Asia Minor masses are!»

13 September 1922

«Report» of Captain ARTHUR J HEPBURN to Bristol (in Bristol Papers, USA N.A.)

«As the situation worsened, I was forced to decide on my own initiative to order the temporary requisitioning of the empty cargo-ship «Winona» which was anchored in the Gulf of Smyrna, into which I loaded approximately one hundred poor Greek-Americans with their wives and children. They were so destitute that they could not pay for their own transport. The order which I gave to the captain of the cargo-ship «Winona» was to take the cargo of refugees and to leave it at Pireus and to return immediately».

Despite the obligation imposed by the regulations of International Law to protect its own citizens from danger and to care for them, rich America, with her intense Turkophile policy, perpetrated yet another wrong in saddling poor, devastated, bankrupt Greece with undertaking the economic burden of a whole shipload of poor Greek-Americans i.e. people who were, officially because of their nationality, its own citizens and its own responsibility.

13 September 1922

Francois Zohrn, the commander of the French naval detachment supervising French garrisons at various points in the city which were placed there to protect French interests and business establishments, sets out the findings of his patrol duty in his daily report to the French Naval Authority with a hard expressive vividness as follows: «The Armenian quarter has been turned into a human slaughterhouse!»

13 September 1922

Lt. Commander H.E.KNAUS

In his daily report, he makes the following revelation: «Today was the day of the biggest slaughter in the Armenian quarter» and he continues: «The original good behaviour of the Turks to American officers is beginning to deteriorate».

13 September 1922

Recorded Nautical Diaries

The fire, which was premeditated and systematically fed with flammable materials and to which the wild roaring and blowing of the strong south-west wind contributed, spread quickly and encircled the whole city of Smyrna. There was a very dramatic exodus, full of Turkish snares, of those trapped and fire-bound inhabitants who could avoid being incinerated in the sudden embrace of the huge fire. At 8 o'clock in the evening, the whole city had been transformed into a vast and truly horrific engulfing pyrotechnic. (For additional details see the testimony of Peter M Buzanski, Chief of the British Fire Service of Smyrna, which reports the systematic frustration of his attempts to put out the fire by the continual augmentation of the flames by Turkish squads with flammable materials with which they rekindled it. Buzanski was forced to abandon his attempts to put out the fires when the Turks tried to murder him, having first terrorised his firemen and cut his fire hoses into shreds).

13 September 1922

At daybreak on the morning of Wednesday, 13 September, Dr Wilfred Post with two nurses and the necessary medical supplies, left the battle-cruiser «S.S. Lawrence» hurriedly in an urgent attempt to stop the spread of a typhus epidemic which had begun to flare up among the homeless crowds who were living under pestilential conditions. Dr Post worked with feverish activity, examining and giving medicines to the sick while, at the same time and nearby, the Turks were brutally slaughtering the Armenians in the area. Late in the afternoon, when the fire had swollen into a huge blaze and was burning the whole of the city, Dr Post continued at the risk of his own life to offer his services to the seriously sick and to ignore the orders of the commander of the «S.S. Lawrence» to go back until, on the order of their leader, the sailors carried him forcibly to a motorboat and took him back to the battleship.

13 September 1922

At 7.45 pm local time on Wednesday, 13 September and while voracious towering flames were burning Smyrna, the battleship «S.S. Simpson» weighed anchor with a terrible sound like the roar of a wild animal and a deep rattle which seemed to be coming from the depths of hell; on board were almost all the American civilian functionaries who had remained and who were serving the USA in Smyrna. The commander of the battleship waited before setting off for George Horton, the US General Consul; although the building which housed the American Consulate was surrounded by the flames of the conflagration and had begun to collapse, Horton had been absorbed in his attempt to save the terribly desperate Greeks from the brutality of the Turks, feverishly writing notes on the headed and decorated with a red ribbon paper of the Consulate in the hope that these would dupe the Turks and save from a fanatical execution those refugees who could show them.

The commander of the American naval squadron in the harbour of Smyrna, Arthur J Hepburn, impatient and anxious for the life of the General Consul, ordered a naval detachment to go to the burning Consulate and bring him out of the burning building forcibly and thence immediately to the battleship. George Horton just had time to hurriedly grab the diplomatic files of the Consulate - this was all except for a rolled-up Persian carpet, which he carried on his shoulder. He left behind in the flames a valuable collection of rare antiques which he had chosen, with remarkable financial sacrifice, over the many years of his travels around the world and which he could have saved if he had not felt in his great philanthropic mind the importance of saving people from danger of extinction and not lifeless objects, however cherished and valuable they might have been to him.

George Horton, having been brought forcibly to the battleship, looked from the deck of the «S.S. Simpson» - which set off immediately - as the huge flames which were being blown violently and ceaselessly downhill towards the masses of refugees. He saw the blazing kiln which was about to burn up a human crowd of unprotected refugees, huddled on the quay in suffocatingly dense masses, a crowd whose volume took up an area approximately two miles (3,200 metres) in length; moved to tears, he voiced his deepest feelings (which he wrote afterwards in his diary) with the following immortal truth: *«One of the most poignant impressions which I am taking with me from Smyrna is the feeling of shame that I belong to the human race»*.

Reports of JAMES WEBSTER and ENSIGN GAYLOR.

13 September 1922

At 4 o'clock in the afternoon, the flames had surrounded the American Institute and all those inside including the naval guard, but without any message or instructions from the Naval Headquarters as to what to do in such a situation. The building at this moment housed around 2,000 refugees and the situation was critical because outside the walls of the building, bomb explosions were making the ground vibrate. The order to the American naval guard came a little later after the building had already begun to burn. Ensign Gaylor drove an American lorry and ordered all the sailors and the Headmistress of the Institute, Miss Minnie Mills, to get into it; it left immediately. James Webster stayed behind with six other sailors, drew up in formation in front and told all the refugees who had been inside the building to follow them. It was only just in time as the walls of the mansion were beginning to collapse with a terrible crash, shaking the ground.

The sailors did not know which way to go to reach the coast, which was miles away. There was great confusion and Webster was forced to stop every now and then so that those following had time to keep up. The Turks were shooting and killing continuously and Webster, to stop the group getting separated, shot sporadically with his pistol protectively over their heads. It is not known how many of these around 2,000 refugees reached the coast. Here however the sailors left them in the great crowd of the other refugees. As Major Claflin Davis, the Director of the American Red Cross, testifies it was past midnight when Bristol's representative, Commander Arthur J Hepburn, was persuaded that it was illogical to continue to remain inactive on the pretext of neutrality, before the immensity of this human tragedy, and he ordered the gathering up of as many refugees as the battleship would hold. The 670 refugees whom he received that evening were transferred later to other ships and finally, when the fire had died down and the immediate danger from the flames was past, they were sent back to shore to join the crowded people who were half burned by the flames with its incinerated buildings.

Bristol Documents, in the *N.A.*

14 September 1922

Report by Lt. A.S. Merrill of the Secret Service to his superior, Mark Bristol: «I am persuaded that the Turks have burned Smyrna except for the Turkish quarters, pursuant to a predetermined and strategically organised plan for the final clearing-up of the problem of the Christian minorities by forcing the Allies to remove all the Christians from the country. I believe that the Turks are planning to attack and to capture Constantinople». It is significant that, on this one occasion, the unimaginable tragedy and distress of the refugees for a fleeting moment awoke a transitory feeling of sympathy in the torpid sub-conscious of the cold and intriguing Merrill to the degree that it militated against the directions he had been given by Bristol, that Turkophile and distorter of the truth, that it was the Greeks who had burned Smyrna, and it made him write in his report the ridiculously untrue reality about who had started the fire.

14 September 1922

The officers and sailors of the American battle-cruisers «Litchfield», «Simpson», "Lawrence» and "Edsall» testify in their sworn depositions to the slaughters and the burning of Smyrna by the Turks. Additional eye witnesses were: «Melvin Johnson; Ensign Gaylor; Officer James Webster; Lt. Commander H.E. Knaus; Dr Wilfred Post; E.O. Jacob; Director of the YMCA and Ed Fisher, Deputy Director of the YMCA; the Chief of the Fire Service, Grescovitch; Vice-Consul Park; John Kingsley Birg, Arthur C. Reed and Ralph S. Harlaw, professors at the American College, and their wives and their American staff.

14 September 1922

Major ARTHUR MAXWELL, of the British Royal Marines, watching the crowd of refugees through his binoculars from the British battleship «Iron Duke», could clearly make out people with buckets throwing a liquid over the people. In the beginning he thought they were firemen trying to put out the flames from the blazing remains of the fire which, with rushing intensity, had reached as far as the coast and was already burning the people. But with horror he noticed that, each time they poured the liquid over the refugees, there was a sudden igniting explosion of flames. «My God» exclaimed Maxwell, «they're trying to burn the refugees alive!» «The British higher government functionaries who were standing next to him, pale-faced at this horrific spectacle, agreed unanimously that they too saw this horrible holocaust of refugees taking place».

In her «witness statement», Madame K. DABANIAN, who was on the battleship «Jean Bart», the French flagship in Smyrna, saw a group of refugees assembled on the northern end of the quay who were trying to get away from the quay on a floating raft which was full to the point of suffocation; with anguish written on their faces they pushed against the stone breakwater on the shore so that their raft could leave dry land. Suddenly, Turks from the shore who were carrying a bucket full of some liquid ran and emptied it over the refugees who were huddled on the raft; then they threw a lighted firebrand into the raft which transformed the raft with explosive intensity into a terrible fireball of flames. Heartbreaking cries of «We're burning...We're burning» could be heard and these reached clearly the battleship «Jean Bart» which was anchored not far away. The officer on duty also saw the tragic spectacle; as soon as the meaning of the heartbreaking appeals «Kegomaste, Kegomaste» was explained to him in French, he was deeply moved and he wrote down the fact in the ship's log together with the other momentous events of the day, which were later rewritten in the official French archives of that period.

14 September 1922

EDWARD FISHER, Deputy Director of the YMCA of Smyrna, «testified» that the flames of the fire, which were driven by the strong blowing of the wind towards the sea and beyond the breakwater on the quay, burned the ropes with which the ships were tied up and which now swung around their anchors. After this, all the ships in the harbour removed themselves to approximately one kilometre from the seashore. At this dramatic and critical moment, most of the foreign warships, including the «Litchfield», took on board as many refugees as they could hold temporarily and until the flames of the fire had stopped; all except the American super-battleship «Arizona» and two others from the same country, which insisted on remaining «neutral» to the end.

This gesture of involuntary compassion on the part of the commanders to receive refugees for a while on their warships did not much ease the incredible pressure of the immeasurable sea of people gathered on the quay. The tragedy being played out on the seashore, with the full suffocating pressure of the enormous crowd of refugees was, according to the picture given by Edward Fisher, indescribable. The refugees lived through unspeakable moments of horror and fear when at that point, the huge flames of the fire, impelled by the violent wind towards the sea, passed over their bodies and literally roasted them alive. «They fell into the sea without knowing how to swim, they wet blankets to cover themselves with so as not to be burned alive by the flames, they hid under dead bodies; the madness of despair had seized the crowds because, on top of all these terrible things, there was the brutal persecution, the wild butchering by the Turks. They had no way of escape. On the one side, the fire which would burn them, on the other the sea which would drown them and, above all, the inhuman murders by the Turks.

14 September 1922

BARNES MAYNARD, US Vice-Consul at another building which had not yet been set on fire and who had taken over the diplomatic duties of Horton after his departure.

In his report he reveals the following: «Turkish officers and soldiers, even children 12 years of age, hurled themselves into the crowds of refugees before my very eyes and, using rifles, bayonets and even knives, killed with wild fanaticism the refugees who were huddled together on the quay». And at another point of his report: «I saw Turkish soldiers who, undisturbed, were pouring large quantities of petrol and starting fires in the road alongside and in front of the temporary Consulate; this made me throw myself with feverish speed into my responsible attempt to save the Consulate Archives. The building caught fire at exactly the same moment that the last files were being removed».

14 September 1922

Returning from Constantinople at maximum speed on the battle cruiser «S.S. Edsall», Lieutenant A.S. Merrill found that, as far as he could see, the situation was indescribably changed within 20 hours compared to how he had left it. The whole city was ablaze from the spread of the fire and the harbour was lit up as if it were daytime. The noise which could be heard was monstrously terrible: an overwhelmingly resounding mixture of noises and an uncanny acoustic mingling of echoes - the thump from the volcanic collapse of the mass of the buildings; a penetrating sound from the sudden explosive sparks being given off by the flames of the fire which was being continuously fed with explosive flammable materials carried by the special arson units; the horrid screaming of the southwest wind which echoed through the air, a screaming which came from the headlong passage of this wind through the huge flames of the blazing fire; the continual rattle of Turkish rifle-shots and machine-gun fire into the crowds of refugees; and worst of all the loud heartbreaking cries from the throats of the thousands upon thousands of refugees who were being burned by the fire and who were beseeching urgent salvation.

14 September 1922

On the bridge of the passenger-ship «Bavarian», grown men of foreign nationalities were crying emotionally on seeing this horrific spectacle of the burning mass of refugees. The English master, Captain Allan, was amazed when he saw on his ship some rich Englishmen who were known to him and who were almost naked, wearing only a fur coat or some other rough and ready covering. The richest foreign inhabitants were the most unprepared for such an unexpected catastrophe.

14 September 1922

From early in the morning, the US Vice-Consuls Park and Barnes, together with their consular assistants, noticed five units of armed Turks with bloodstained bayonets going round among the crowds of refugees and systematically gathering the men of 17 years of age and over. They put them into groups of six and sent them with an escort into the interior, using the word «deportation», but for the Turks this had the hidden meaning of «execution».

14 September 1922

Deposition by the crew of the battle cruiser «S.S. Simpson» which on the evening of 14 September weighed anchor and, on the orders of Captain Hepburn, took on board the last American civilian functionaries and their families.

14 September 1922

«From 140 miles out (259 kilometres)» reports the crew of the «Simpson», «the smoke from the fire could be seen from the Marmara Sea (Constantinople) and the gleam from the fire was very clearly visible in the evening from 50 miles out (80 kilometres). The Europeans in Constantinople thought that the smoke they could see from such a long distance away was from the eruption of some volcano in Asia Minor».

Horton writes his impressions in his revealing book *Blight of Asia* and in his *Memoirs*: «Huge sky-high flames in the shape of a horseshoe circled upwards and surrounded the vast sea of refugees on top of whom they fell like a rain of burning pieces which had broken off and had been brought with the rushing violent wind. All along the quay, a length of approximately two miles (three and a half kilometres), there was a black verge of packed masses of refugees».

14 September 1922

Captain ARTHUR JAPY HEPBURN was awakened (on the battleship) by the rattle of a loud explosion at midnight on Friday 14 - 15 September. The explosion came from a direction in front of the point where the battleship «Litchfield» was anchored far from the shore. In the morning he saw the burned and still smoking ruins of the building which housed the Customs House and the Passport Department which the Turks had blown up during the night with incendiary bombs.

15 September 1922

The Vice-Consul of Smyrna, MAYNARD BARNES, testified that he was an eye witness and was watching in person from the balcony of the temporary American Consulate while a Turkish officer, who was accompanied by an escort of fifty or more Turkish soldiers, doused the large Smyrna Customs and Passport Offices Building with petrol and burned it down with explosive bombs.

15 September 1922

Lieutenant Commander H.E. Knaus reports: «Every day they gathered up thousands of bodies (of those killed) and cremated them in a burned-out area behind the building which formerly housed the American Consulate. This macabre cremation gave out into the air a disgusting sickly smell. The smell of burning flesh can easily be recognised».

Jacob, H.O., *The Historical Reference Library*, YMCA, New York, N.Y.

«Foreign observers agree that the clear thefts carried out by groups of Turks, the heartbreaking grabbing and wresting of girls from their mothers» arms, the bestial rape of the women, the looting, the wanton destruction and ruination of everything was a freedom officially given to the Turks as a suitable reward for their great victory».

Journal of Captain J.B. RHODES on the battleship «S.S. Lawrence».

«When I awoke on the morning of Friday, 15 September 1922, after a sleep which was very disturbed by the shocking events, I noticed that the flames of the great fire had been half extinguished and were nearing their end. The whole of this beautiful city had been transformed into a horrid black charred apparition, smoking among the ruined skeletons of the once shapely buildings. Really, there was nothing left to burn».

JAMES WEBSTER, Revealing letter published in the *World Herald* of Omaha, Nebraska.

«Three quarters of the buildings of Smyrna which were in the Greek, European and Armenian quarters had become a vast mass of black skeletons which were still smoking after three days of encircling fire. Only the Turkish quarter on the hill to the North-west of the city remained untouched, as did the area around the complex of warehouses of the big foreign businesses in the French Railway network, and the enclosed area of the big American oil company Standard Oil Co. which was guarded by sentries of the American Navy until the end of the fire - these still remained untouched by the arson».

Churchill, Winston, *Memoirs. Smyrna Affair,* pp 116, 117. Hemingway, Ernest, *The Silent Procession,* et al.

Following his tremendous military victory (after a Greek collapse and rout which took place with unhoped-for ease and speed), the victor Kemal lost no time in planning his next action to complete his ulterior aims. He was aware of the profit-seeking rivalries of the victorious Great Powers and of their competitive ambitions in Turkey and he handled their conflicting interests with artfulness, playing his premeditated game with them with great adroitness and with the eastern instinctive cunning of his far-off ancestors the Huns. (Actually Kemal was not a Turk of pure blood. He was a Donmé from Salonika, which in the then official Turkish language of the area meant that he was of mixed race. He was in other words a half-caste whose father was a Turk and whose mother was a Jewess from Salonika, where he was born. He inherited from this miscellaneous atavistic mixture the eastern cunning and the savage brutality of his Turkish father and the agile dexterity of his Jewish mother. He was clever and he managed to attract the attention of the German propaganda machine and to be sent to Germany, there to study high military art). After his significant victory over the Greeks, he declared with cunning bluff that he would continue to pursue the Greeks from Constantinople to Thrace and that he would push them as far as Athens, there to impose his terms.

This proclamation kept the Allies in anxious suspense as they did not know his real intentions. But it was a cleverly thought out bluff on his part which he had unleashed deliberately to pave the way for the blackmail he was planning against the Allies. But in his innermost thoughts, Kemal had serious qualms and wondered: «Since the Allies blackmailed the Greeks (who were their allies) and stopped them from capturing Constantinople, which these same Allies themselves had jointly declared to be a «free» zone, would they allow him to take it - he who represented a Turkey which had been defeated by the Allies in the European War?

He could see clearly that it would not be desirable for the Allied Powers, whose demobilisation was by now almost complete, to fight a new war with the now victorious and triumphant Turkey, which however the same powers had armed and strengthened and which was already provocatively aggressive. But neither did he want to get involved in a war with one of them or with all of them together. But he knew well the exceptional interest of the Allied Powers in the strategic area of Constantinople, and especially in the key point of the Dardanelles and the free naval passage of the Straits through them. He was afraid that Great Britain might not hesitate to declare war on him since for her the Straits were of vital significance and importance and she might act provocatively in order to obstruct the eventuality of their being blockaded by the victorious nationalist New Turkey, And so he played his game of bluff with a cunning and very adroit hand.

With great diplomatic agility, he notified the ruling parties of the Allied Powers in Constantinople of his covert threatening bluff in an proposal which invited them to choose. They could choose to take the attractive and desired bait of peace and end the war - this peaceful choice was a definite one but it had a dual outcome. His proposal was formulated more or less like this: I am strategically obliged to finish off the war with the Greeks, to capture Constantinople and the Straits with my army and to rule and fortify them and to send my army into Thrace so as to force the government to accept my peace terms or else I will go on to take Athens; but on the contrary, I shall respect the current regime of neutrality in this area and I shall not take Constantinople, neither shall I overthrow the current situation of free navigation in the Dardanelles if the Allies accept my proposal for a compromise and act to give me Eastern Thrace, free of its current population just like the Christian minorities which remain to be finally removed from Turkey.

For some time, the Constitutional Assembly of nationalist New Turkey had declared the chauvinist principle: «Turkey for the Turks». Kemal's bluff, with its seemingly moderate demands, «succeeded» since basically the Allies won the most important part of what they wanted without a war with Turkey, a war which none of the three Allied Powers sought. Kemal felt inexpressible pleasure at the outcome of his bluff by which he got what he had aimed for without unpleasant belligerent intervention against him by the Allied Powers. The unexpectedly pleasing outcome of his bluff was especially satisfactory for his egocentricity since, although the bluff seemed to have the intention of continuing the war, his shrewd mind had never seriously thought of doing anything like that. His army was tired and exhausted and angry at the strict dictatorial discipline which Kemal enforced with execrable violence but to which the Turk, with his primitive tendency to act on his own free will, was not accustomed to submit for long. He also had to think of the very worrying desertions of soldiers which had already begun to take place.

At this point the great and shocking drama of the uprooting and flight of flocks of Greeks from Eastern Thrace begins to unfold.

Smyrna Affair pp 152, 153, 154. Hemingway, Ernest, *The Silent Procession*. Ibid: *The Wild Years*, by Harrahan, G.Z., pp 10-20 and 11-14. John, Clayton, *U.S.A.* print, Constantine Brown, *Chicago Daily News*.

The stirring drama and the unspeakable misery of the violent removal of the refugees from their houses and lands unfolded before the very eyes of certain journalists (named above); they awoke from the depths of their venal consciences and reacted against the intolerable oppression imposed on them by the State Department and by Admiral Bristol who was intimidating them and forcing them to falsify the grisly reality in their reports. But these shocking circumstances, this same reality, broke out in violent, dynamic and honest self-expression and impelled them to reveal the horrible truth.

JOHN CLAYTON wrote a report from Athens, which was sent by the battle cruiser «S.S. Simpson» in the following telegram: «Apart from the dirty Turkish quarter, Smyrna no longer exists. The problem of the Christian minorities has been solved by the Turks in this inhuman way for ever. There is no doubt about the origin of the fire. The conflagration was started by disciplined Turkish soldiers who were obedient to their leaders» it slipped easy the State Dept. vigilant press censorship because Clayton was well known to the censors of his keeping up the State Department's line of the pro-turkish policy. Clayton's report, sent in the morning from Athens, was the first tragically shocking news about the holocaust of Smyrna to arrive in America and it was published immediately. It was widely circulated both in New York by the *New York Times* and in all the other states, and it made a great sensation and produced great emotion because it overtunred all the previous false and devious reports from Turkey.

CONSTANTINE BROWN, in his report for the *Chicago Daily News*, was not far behind in disclosing and restoring the truth with his laconic description: «A crime which will mark the Turks for ever for their brutal inhumanity was carried out yesterday, when the Turkish soldiers, having firstly completely stripped the city and its inhabitants by freely killing and looting and plundering every valuable object, proceeded to start a fire all around the city and burned it».

Horton notes in his diary: «Only the destruction of Carthage (the most developed and richest city in the Mediterranean at the time) by the Romans can be compared with the devastating end of Smyrna, as regards the horror, the savagery and the martyrdom which its inhabitants suffered». And he continues: «But in the case of Carthage there was no Christian war fleet of great and strong battleships which could have given active protection but which stood by inert in the face of this ruthless, steely and powerful threat without giving help in a calamitous situation for which the governments of their countries who caused it were responsible».

Kemal's Proclamation

16 September 1922   On Saturday 16 September 1922, an official proclamation made by Kemal himself was displayed at the most obvious points of the burned city of Smyrna and was dropped from the air by aeroplanes along the quay, where the refugees had chosen to crowd together. This proclamation contained his ultimatum: «All Greek and Armenian men between the ages of 7 and 45 years are considered to be prisoners of war and will not be allowed to leave. All other refugees must have left Turkey by 1 October. All those who have not left by then will be forcibly deported to the interior». The Commander of the «S.S. Edsall», Captain Halsey Powell, who had on the orders of Admiral Bristol undertaken responsibility for protecting American interests in the area of Smyrna, says in his «report» which he submitted to Admiral Bristol: «The Turks have stated pointedly that if these people are sent to the interior of the country they will be killed. If you want to do something for the refugees, send ships and get them out of here».

Captain H. Powell, when he went to Salonica in the battleship «S.S. Edsall» loaded with Greek and Armenian children under the protection of American Organisations, asked the Greek officials there to tell him if they could send ships to the burned city of Smyrna to take refugees. The answer he received was that the Greeks would willingly send ships for this purpose if they received a guarantee that the Turks would not confiscate or interfere with them. Powell reported this statement to Bristol, asking him to ensure that the Turks would give such a guarantee. The Italian Admiral «Pepe» discussed this matter with Kemal and informed Captain Powell. On Monday 18 September 1922, Powell telegraphed to Bristol: «Kemal stated to the Italian admiral «Pepe» who was discussing this matter with him that he CANNOT take any responsibility if Greek ships are allowed to enter a Turkish port».

16 September 1922

Note written by Captain Halsey Powell in the log of the battleship of the «S.S. Edsall» when he took the children to Salonica.

«The spontaneous gratitude of the people was something I did not expect. The Harbourmaster who came onto the battleship with tears in his eyes thanked America on their behalf for her help towards his victimised and unhappy compatriots. America, he added, is the best if not the only friend of Greece; it was a very moving scene which made me feel embarrassed. From then on, this impoverished country which has been abandoned by everyone, took in every refugee from Turkey irrespective of his national origin. This expression of such great spontaneous gratitude was deeply moving both to myself personally and to all the members of the crew of the battleship».

16 September 1922

French Records.

The French admiral Dumesnil left at top speed for Constantinople on the French battlecruiser «Edgar Quinet» to communicate with the French General Pelle concerning Kemal's immediate threat, of which he had been informed during his meeting with him on the previous day, that he would march against the Allied zone of Constantinople. Kemal had already decided on this threat during his meeting with Admiral Dumesnil on 15 September 1922 in Baldjova, a suburb of

Smyrna, where Kemal was staying as a guest at the mansion of Latife Hanoum, the rich woman whom Kemal later married and divorced shortly after that. The frightened thoughts of the French admiral about the very damaging consequences for France were as follows, as he said to General Pelle: «If the obstinate British decide to stop Kemal from going on to take Chanak by fighting a stubborn battle with him, this means that Britain intends to begin a war. This will put France in a very difficult position. If Kemal is not bluffing and if he carries out his threat, this war will result in a loss of all the hard work put in over two years and of the abundant military help given by France to Kemal's nationalist movement, plus the tremendously large amount of money spent for this purpose».

18 September 1922

Article by Mark Prentice, journalist.

On 18 September 1922, in an article published by the *New York Times* and in other American newspapers, Prentice candidly revealed the following: «Many of us (journalists) have seen with our own eyes - and this is why we are certain and we can confirm it on oath - Turkish soldiers, often led by their officers, throwing petroleum over the streets and the houses». On the 20th, i.e. two days later, Mark Prentice was forced by state Dept. imposed censorship to change his tune and once again to cease his objective and candid quoting of the facts after receiving violent threats from organs of the State Department of very unpleasant consequences for himself and of being charged with militating in his articles against the official Turkophile policy of the US Government and thus endangering American interests in Turkey. The truth however continued to slip out in the various reports which were made by official naval military authorities by many serving officers in command and by other political officials. An example was the naval patrol which reported that it clearly saw a horseshoe-shaped fire, which had been started by the Turks, burning around the American College. The government of the day managed to smother all these anti-Turkish articles which had escaped the censor and which had been published and to hide them from the American public in a systematic attempt to falsify the official history of that period and to overturn the true facts by employing clever wielders of the pen. The truth is however that the articles which escaped the censor and which were published, like Prentice's report of 18 September 1922, remain and anyone can now ask for a copy. This anti-Greek policy of the US government was sustained until 1927.

18 September 1922

Jacob, H.O., *The Historical Reference Library*, Y.M.C.A., New York, N.Y.

Jacob, a former Director of this Organisation in Smyrna who was designated at that time to care for the refugees, writes in an essay, a historical document which proves the atrocious reality and which reports the historical facts as he himself saw them: «My work in bringing relief to the refugees of the burned out city forced me to leave the central point where the Organisations»s temporary offices are situated, to points somewhat removed from the coastline, to the interior, to camps of refugee prisoners who had been unspeakably badly treated. Baldjova was one of the large camps where I went with my assistants to give what little help we could at those difficult moments. There I found more than 8,000 old men, women and children, enclosed and surrounded by Turkish guards. This enormous crowd of refugees in the prisoner-of-war camp was striking for the absence of men». Some refugees who spoke English gave an account of their Odyssey. «They forced us with bayonets and whips to march from the far-off places where they had arrested us, a march of between 10 and 20 miles (approximately 16 - 32 kilometres), pushing us into various Turkish camps from where they divided us up. They separated the men and they took them away from us with a Turkish escort. The rest of us remained abandoned to the hostile fanatical mania of the military and civilian Turkish riff-raff». Jacob reports in his historic and revealing account that there was no water at the refugee camp at Baldjova and that the refugees there had eaten nothing for many days. «I shared out flour and took care to send a technician to mend the water-pump. The Turks without hindrance grabbed girls in our presence, in the camp, on the road, wherever they could find them».

18 September 1922

Report of Maynard Barnes, US Vice-Consul in Smyrna, to the State Department.

«The very torturous execution of their victims in this criminally inhuman action on the part of the Turks was done with a brutal savagery which was incredible».

19 September 1922

Report to the International Red Cross from the island of Lesvos from refugees who managed to get away from the Turkish collar and to escape at risk to their lives.

«At bayonet point and by shooting at the recalcitrant and at those lagging behind, they pushed us into the interior which stretched ahead of us and into small scattered settlements in the country areas of Mersinli and Chalkabounar. There they separated the men and took them to remote ravines from where later could be heard the rattle of intense machine-gun fire. Everyone else in our large group which remained behind understood their fate; they had killed them one after the other with bloodthirsty savagery. Some of us who had been able by trickery to save some gold sovereigns secretly bribed the guards and they let us escape; as a precaution we hid inside brambles during the day and by proceeding very carefully at night we reached the sea from which we got away. After murdering the men, they returned and grabbed most of the girls. They shut the older women and the unattractive girls inside walled areas without food, shelter or water and they died slowly of hunger and thirst».

21 September 1922

Smyrna Affair, p 169.

During the afternoon of 21 September Admiral Pepe of the Italian Navy, with the special information which he had, as a confidant of Kemal, concerning the domestic political line which the Turks would follow, was greatly shaken with fear about what was going to happen - to the point where his anxiety caused him to invite the official representatives of the Allies and of the USA to a meeting. The warning from Turkish headquarters could not have been clearer. «If the refugees have not left by 1 October, they will all be deported into the interior». There was no need to tell Admiral Pepe what «deportation» meant (to the Turks it meant death) and he called a meeting for five o'clock in the afternoon on the next day Friday 22 September on the cabin- cruiser «Galileo».

The following were present at the meeting: the Americans Major Claflin Davis, Deputy Director of the American Red Cross and Captain Arthur J Hepburn, local US representative and chosen by Admiral Bristol; and the British and French Consuls. The British and French Admirals Sir Osmond Brock and Dumesnil were conspicuous by their absence. They all agreed that the noticeable reduction in the mass of refugees, which could be seen with the naked eye, meant that large numbers had already been deported. Everyone except the French representative agreed that immediate action was an urgent necessity for the survival of the remainder.

The refusal of the French representative, who was carrying out orders and speaking on behalf of Admiral Dumesnil, was the reason why the meeting was cut short without any result but with the intention of reconvening it later. «There will be no more refugee problem to cause mental discomposure and to warrant a solution by the time we've finished our meetings» observed the Italian Admiral Pepe in an ironic tone of voice as he saw the American Commissioner Hepburn to the door. The prospect of «immediate action» seemed even more remote the next day, 23 September; Hepburn, the local head of the U.S.A. naval squadrom of battleships and representative of the US position, managed hurriedly to meet Admiral Dumesnil who told him frankly that other problems had prior importance for France at that moment and that he did not see the question of the refugees as such an urgent one. Hepburn decided to leave immediately for Constantinople and to pass the whole problem and the responsibility for it over to Bristol.

Jacob, H.O., *The Historical Reference Library,* Y.M.C.A., New York, N.Y.

In the historical documents which are kept at this library, Jacob gives an eye witness account of the most dramatic events which took place during this horrid catastrophe. He writes: «Tuesday, Wednesday, Thursday 19th, 20th and 21st September. Still no ship to take the refugees. Kemal's ultimatum, which has until 1st October, is running out. In ten days the expulsion will begin (the Turks prefer the word «deportation» for pushing the refugee mass out to the inhospitable wastelands, stony arid internal stretches of land where total destruction awaits those who have been condemned to death).

21 September 1922

Asa, Jennings, *Diary,* Assistant Director of Y.M.C.A.

«I myself saw men, women and children being flogged, robbed, shot, knifed and drowned in the sea». «Although I helped to save some, my assistance was as nothing compared to the extent of their distress and their need». «It seemed to me that the fearfulness of the events, those anguished moments when the horror of it shook them bodily, the desperate, heart-breaking screams for help which they brought out of their throats in agony would remain with me like bad dreams and would pursue me for ever».

Smyrna Affair, pp 179-185

Jennings actually saved many and he was very soon to carry out a rescue incredible in its result although, judging by his plain and insignificant appearance you would have thought that he was the last man in Smyrna to play the role of the hero, but his physical characteristics were deceptive. He was a sickly, of short stature unattractive man, about forty-five years of age, who had given up the pulpit (he was an ordained cleric of the Methodist faith from a northern part of New York State) and he did administrative work at various foreign Y.M.C.A. centres. He appeared to be a small, insignificant man, just five feet tall (one and half metres) and seemingly condemned to second-rate jobs. But as soon as he arrived in Smyrna at the end of August with his wife and two children, to be the secretary of the Y.M.C.A, the young people's organisation, Jacob and Fisher (the Director and Deputy Director), who were the administrators in charge, had left for their holidays leaving the whole administration to him. By the time the other two had returned at the beginning of September, Jennings had accepted the offer of a Greek trader who gave him his house (No 490 on the quay) which had not been burned and which was full of supplies which the Greeks had left; Jennings began to use it as a food warehouse for the refugees. When the plans of the Turks to exterminate the Christians became clear, Jennings raised the US flag on this house and began to fill it with refugees, not caring about the disapprobation of Hepburn, Bristol's general representative.

After the holocaust of Smyrna and again without any order or approval from Bristol's representatives, the political and naval leaders, Jennings quickly took over another house which had not been burned, one of the few houses which remained on the northern line of the quay, and turned the first (which also had not been touched by the fire) into an emergency hospital to which the sailors and the care workers brought pregnant women and small children who had lost their parents (there were many, according to Jennings» testimony, whose parents the Turks had killed before their eyes). The naval patrols found that it was often possible to save young girls «from a fate worse than death» by running after the Turkish officers and soldiers who were dragging them away and by insisting that these girls were their own girlfriends. It was estimated that all those who were brought to those two houses by some urgent need amounted to more than one thousand souls. Jennings named these houses «my own concentration camps». Captain Powell, who was now the appointed by Bristol new Governor in Smyrna, was less authoritarian and precise than Captain Hepburn in quibbling over the meaning of the diplomatic words «strict neutrality» and he seemed to want to close his eyes to such small philanthropic infringements. Under Powell's humane orders Jennings found the naval world exceptionally kind-hearted in every matter. «In my attempts to save people from drowning, as in many of my other actions, the navy left me free to go ahead at will. I was not even obstructed from giving orders». Jennings, a devout man, prayed for ships to be sent as did every refugee. «I did not try to obtain ships for the refugees because permission for such an attempt had not been given to me, neither had any competent Committee sought my help in this».

But on 20 September, Jennings awoke with his mind

made up to do something. As he later said: «I was seized with an irrepressible urge to save at least those people who were under my care». Thus motivated, Jennings hurried furiously to the battleship «S.S. Edsall». He writes: «I borrowed Captain Powell's motor-boat and started it up with the following earnest and encouraging exhortation of the compassionate captain: «Go and try to achieve your aim, using all the skill you have». I set off and went through the harbour with a fine-toothed comb». First he approached the French passenger-ship «Pierre Loti», but he was unlucky and received a curt refusal from the captain. He then approached the big Italian cargo steamship «Constantinapoli». To save time, instead of going up onto the ship, he stood up in the motor-boat and shouted: «Has the captain got any refugees on board?» «No» was the answer. A huge ocean-going vessel lay there empty. «Will the captain receive refugees?» The captain, whom they had called to draw near, expressed his regret. He had orders to take cargoes for Constantinople. He did not have orders to receive refugees. Jennings insisted with the question: «Can the Italian Consul here change your orders?» The captain seemed doubtful. «Has he the authority» repeated Jennings «to change your orders?» Then, with a «yes», the captain agreed that «he has». Jennings climbed on board. «Fine, I will pay you 5,000 sovereigns to take 2,000 refugees to Mytilini. I shall pay you 1,000 sovereigns more for your trouble».

Jennings worked throughout the afternoon and night to make preparations for sailing. He had to obtain permission both from the Turkish authorities and from the Italian Consul. The next morning he found that the Turks had placed two rows of soldiers from the door of the house where all the refugees who were about to leave had gathered, to the pier where the ship had tied up. «Although it had been made clear to us that no man of conscription age could hope to leave, a few tried to escape dressed as women» writes Jennings in his account. «It was heartbreaking to see the grief caused to their loved ones who were accompanying them when the Turkish scouts discovered the tricks to which their men had resorted and they pulled them off the ships for this reason». Jennings was completely exhausted when finally, in the afternoon, the ship set sail. As soon as the ship's engines were started and its propellers began to churn up the water, the refugees gathered around him on the deck. "They kissed my hands and my clothes and some grabbed me, falling prone at my feet and kissing my shoes. This demonstration moved me very greatly» he writes. «With difficulty I opened up a passage through them, tearing myself away from the adoration which the grateful refugees were expressing, and I went to my cabin, flooded with emotion; I fell onto the bed, broke down in convulsions and wept uncontrollably».

Eight days later, when the «Constantinapoli» arrived at Mytilini, Jennings was seized by another internal urge. In the harbour, even in the shadow thrown by the approaching darkness, he could make out ships. Twenty large, beautiful, empty passenger ships, moored in a line one after the other. It was the fleet which had transported the Greek army.

Before his ship had left Smyrna, Captain Powell had informed Jennings that the Italian Admiral Pepe could in the end got permission from Kemal to let Greek ships enter the port of Smyrna to pick up refugees without Turkish interference. Powell also gave him two telegrams from Major Claflin Davis, local Director of the American Red Cross. The first ordered him to get refugees out to Mytilini under the protection of the Red Cross. The other authorised him to act as he himself thought fit and according to the situation to meet «whatsoever emergency need». Using the second of these telegrams, Jennings now went to General Frangos, Commander of the Greek Army in the South and Commander of the ships in the port of Mytilini, and asked him if these ships could be sent to Smyrna. The General was willing to lend him six ships on condition that he would provide him with a written guarantee that they would be under American protection and that they would be allowed to return. Having officially delivered the refugees to the General Administrator of the island who offered to accept more, as many as he could feed, Jennings boarded the battle cruiser which had escorted him on his journey and returned to Smyrna, covering this distance by sea in less than three hours. On arriving there, he immediately got a written statement from Powell and returned at once to Mytilini and to General Frangos, who read Powell's document but who placed more difficulties in the way. The Americans offered «to escort the ships on their entrance into and their exit out of the harbour» but the document said nothing about protection in the event that the Turks attacked them.

«The Turks do not have a navy» observed the General «and they could well confiscate the ships, board them and set off to seize Chios and even Samos island and Mytilini» (two other close-by islands). «General Frangos did not believe that the Turks had given permission and he sought additional proof Jennings testified later to Commander Powell; he continues his narration: «I appreciated the logic of the general's wariness, but I felt that something had to be done immediately and I told him that I would escort the ships in person during their entrance into and exit out of the harbour. However, this was not sufficient assurance for the general».

Outside, in the vapour of the morning mist, the shape of a familiar battleship could be faintly made out. To Jennings it seemed like an American warship, but he realised that there were no American warships of large tonnage around in these waters. Someone whom he asked told him that it was the Greek warship «Cilcis». «Then I remembered that somewhere, sometime, before the war, I read that the United States of America had sold to Greece the old giant war ship «Mississippi». And now here it was under a different name and flag. «I felt a strange sort of confidence that, with the mediation of this ship, I would get help» he writes.

Jennings found the captain of the «Cilcis» willing to co-operate. «Together we phrased a message to the state authority in Athens, which the captain sent by the ship's wireless, using a cryptographic code, and which said: «In the name of humanity, give the order to send without delay the twenty ships which are moored here to pick up from Smyrna Greek and

Armenian refugees who are dying of hunger». He signed it «Asa Jennings, US citizen». Within a few minutes came back the answer with the question: «Who the devil is this Asa Jennings?» "I identified myself as the President of the US Committee for Social Relief in Mytilini. I didn't bother to explain that I was in this position solely due to the fact that I was the only American there who was arranging the transport and care and doing everything possible to save the refugees». He told an indubitable lie but it was an important one. With what real authority could Jennings have assured the Greek government that America would support Greece to the end if the need to counter a Turkish attack turned out to be unavoidable? The second question on the wireless: «Will the American warships protect the ships from such a Turkish attack and confiscation?» Jennings dodged out of this one: «There was no time to discuss the precise details of how the ships would be protected. His statement of guarantee should completely satisfy them».

But the Greek government at that moment was in a condition of great instability after the terrible domestic turmoil caused by the great national disaster of having been overthrown, just four days before, in a consolidated popular uprising which resulted in a new revolutionary military government being formed. However it was very guarded and felt intimidated by the terrible disaster caused by the Turks and it found Jennings» guarantees somewhat poor and inadequate. At four o'clock (local time) in the afternoon on Saturday, 23 September, with his communications at a completely unmanageable impasse, Jennings was in despair and his despair made him reckless: «I threw all reservations to the wind» he wrote. «And in that act, I risked everything. I sent by wireless, in code, the following threat: If I do not receive a favourable answer by six o'clock in the afternoon, I shall telegraph openly and without code in such a way that every wireless station will be able to receive my message and to publicise it: that although the Turkish authorities gave their permission and although the US Navy guaranteed the ships its protection, the Greek government stalled and would not allow Greek ships to save Greek and Armenian refugees who were awaiting death or something worse».

It was not yet six o'clock when the answer came. «Asa Jennings: all the Greek ships in the Aegean Sea have been placed under your command to transport refugees from Smyrna!» The captain of the «Cilcis» began to ask for instructions from his new commander but Jennings, now admiral of all the Greek fleet, was dazed with surprise. «The only thing I knew about ships» he wrote later «was that I get seasick on them». He came to his senses quickly however and summoned all the masters of the passenger ships to a meeting on board the «Cilcis», and discovered that ten of the ships could be ready to depart by midnight. Jennings then remembered that the admiral, as leader of the fleet, should have his flagship. He chose the ship bearing the name «Propontis», chiefly because its captain spoke a little English. «I was carried away with the pleasant surprise of thinking that my leading ship had already been selected» wrote Jennings later. «I don't know if the Greek captain realised the danger he was facing by going first into the Turkish harbour with his flagship» says Jennings in his narration. «I didn't insist on telling him all the details».

«At twelve midnight everything was ready and I ordered the Greek flag to be taken down and the US flag to be flown in its place on my ship as well as the signal flag which means «follow me» and which was flown on the rear mast. I went up to the bridge and gave the signal: «Full speed ahead». Half way along the route to Smyrna, the convoy met the battleship «S.S. Lawrence», which approached abeam and its captain asked Jennings if he would prefer to go the rest of the way on board the battleship. The truth is that Jennings was not feeling well and had symptoms of nausea and he would have preferred to board the battleship, which was more stable and faster, but glancing behind him and «seeing my nine ships following in well disciplined formation, and also with the reinforcing memory of the promise I gave to the Greek government that I shall be personally with the convoy on board the first ship, I refused the invitation and stayed on the bridge of my flag-ship».

The convoy with the frigate escort continued at full speed and without any undesirable happening to stop its onward course. When the dawn melted the shadow of darkness, every-one could see thick black clouds of smoke over their destina-tion. The smell of smoke, which was noticeable during the whole of the passage to Smyrna, became more penetrating as the sun rose behind Mount Pagos. Jennings was destined to remember this moment until the end of his life. «Straight in front of us appeared the ugly remains of the stone and brick skeletons of the previously beautiful buildings, and now they rose over the charred rubble and ruins which covered the earth. It was» he writes «the most horribly desolate and terri-ble picture I have ever seen in my life». And at the curve of the shoreline which separated the water from the land and which extended for miles, there was an uncanny something which looked like a lifeless black adjacent verge. «But I rec-ognised that the seemingly lifeless line of black which I could see was a verge not of the black remains of death but of the living victims of an unspeakable disaster who with hopes and prayers were waiting for ships....ships........ships ....». «As we approached and the length of the shore spread out before our eyes, we could clearly see every face on the quay turned towards us, every hand outstretched as if trying to bring us in as quickly as possible. The air was filled with loud voices coming from thousands of throats, voices of delight which spilled out into the air, yearning for salvation, so vibrant with the uttermost joy that the sound of them penetrated, burrowed and reached deep inside my being, touching the most sensitive chords of my spirit».

Smyrna Affair, p 186.

24 September 1922

On Sunday 24 September 1922, the curtain rose on the last act of the ghastly tragedy which was played out in Smyrna, when that small fleet of Greek passenger ships, commanded by Admiral (as he was called by the Greek authorities) Jennings, saved 15,000 old men, women and children from the hell which the once great, rich and famed city had now become. This was managed inside two endless periods of twenty-four hours (going back and fore).

Two days later, Jennings returned with seventeen ships and took another 43,000 refugees to Mytilini. A convoy of cargo ships under British charter was added on the third day in the attempt to save the refugees. By 1st October 1922 around 180,000 refugees had been taken out of Smyrna alone, according to the estimates of N.E.R. The last ship set sail from Smyrna six hours before Kemal's ultimatum deadline ran out. The insistence of the leaders of the Allies and of the Americans finally prevailed and the Turks were persuaded to extend their deadline for eight more days so that the Greek and British ships could evacuate other coastal towns where refugees had gathered. Another 60,000 refugees were taken from the coastal towns of Vourla, Tsesme and Aivali to where they had flocked in the space of two weeks. This brought the total number of refugees shipped to approximately a quarter of a million.

N.B.: The figures given by Near East Relief are a gross estimate and do not correspond to reality. A count was not taken at those very critical moments of commotion. The calculations were done by means of the weight of the cargo shown by the ship's draught, from its Plimsoll Line to the height of the water-line, which shows the water displaced by the weight of the refugees, divided by an arbitrary average weight for each passenger. But the human bodies, skeletal from weakness, starvation and the unimaginable privations of 15 days, were bodies which were amassed like amorphous piles of sardines compressed into a sardine tin can, in comparison with a human being of normal weight. A meticulous analysis leads to the irrefutable and logical conclusion that two of those skeletal, anaemic bodies together must have weighed as much as one healthy body. The systematic count which took place later in a census of the refugees who fled to Greece shows a huge comparative difference from the arithmetic totals given by Near East Relief. A conservative total exceeds one and a half million refugees, including the refugees immensely crowded and temporarily sheltered in Constantinople.

Another dramatic adventure had arisen in Greece and was being played out violently on Greek soil during the transfer of the refugees. A turbulent political lightning storm broke out suddenly, led by military officers with moral prestige; it was a spontaneous revolution against the catastrophe, so inestimable in its consequences, which the government leaders of the day had brought to the nation; the military took office in Mytilini and, four days later, annulled the Parliamentary national government in Athens. After a brief hearing in a Military Court, the Revolution shot the government royalist leaders who had contributed to the unimaginable disaster. The revolutionary government sanctioned the act of shipping the refugees and showed fraternal and compassionate care for the refugees who were very poor and sick after the horrible hardships of 15 days.

In the USA, the Secretary at the State Department urgently appointed by those ruling at the time the external affairs of America was now the well-known businessman, Charles Evans Hughes, the executive head of S.O.C. who on this occasion had resigned his post to be placed by the then U.S.A. Government Head of the State Dept. to promote its policy with the advantageous intent and purpose to protect and facilitate every U.S.A. enterprise doing business in Turkey, and who had clear and unchecked speculative ambitions in Turkey; the Turkophile Bristol in Constantinople was his meek instrument. He proved to be more of a Greek hater than the previous Secretary of State by his actions which have been officially recorded and clearly shown in history books written by internationally recognised historians. In the interim period in Constantinople, the half million or so Greeks who had fled there and who were suffocatingly stuffed into Greek houses and hotels were very agitated and afraid as they expected at any minute the capture of Constantinople by the Kemalist troops, who had already surrounded it. The disaster which befell the Greeks in Smyrna with their slaughter at the hands of the fanatical Greek-hating

Turks provoked in them a feeling of panic. They were especially terrified when it was learned that, on the previous night, the British had secretly helped Hamid, the last Sultan, to escape on board a British battleship and they took him to the island of Malta for his own safety. The Greek and Armenian traders sold off their goods for as little as was offered to raise the necessary expenses for their repatriation to Greece and fled in panic with their families. There were more than a few various foreign and Turkish speculators at that panic-stricken moment. When Bristol learned that Kemal's new nationalist government had begun to distribute guns to the local Turks, he became worried and afraid of the eventuality of mass bloodshed like that which had happened in Smyrna and he asked the British General Rumbold to reinforce the garrison inside the city from the British and French military command in the region. The commanders did in fact send some small units which remained on stand-by around the city boundaries.

26 September 1922

Bristol Documents

Admiral Bristol authorized to do so by the State and Naval Departments and sent his subordinate naval representative of the US Navy in Athens a warning telegram, the contents of which were encrypted in code, with the following order: «If the Greek authorities ask you about the extent of the naval military protection given by the US to the Greek ships which are transporting refugees, you are ordered to give them to understand that this act by the US is limited only to a favourable mediation with the Turkish authorities so as to allow the entry of Greek ships into the port of Smyrna to pick up the refugees. You will make it clear that we did not promise, I repeat, we gave NO promise of naval military protection to the Greek ships which are carrying the refugees, nor any assurance regarding the care of the refugees after their transportation».

26 September 1922

Captain Halsey Powell, Commander of the Smyrna region after the holocaust.

Powell writes in his report: «Systematic kidnapping of girls, seizure of articles which the refugees had saved and brought with them, arrests of men and even of youths whom they take every day into the interior, murders and inhuman acts - all these are being carried out continuously by the Turks. Even at the last minute, during the embarkation of the refugees onto the ships, the Turks in my presence were hitting old men, women and children in a paranoid frenzy and stealing whatever they could get their hands on. It was the greatest and most dastardly brutality and an inhuman show of criminality which was unfolding before my very eyes. They showed total indifference to the presence of Allied officers. I telephoned the Turkish Governor of Smyrna, Noureddin Pasha, and reported the events, but he showed indifference. It is clear that the tolerance shown by all their middle-ranking officers and all their officers is due to the freedom given to them by a higher authority», which was none else but Kemal himself.

27 September 1922

Certain Samaritans, by Dr Esther P. Lovejoy.

She writes with emphasis: «I am annotating my narration with extreme caution because my trust in the official history has been so shaken by the deceitful, false and manipulative descriptions which are circulating concerning the real destruction which happened at the hands of the Turks - the destruction of the Christian minorities in the whole of Asia Minor with the forbearance of the great and strong so-called Christian Powers». «Even at the last moment of embarkation of the refugees onto the rescue ships at the evacuation of the burned city of Smyrna, the Turks were inhumanly hitting out wherever they could at old men, women and children, stealing whatever they were holding with unimaginable savagery and with the brutality of rabid wild beasts - all this was before my very eyes and ignoring my presence. They bayonetted and shot at the slow-moving sick people and recalcitrant men and youths whom they grabbed and who tried desperately to slip out of their hands and to run back to their people who were waiting for them and who were crying and shouting out desperately. The greatest, most dastardly and brutal inhuman crime which the heavens have ever seen was unfolding before my very eyes».

27 September 1922

Horton, George, *Blight of Asia*, also in his *Diary*.

«Fire broke out in that ill-fated city which was systematically burned by Kemal's soldiers». And he continues: «With characteristic apathy and reluctance on the part of their crews (irrespective of whether this was intentional or unintentional), the all-powerful and supposedly Christian Allied and American warships watched with criminal inaction the most heartbreaking tragic scene of the slaughter of the inhabitants of the city and their incineration by being trapped inside the terrible holocaust of the fire; they showed a stony lack of all conscience towards the countless thousands of Asia Minor Christians. It was the most revolting feature of the whole picture».

29 September 1922

Dr Esther P Lovejoy, «*Certain Samaritans*». Captain Halsey Powell, *Commander of Smyrna after the fire*.

Dr Esther Lovejoy was the heroine of the second fateful week. She was the only American woman and one of the three doctors in that tragic disaster who offered their valuable services in the distress. The other two doctors were the English doctor Dr. Post and a surgeon of the British Navy. These three doctors were the only merciful medical unit which stayed behind and offered valuable emergency services at those most critical moments. Dr Lovejoy writes in a letter that words were inadequate to express and to describe the picture «of pain, of torment, of despair; and finally there was a horrific stony silence which surpasses the limits of despair and which cannot be expressed in words».

Marjory Housepian describes in her revealing book *Smyrna Affair* pp 191-196 that these three doctors, who stayed up to the end with the refugees, sacrificed twenty out of every twenty-four hours caring for the sick refugees, women who were giving birth and people who had sword and bayonet wounds inflicted by the Turks, and made a desperate attempt to stop the typhus and other pestilential diseases which had made an appearance and were killing off the refugees. Dr Lovejoy also describes vividly in her profound work, uncovering the bitter truth with pain and anger, how she «came up against many obstacles from Americans with official status who told her harshly that being seen by the Turks obviously helping the Christians, who were the enemies of the Turks, she was violating «American neutrality»!!! Dr Lovejoy was the last to leave on the battleship «Litchfield», trying to save two young men of 19 and 20 years old whom she smuggled onto the battleship but who were thrown off by the cruel captain of the ship when he discovered them. Her appeal to him to let them stay on board to be saved was a waste of time. The boys were educated and well-behaved and spoke English and there was no other pretext except for the unforgivable defect that they were of the Orthodox religion and Greeks. «"US neutrality" he replied to my fervent appeal "prohibits me from violating the Turkish order which forbids refugee men to leave. The law is The law...», he answered to my appeal.

This dramatic scene took place on the evening of 29 September and the ship arrived in Constantinople at daybreak on 30 September, which was also the last day of the deadline of Kemal's ultimatum for the completion of the removal of the refugees. At Constantinople, which was the battleship's final port, Dr Lovejoy set sail immediately for America to raise funds for the refugees. The tender-hearted doctor however returned to Athens and with the money which she had raised she started building the American Hospital for women in Athens, later helping with its maintenance, where thousands of poor unfortunate refugee women were treated, neither were local poor women excluded.

29 September 1922

Current History, by Abdul Hamidi, Turkish English-speaking inhabitant of New York, N.Y.

«The burning of Smyrna was the work of the Greeks» (published in this history book with the approval of the State Department, and in a plethora of other misleading and untrue accounts by means of which the then United State's leaders falsified historical fact).

4 October 1922

Bristol Documents, in N.A. *Smyrna Affair*, pp 187, 203.

On 4 October 1922, Bristol sent a verbal note to the leaders of the Greek government saying that Greece was obliged on her own to take care and to arrange for the needs of the refugees who fled there and not to expect any relief from the US, who would not bear the financial burden. In the *United States of American National Archives,* there is a classified coded telegram from Bristol to the State Department carrying a previous date in which he was at great pains to point out that, as he maintained, the creation of a precedent for other similar situations should be excluded, and that Greece should be left alone to meet the financial burden of the care and settlement of the refugees and not to expect America to shoulder it. The State Department was of the same opinion and adopted Bristol's suggestion, ordering him to announce America's decision to the Greek government.

But that pathological Greek-hater and Turkophile Bristol did not stop at this hard and unfeeling anti-Greek act. With the like-minded collaboration of his colleague Allen Dulles, (of the Secret Service of the State Department and also a hater of Greeks) he concocted and launched an officially formulated document (which was widely circulated at that time in a U-turning in policy aiming at Europe which was, for financial and business reasons, Turkophile) and which contained the unscrupulous and inhumanly sick sarcasm: "Let Greece simmer in the frying-pan in her own grease».

6 October 1922

USA National Archives (from the archives of the Minutes of Congress).

Telegram from the new Secretary of State, Charles Evans Hughes, to Bristol (US representative in Constantinople), specially marked «urgent» and with an order to send a copy to Kemal: «The State Department assures Turkey that the outrage of the American people about the supposed atrocities committed by the Turks during the fire of Smyrna has not changed the policy of friendship of the US towards the Turkish nation».

6 October 1922

The Allies, intimidated by the Turkish army which was gathered threateningly on the edge of Constantinople, were won over by the false threat expressed by Kemal that he would capture Constantinople and the Dardanelles if they did not put pressure on Greece to return Eastern Thrace to him. And to gain time from the possibility of a Turkish coup, they invited Kemal to a meeting to discuss the terms of peace. This meeting, greatly delayed by Kemal, took place at Moudania, a small coastal village, a hole in the mud, as the Allies called it, on the Marmara Sea and it lasted two days, the 3rd and 4th of October. The Allies and the US agreed to almost all of Kemal's demands in order to avoid his capturing Gallipoli, the Dardanelles and Constantinople (as he maintained) and to proceed with his army into Thrace and the rest of Greece. And although they themselves had awarded Eastern Thrace to Greece in the Treaty of Lausanne, they pusillanimously (cowardly) now in their new decision granted it to Turkey and ordered the Greek government to evacuate all of its Greek population and to cede it to Turkey.

But Kemal had no intention of starting the war he was threatening with any of the Allied Powers who all on the contrary, with cowardly compliance but also with profit-seeking expedience, showed him their obvious friendship. He realised that he would achieve his aims without a war, but he bluffed to gain time and to seek to formulate the treaty in his own way in terms whose form and extent would favour his ambitions. He could see that the apple on the tree was ripe and that it would fall into his hands, so why should he wage war? He specified expressly that, if they forced his defeated enemy to evacuate Eastern Thrace, he would not resort to military operations. And such a cruel and merciless order of betrayal was immediately sent to the Greek government by the US and the three Allies. But Kemal succeeded in doing something much worse to Christianity. On 4 October, when he convened the National Congress of Turkey in Ankara, he announced that «we must throw our enemies out of every part of our country» - he meant the permanent Christian inhabitants who were none other than the Greek and Armenians - as was said at the Congress, it was easy to make the Jews leave by means of heavy taxation which they would not tolerate.

A mass exodus of Greeks from Eastern Thrace began immediately as soon as the terms of the Treaty of Moudania were learned. Terrified by the disaster of Smyrna, the people tried to act in time to avoid something similar happening to them. Most of the inhabitants of Eastern Thrace were newly-settled peasant farmers who, within a short period of time, had transformed a barren area of heath into a breadbasket and a beautiful green paradise. The mass exodus from a piece of land with an area of eleven thousand square miles (a mile equals 1,609 metres) took place on foot due to the absence of means of transport and under unspeakably dramatic difficulties, in the rain and via almost impassable mud-tracks. It was a very hurried and heartbreaking march, similar to the agonising foot-marches of the Greeks from the interior of Asia Minor towards Smyrna.

However, more ordeals awaited the refugees in Greece. With the coming of winter, many infectious diseases appeared among those who were crowded into unhealthy places which were unsuitable for human habitation. Pneumonia, tuberculosis, malaria, infectious trachoma and manifestations of other pestilential diseases had reached epidemic proportions. These hard blows did not stop falling on the unfortunate Greece, one after the other. On 29 September 1922, plus and over those heartbreaking misfortunes the American organisation Near East Relief announced that it was stopping its aid to Greece for adult refugees and that for an indefinite short period aid would be limited to orphans.

During the continuing and ceaseless transit of refugees in December 1922, deadly diseases broke out on board the overloaded ships which were bringing the unfortunate refugees from the Pontos, the large Turkish northern region of Asia Minor which borders onto the Black Sea. A long line of ships, one after the other, was stationery off the coast under sanitary quarantine and forbidden to unload. And these ships, with their masses of refugees and with their anchor down in the rough and stormy sea, were all transmitting the same hardship signal on their wireless: «4,000 ... 5,000 ... 6,000 refugees aboard-ship, without water, without food, cruelly tormented by smallpox and typhus fever». The Greek government made an appeal to the US High Commission in Constantinople to intervene and to persuade Kemal to stop the transportation for a while «until it is practicable to disperse the crowded refugees». Up to that point, approximately one million refugees from Asia Minor had been transported; they had no shelter and epidemics had broken out and were spreading at an alarming rate.

But there was no more pity for the Greeks from the official circles in the State Department which directed US foreign policy, neither was there any sympathy for the Greek government of the day. If, they stressed flatly, the Greek government insisted on obstructing the transportation of the refugees and if these sick refugees began to gather and to mingle with healthy people in Constantinople and the areas of the Black Sea, then the Turkish government, acting «very thoughtfully» (as ruling circles in the US inhumanly stressed) would deport them to the interior of Anatolia to stop them from passing on to others the epidemics from which they were suffering.

«And everyone knows very well» stressed the American representative who conveyed the message «what the results of such a deportation mean and no reminder is necessary».

After this reaction from the US High Commission, the Greek government again convened a Council of Ministers which decided to repeal its prohibition. Since the news from Greece was not censored, the scorching reports on the imminent death of one million refugees from hunger became known throughout the world and contributed to a common outcry and anger which broke out in many social classes in certain nations and in the religious conscience of a large number of US inhabitants. This worldwide uprising pushed the State Dpt. to authorize the American Red Cross into giving three million dollars which were earmarked for six months» aid to Greece. The Red Cross and Near East Relief, both of which were semi-official organisations of the US government, in some consciously directed if doubtful and hypocritical way, seemingly unconnected with the events but deluding many ignorant people, had worked together against Greek predominance in Smyrna and had actively helped bring about the total defeat of the Greek army and its catastrophe.

In January 1923, under the direction of Dr Esther Lovejoy, the organisation «AWH» (American Women's Hospital) set up a quarantine station on the small bare island of Makronisi, where the Pontian refugees underwent a careful examination before being given an exit permit. Dr Lovejoy returned to America and collected the necessary money from contributions and fund raising activities to continue the charitable work of this Hospital for poor women - it was known by its initials AWH (the American Women's Hospital in Greece). In 1924, when the Athens Hospital was still in operation, the *National Geographic Magazine* (the organ of a large world-famous geographic organisation) published photographs of the Women's Hospital on the island of Makronisi showing historic snapshots.

On 23 March 1923 the US Red Cross notified the Greek government that it was withdrawing its emergency work from Greece. The Greek Council of Ministers, in a decision taken after a prolonged meeting, asked Dr Fridtjof Nansen, a famous Norwegian explorer who had been sent to Greece by the «League of Nations», to undertake the attempt to give aid. Nansen asked Greece's former Allies, the three Great Powers of Italy, France and Britain, to contribute aid but they all refused in turn. America had already stated its decision, in the order of the State Department to Bristol (who was the principal person who had instigated the decision when it was proposed to the US government that the Greek government should undertake all the burden of the work and the expenses of the settlement and care of the refugees in its country. And he also suggested something incredible - that American aid should change direction and should now be given to the Turks who remained behind and that the final cutting off of this aid should be announced to the Greek government.

October
1922

Congressional Records

«The Congress of the United States of America, on the strong recommendation of the State Department» and with clever excuses (their health and moral turpitude, the passing on of supposedly pestilential diseases and the moral corruption of the character of the Greeks), passed a law which excluded immigration to America for Greeks without relations there - as if Greeks had infectious leprosy or the plague or as if they were immoral and indecent debauchees. This ban, lasted until 1927 when the law on immigration was amended.

The new refugees from Thrace, most of them country people, left their vineyards, their groves of fruit-bearing trees and their wheatfields, which that year had produced an unprecedented harvest and had filled their wheat stores so that they were spilling over with the abundant amount of cereal gathered in; these resources had been produced by hard work and sweat but, in the hurried evacuation and with the lack of means of transport, they were forced to leave them behind in their rush to save their lives from the bloodthirsty Turks - understandable after the Smyrna massacre.

The French had already with obvious enmity for Greece, brought in two regiments of the brutal enemy, with total disregard for the Treaty of Moudania and trampling on its terms, using their transport ships to bring them oversea in the harbour of Alexandroupolis in Eastern Thrace to this end.

The flocks of sheep and cows went in front and the mass of refugees followed in terror. They had hand-carts, small open loaded carts, mules, donkeys and oxen and many carried on their shoulders whatever they could save of their belongings. Small children stumbled under their huge burdens and fell into the gutters which were muddy from the rains. Pregnant women were trampled in the mud, having slipped and fallen and stayed lying in the mud until the loaded oxen had passed. It was a spectacle which presented a harsh and mentally shocking picture which could have come from medieval times. It was a repetition of the exodus from Smyrna but this time the exodus seemed greater because of the sheer mass of the very hurried flight of all the inhabitants who had left simultaneously, and because of the very long lines which the crowds formed on the narrow paths in their mass tramp. On top of everything it was a season when the rains had transformed the primitive paths of Thrace into rivers of mud. The

Turks had never built roads. The Greeks had never had the necessary time at their disposal to create a road network.

The Allies, via their official representative, now got in touch with the Governor of Eastern Thrace; by an ironic accident, a very interesting and devilish coincidence under the circumstances, his name was, of all the names in the world, Xenophon (named after the general and historian Xenophon who, around 2,278 years previously, had led and saved his army who had become completely lost - the «myriad» Greeks, an army of around 12,500 to 13,000 men according to the internationally recognised historical researchers of the world-wide publication *Encyclopaedia Britannica* (1911-12)). Xenophon was informed that within a month he was obliged, in accordance with the Treaty of Moudania, to evacuate Eastern Thrace of all Greeks and to give it to the Turks. Upon this, Governor Xenophon broke out in anger and answered: «And where the devil shall I take and settle four hundred thousand people?» "That is your problem» replied the representative of the Allies with inhuman cruelty. The Thracian refugees made for Macedonia. But when journalists asked them «Where are you going?», they got the stereotyped answer: «I don't know». The instinct of survival pushed them in the direction of Greek Macedonia but they walked blindly without any plan. They did not know where they would end up, how they would be received, who would take them there, what awaited them, if they would find accommodation, food or somewhere to lay their heads. (This description comes from the famous pen of Ernest Hemingway).

20 October 1922
Ernest Hemingway, in the *Toronto Daily Star,* 2 October 1922; also in *The Wild Years*, Gene Z Hanrahan (ed), New York, 1962. Oeconomos, Lysimachos, *The Thracian Exodus, Compilation*, London, 1922.

«The Christians of Eastern Thrace walked falteringly in an endless line, making for Macedonia, crowded into the narrow dirt roads which led in that direction. The longest line which is crossing the River Maritza towards Adrianoupolis is twenty miles long (almost 32 kilometres). Twenty miles of two-wheeled carts pulled by cows, bullocks and water-buffaloes together with exhausted and stumbling men, women and children with their heads covered in blankets. They are walking blindly in the rain beside the carts which are loaded with all they could save of their worldly possessions».

There was no aid from Near East Relief All at any point of the line of refugees nor any medical help from any other philanthropic organisation, only the Greek cavalry which had also been thrown out of the region, whose cantering horses sprayed the bent figures of the refugees with mud. Immediately after the Treaty of Moudania, Turkish gendarmes moved into Eastern Thrace and took from the refugees their farm animals which they were taking with them, saying that it was against the provisions of the Treaty to take these animals with them as they had been fed and grown up in the region of Eastern Thrace and thus belonged to Turkey.

20 October 1922

Marjory Housepian, *Smyrna Affair*, pp 200 - 203.

Admiral Bristol was so angry about the so-called predatory greed with which the refugees tried to steal all the herds of cattle, fowl and other farm animals there that he promised the Turks that the Allies would do all they could, with the authority of their strength, to force the Greeks to return all the stolen cattle which they had taken in this «misappropriation» (as he rapaciously said to the Turks) during their final departure from those regions - they would force them to send them back to Turkey and to the land of Eastern Thrace where they belonged (as this was supposedly the land where they lived and which fed them)! Bristol used on the occasion ridiculously absurd lies.

20 October 1922

Barnes, Maynard, US Vice-Consul in the incinerated but now Turkish Smyrna. His message to Bristol (*National Archives of USA in Bristol Documents*).

«Our generous behaviour to Turkey, which has been lavish up to now in order to achieve the successful outcome of the Turkish national question and the warm, friendly and watchful support of America in their current vital interests have begun to bear fruit and to pay off. The Turks who are in power now actually facilitate with their clear offers of help the penetration and spread of American trade and the business operations of our compatriots; while at the same time such facilities and preferences are not being given to foreign businessmen of other nationalities».

22 October 1922

Bristol Documents, N.A.

The biggest headache faced by Bristol and by the responsible authority at the State Department which directed American foreign policy was the attempt to calm down the great excitement and vengeful anger shown by Kemal at the systematic revelations which were coming to light in articles in all the European newspapers concerning the massacre of the Christians and the inhuman savagery of the Turks and the Smyrna fire which had been started by the Turks; these events were confirmed by many eye witnesses both officially and unofficially in judicial decisions in British courts. The rulers at the State Department made desperate attempts to falsify the facts with official government statements in the Press which, by overturning the truth, maintained with total lack of conscience and without any shame that the Greeks and Armenians had started the fire, that there had been no massacre or abuse of the refugees and that many European newspapers had published fantastic and malign accounts given by the Armenian and Greek refugees who had been taken in by certain European states in which their relatives were settled and who, by means of such hostile and completely fantastic stories, tried to give the Turks a bad name and to present Turkey as being a barbarous and uncivilised country.

28 October 1922

Smyrna Affair

The Turkophile and profit-seeking policy of the State Department has remained unchanged during the period between the beginning and the end of the twentieth century. But during the second and third decades of the century, the conflicting interests of the then Allies had become so acute that they disagreed on their basic original directions and actions and each of the Allied countries secretly plotted by means of the machinating actions of their cunning double agents, each trying by acting more quickly to supplant the other. And trying their utmost by means of attractive exchanges and seductive promises, each tried to succeed in being the first to win rich privileged concessions on Turkish soil. These were concessions which they coveted to the same competitive degree and which all the Allies spared no effort to acquire, all using the same intriguing, infernal and reactionary hostile means against each other to achieve their purpose.

France and Italy had broken the united tactic which they had maintained and in reality had withdrawn from the Alliance, although formally and for the effectiveness of their own interests they continued to take part in the conferences so as to have a decisive vote in the resolutions taken by the Council. It is worth mentioning that at the Council which had been convened at Constantinople on 24 September 1922 with the aim of cooperating over the removal of the refugees before Kemal's ultimatum ran out, all sending ships for this purpose to Smyrna, both the French who were led at the conference by General Pelle and the Italians who were represented by Marquis Garroni refused any participation on the part of their nations in such a joint effort. The British and the Americans followed their example and so the urgent rescue and act of mercy was cancelled.

Those refugees who happen to be still alive have never learned that their salvation was due to a small and sickly but lion-hearted civilian named Jennings who risked his life without having been given any lead or authority but simply because of his strong and determined will and pure spontaneity, impelled by the distressing unwillingness of the Great Christian Powers to prevent the slaughter of the refugees In a spontaneous and unimaginably great bluff which he played against Athens, he terrified the choleric Greek government which was still royalist at the time and had a German dictatorial mentality and which was unmoved by the destruction of the refugees, making no attempt at this time of unimaginably urgent national need to save countless thousands of souls from a Turkish massacre; these people had been waiting with terrible mental anguish under unimaginable privations for fifteen days to be saved by ships which however were sent neither by the Greeks nor by the foreigners. A horrific misery for which the thoughtless and unfeeling policy and action of the then royalist Greek government was responsible; fortunately they believed the intimidating and threatening bluff which Jennings had let loose at them and immediately made him commander of all the available ships in Greece and made him personally responsible for bringing the refugees to Greece.

On the other hand, the Turkophile policy, so favourable to Turkey, now became obvious with the now added rich financial aid given to Turks by the charities (Near East Relief and the American Red Cross) which had already by order of the US government and with incredible lack of sentiment finally cut off all financial aid to the unimaginably pitiful misery of the Greek refugees and to refugees of other nationalities. However, in striking contrast and by order of the State Department, they made their financial resources available for the care of the supposedly suffering Turks, an act which pleased Kemal so much that he showed his favour clearly by readily agreeing to give an audience to Clayton, the then well-known correspondent of the American newspaper *The Chicago Tribune*; he assured Clayton, in answer to his question, that the oil-fields of Mesopotamia which belonged to Turkey were now accessible and available to American businesses on his order because, as he said, he recognised that America had no ambitions on Turkish land. (People had already begun to realise that America's profit-making interests had basic priority on the international scale of her aims and decisions and were more fundamental and much more pressing than any basic humanitarianism which, for the State Department, was of extremely minor importance).

Smyrna Affair, pp 203, 204

October 1922

In Athens there was no room to accommodate and house the refugees. Many of them spent the nights half-asleep on the pavements; refugees were put into all the houses which had been commandeered and into all the empty spaces. The royal palace was full to suffocation point; the refugees even went to the ruins of the Parthenon, to all the theatres, cinemas, dance and entertainment halls etc. At the National Opera every velvet carpeted box housed a large family; the orchestra pit, the stairs, the dressing-rooms, the stage and the wings and all the other areas were full of refugees who needed to rest and to sleep after the dramatic moments through which they had lived. Temporary tents were erected and they could be seen spreading out along all the coastline for kilometres. Useless abandoned vehicles had also been taken over for shelter and sleep.

With the coming of winter, this tragic situation worsened suddenly. Under such incredibly insanitary conditions, almost every refugee was ill. The image of this gloomy situation suddenly cut off and put a stop to the small amount of tourism and the small inflow of money which it brought and on which Greece was greatly dependent.

December 1922

Smyrna Affair, p 207

Faced with the tragic impasse in which Greece found itself with the sudden cutting off of American aid, the Council of Ministers of the government agreed to the «Nansen» plan for a Committee for the Settlement of Refugees under the umbrella of the League of Nations. But the US government, represented by the State Department, refused to send a delegate to this Committee; this forced the League of Nations, using the right given to it by its constitution, to make its own choice of representative and it appointed the former US Ambassador Henry Morgenthau to be President of the Committee. Morgenthau made an appeal to America and asked the American Red Cross to continue sending aid (it had cut off all aid to Greece since 29 December 1922) because, as he could confirm, the health conditions were dramatic. The State Department played its game by extracting a false answer from the Red Cross (the same government funded the Red Cross) which Allen Dulles, who had been promoted to Deputy Secretary at the State Department, notified in a dry and formal note. This answer was an irreversible decision which said, with inhuman harshness: «The situation in Greece is no longer of an urgent nature».

But Greece's urgent financial needs were extremely large. With the favourable contribution of the League of Nations, the Committee for the Settlement of Refugees could at last contract a «Refugee Loan», as it was called, at a rate of interest of eight point seven one per cent (8.71%); this was a very high rate of interest for the time and was unusually extortionate in the borrowing conditions of the financially depressed money market. There is never a shortage of lenders to take advantage of such opportunities, however. A loan paying such an exorbitant rate of interest was bound to be a success. It was oversubscribed approximately five and a half times in Athens, almost 20 times in London and at the Merchant Bank of Sprayer and Company in New York, it was completely oversubscribed immediately.

End of November 1922

«Minutes of the Conference», from the Resolutions taken by the Council in the Treaty of Lausanne.

After a delay of five years, the representatives of the Great Powers who had won the First World War gathered at Lausanne in Switzerland at the end of November 1922 to settle the terms of Peace with Turkey in a joint decision. The Conference took place at the Ouchy Hotel, near to Lake Leman, and as soon as the discussions on various matters reached the point which concerned the arrangements for those matters remaining to be decided about Greece and Turkey, the Council decided unanimously to accept the proposal of Dr Fridtjof Nansen for an obligatory exchange of Greek and Turkish minorities, but on condition that this would be mutual and under the supervision of a joint Committee appointed by the Conference of Lausanne.

Dr Nansen recommended to Greece that she should accept the proposal as it was in her interests but also because this term would force Turkey to send to Greece the countless thousands of deportees who had been sent to their deaths in the waterless wastelands deep in the interior of Turkey and the men who were being detained as prisoners of war, at least those who were still alive out of those who had been living under such inhuman and life-threatening conditions. There was also the fact that Greece was pressed by the circumstances and needed to take into her possession all the agricultural land which belonged to Turks in order to settle the refugees.

The Western Powers carried on a profitable trade with Constantinople but since this had always been controlled and distributed by Greek traders in was in their interests to agree to Greece's demand that the Greek population of Constantinople, amounting at the time to approximately 400,000 souls, should be exempted from the exchange and counterbalanced by exempting the Turks of Western Thrace. The Turks accepted this condition because, whenever they wanted to, they could easily blackmail the Greeks in Constantinople to leave Turkey by means of oppressive measures, heavy taxes or even by expulsions whenever they found some superficial illegality or something else which obstructed them in their aims or they could always fabricate a reason. (See an analytical account of the unchecked violations and infringements of the terms of the Treaty concerning the Exchange of Populations of Greece and Turkey, in the revealing work by Steven P Ladas in the publication *The Exchange of Minorities, Bulgaria, Greece and Turkey*, New York, N.Y., 1932).

The Treaty was signed after a long delay in July 1923 and the Turks, in accordance with its terms, should have left Greece by May 1923, but the Joint Committee which had been appointed at Lausanne by the jointly signed Treaty «Concerning the Exchange of Populations» did not come together in a meeting until the end of October 1923. This great delay was disastrous for Greece because the Turks had not cultivated their land in the spring or the autumn and it was winter before the Greek refugees could be settled. They found that no agricultural crops had been sown to enable them to gather in a harvest as the fields were uncultivated. But the season had passed and it was too late for them to do any sowing themselves. Another important infringement by the Turks of the terms of the Treaty of Exchange of Populations was that, apart from the women and the children, very few of the male population which had been kept in Turkey were returned to Greece. Most of these had been machine-gunned in mass executions. The few who survived this martyrdom were finally freed in January 1924.

But in addition all those who were able-bodied and useful to the Turks were kept back because they had many necessary specialisms which the uneducated Turks did not have. These people were not allowed to be repatriated and most of them eventually died there. The Committee of Exchange set up by the Treaty of Lausanne showed from the start its total inability to impose the exact performance of the terms set down. The neutral members of the Committee showed great forbearance to the Turkish violations. According to the estimates of the Committee, the total exchange amounted to almost two million people but without this number taking into account the hasty compulsion on Greeks to vacate the Turkish-held areas and the real movement and flight which took place during these five years because of Turkish blackmail and oppression.

Beginning
of 1923

Smyrna Affair, pp 212-215

For some years after the unimaginably violent destruction of Smyrna (in truth due to the Europeans and to the unscrupulousness of American capitalist profit-seeking tycoons), a desperate and truly ceaseless attempt was made, vast in its extent, to rewrite the history of the period 1919-1922 and after, up to 1927, reversing the true historical facts and refuting the publications which had been made up to then; they calculated that this would be a vital contributory factor to their plutocratic aims in Turkey.

Distinguished and well-known diplomatic and financial personalities of the day in the American political arena took part with joint and unanimous approval and like-minded cooperation in this unspeakably colossal attempt to pervert the truth. People like Warren Harding, the then President of the United States of America; Charles Evans Hughes, Secretary of State and former Executive Director of the Standard Oil Company; the Dulles brothers, Allen and Foster, those well-known

American functionaries with corrupted political consciences in regard to their adopted «immoral motto» that profiteering and philanthropy are two thoroughly incompatible things; Herbert Hoover, later President of the USA; Admiral Bristol; Richard Washburn Child, a magazine publisher who later became distinguished on the diplomatic scene and whose name became known for his vulgarity of expression at the Peace Conference (Washburn, as representative of the USA at the Peace Conference at Lausanne, Switzerland in 1923, shocked the delegates with his crude and provocatively foul mouth, making the British Foreign Secretary and respected British representative Lord Curzon shed tears when he accused and offended him with obscene barbarity of plotting with the other two war Allies (France and Italy) and of aiming, by his attempts to add terms to the Treaty which were in Britain's interests and by the final binding provisions of the Treaty, to seek to exclude the participation of the United States in the exploitation of oil and to stop the benefits to US oil companies gained from its abundant export and the profit yielded by the rich deposits found in and produced by the subsoil of Mesopotamia.

The majority of missionaries and foundations which were financed mainly by the US Treasury also took part in this attempt, as did many others in opinion-forming literary circles and in the intelligentsia. A very important role was played in this intensive attempt by the American Board of Commissioners for Foreign Missions, the then all-powerful United States Chamber of Commerce, the Standard Oil Company which, together with the three other large oil companies Sinclair, Texas and Gulf made up the United Petroleum Companies of America (at that critical time when, at the Lausanne Conference, they decided the fate of Mesopotamia and its rich oil deposits).

In charge of all these official efforts was the American Turkophile Admiral Bristol, General US representative for the Turkey which had been defeated in the First World War. He had been given a very wide jurisdiction together with the impressive title of High Commissioner that is Governor vested with broad prerogatives and a base in Constantinople. Following a clear order from the State Department which was accompanied by an unqualified approval from the US Treasury to provide the large sum of money which was needed to secure the aim of the order, he undertook in a masterly way to employ under his authority and on behalf of America, whom he represented as High Commissioner, the best-known private citizens who had the skilful writing abilities he was looking for.

To attract the naturally gifted people whom he sought, he resorted to the cunning device which attracts like a magnet and which often seduces the strongest and most resilient will. It is the trick of a provocative temptation which arouses a keen desire and which uncontrollably pushes the person into giving in to this strong mental lust. In other words, it is the very attractive bait in the trap which has been set, a bait which tempts and which instinctively pushes the person and almost always creates in him the irresistible desire to want to benefit from the situation, to exploit the wealth-producing opportunity so suddenly presented to him out of the blue to improve his living conditions from now on, to have something which he has always yearned to enjoy; such an opportunity is now presented to him in the form of a very tempting and undreamed of rich reward offered by Bristol.

In this way he achieved his ambitions and succeeded in bringing the services of a large group under the jurisdiction of his span of control, people who were available and capable of being guided, who had the specialisms which he sought and which were necessary for his purpose i.e. the cream of intellectual thought, famous men of letters, recognised historical writers and eminent journalists. These hired pen-pushers undertook an interrelated attempt to rewrite, on Bristol's orders and under his guidance, the recent history of the events which had taken place in Asia Minor between 1919 and 1922 and afterwards, but this time it was a totally falsified history, monstrously distorted and with the true events turned completely upside-down. In other words they undertook to replace the naked truth and to completely twist it with loose lies and conscienceless vile suggestions made by Bristol, the US High Commissioner, who in this action clearly supported by the State Department, was fully aware of, and lovingly contributed to all areas of Turkish propaganda with his truly monstrous lies and fully falsified depictions of those tragic and historic happenings.

All these scribblers were engaged to write, on Bristol's behalf, a narration which was completely divorced from reality and totally manipulative. It related the unspeakably bloody drama and crime against humanity but with the mastery, the persuasiveness and the elegant speech of the clever pen which can inspire people to accept the recorded events and can impart confidence in the events narrated. This can be done by someone with a charismatic, agile and experienced mind, even if he does turn the events upside down in a monstrous distortion of the truth; events which concern both the dramatic history of the Asia Minor catastrophe and the extermination for ever of Christianity from the majority of the Asian continent.

Shamelessly praising the Turks, they callously excused their acts against the Christian minorities with the elaborate persuasiveness of a completely inverted and misleading picture, something which can easily be achieved by the internationally recognised and artfully intellectual agility of the written word. They subsequently rejected the accusations made against the Turks concerning the terrible burning of Smyrna; they maintained that it was a case of shouting libel and of hateful and hostile inventions by the Greeks and Armenians who were (as they have insisted on maintaining in all their publications both then and now) the real offenders who started the fire in order to burn Smyrna and the victorious Turkish troops who were there. And on top of this they proceeded in their odious addendum to impute this insult to shame by lauding the strength and the blooming refreshing spirit of civilisation and recovery which inspires and excites the new Turkey.

The success of this giant attempt made those in charge at the State Department, whose Secretary at that time was

Hughes together with all the cooperating tycoons and businessmen at the US Chamber of Commerce, smile with pleasure at managing to change so completely the true story of the catastrophe and to turn the former severe antipathy and repugnance of American public opinion for the Turks from the nadir of their policy into a moderate sympathy. They did it with a truly abundant flood of publications, full of manipulative descriptions (in magazines, history books, accounts of so-called eye witnesses, newspaper serialisations and in the articles in the daily Press, which was being intimidated by the pressure exercised by the Secret Service which censored every publication at that time by a direct threat to remove the licence to publish in the event of recalcitrance, disobedience or nonconformity with government instructions). They did it in the widely circulated propaganda which flooded every area, a whitewash of their original feelings of hatred against the Turks for the American stance which occurred slowly in the minds of a large proportion of people.

A very helpful fact which helps us to understand the picture of the completely uncontrolled and predatory tendency of the capitalist oligarchy of that time is that the US Secretary of State, Charles Evans Hughes, was president and executive director of the Standard Oil Company of New Jersey before he became responsible for US foreign affairs. Hughes, as soon as he had successfully achieved the objectives of his capitalistic group, returned to his much more lucrative high management position, that of top executive, simultaneously taking on the presidency and the job of planning the general forward direction of the worldwide oil-exploiting business activities of the giant Standard Oil Company.

As for the seemingly irresolute stance of American public opinion, the truth is that the majority of the American people were in ignorance of the facts and in real darkness as to what really happened; apart from sporadic indications by a very few whose rebellious consciences exploded spontaneously because of the vicious suppression of the truth by the government and its total indifference to the horrific drama of Asia Minor; and apart from the reprisals and the persecutions which those few people with a conscience suffered later as a consequence of innocently and daringly revealing the truth, interpreting what they stated and writing the terrible and irrefutable truth.

Much later, however, after 1929-1930, in a harsh, crude and vulgar revelation, the unimpeachable and incontestable truth which had been hidden for so many years broke out unrestrainedly and came to light. Those who had suffered and eye witnesses who knew the terrible reality from personal experience had been kept silent until then by the fear of reprisals and of invidious persecution which had caused them to hold their tongue; these reprisals had been launched by the State Department via its executive bodies against whomsoever should contradict in their revelations the vicious and inhumanly hardhearted official foreign policy of the government (which sought to further by every means the victory and domination of the nationalist and barbaric Kemalist Turkey so that their vile profit-seeking monopolies would gain the wealth-producing concessions and other rights which they secretly sought in exchange for their effective aid). These people, unfettered now by the oppressive muzzle of fear which had kept them mute, proceeded to make sworn statements exposing horrific details which shook public opinion.

This freedom to express their opinions was achieved by a change brought about by a legal act. An incontrovertible decision was taken which was beneficial to the public and which concerned an ambiguous constitutional interpretation by the US Supreme Court in accordance with which, by an express provision in an article of the Constitution of the United States of America, all classified documents concerning historical events in the National Archives were to be made accessible to the public. From then on, the unadulterated and true portrayal of the facts which had taken place during that dramatic period of history began slowly to emerge in sworn depositions - revealing articles in newspapers and magazines, history books, newspaper serialisations and historical sources - which gave up the grisly but unfettered truth.

23
April
1923

Churchill, Winston, *Memoirs. Lausanne Treaty Records. S.O.C. Historians. Smyrna Affair*, pp 212, 214.

On 23 April 1923 at Lausanne in Switzerland, the Executive Committee of the representatives of all the Great Allied Powers of the First World War of 1914-1918 was convened to draw up the final terms which the delegates would agree should be contained in the Peace Treaty for the cessation of hostilies and the imposition of reparations on all the defeated peoples of that long and bloody war. This conference (which took place five whole years after the original conference in the town of Sevres in France in 1918, which had resulted in final decisions being made concerning the defeated peoples which were couched in widely stated terms), was one of the blackest pages in history because of the conflicting interests of the allies which had sprung up during those five years and which, with a diplomatic acidity unusual in history on the part of the representatives of their nations, resulted in a very unpleasant and bitter expression of disagreement.

The Council at the Lausanne Conference had to get down to publishing final decisions regarding the many important and pending matters which had cropped up during those five years. But the stormy discussion on the problematic question of the claim to the oil exploitation concession had priority and took up most of the time at the conference, pushing aside all other questions. A fundamental principle which prevails in western nations as far as the rate of the successive examination of each question is concerned is the degree of importance attached to each question in the scale of priorities. But the greater the theoretical show of agreement on what one nation accepts as being correct and just, in comparison with what it seeks to achieve in practice by using totally heterodox and indirect means, the greater the need for that nation to justify this contradictory policy!

Teachers of political science may maintain that morals are completely irrelevant to national interests. However experience of observing history over a long period, with the repeatedly unpleasant consequences of this tactic, condemns and emphasises this self-evident delusion, and confounds this principle.

The United States of America had sent to the conference at Lausanne three additional observers apart from their official representative: Admiral Mark L Bristol, Joseph C Grew, later Ambassador to Japan, and Richard Washburn Child, a magazine proprietor who advocated America's claims with harsh continuous monotony with the refrain «Open Doors» for oil.; the USA was governed at that time by the agents of financially predatory oligarchy. According to the annotation in the book by the English writer Harold Nicolson, Child declared harshly and abusively as far as the others were concerned that «the whole Lausanne Conference was an obvious plot planned and executed in the mould of the «tactical manoeuvres of the Old Diplomacy» to deprive American companies (S.O.C. and its US associated companies) of their oil concessions».

As the oil scandal came to light in 1924, the State Department, in a strong demand by the American government which was formulated in the Council of the 1924 conference, succeeded in *having all the intense discussions regarding the demand which were formulated concerning oil, and dissents from them, struck off from the Minutes of the conference.* After this demand all these deplorable incidents, which were so degrading to the dignity of the delegates, were struck off from the final engrossed text of the Treaty of Lausanne. But they remained in the «delegates» files and were later given to the press.

Turkey had sent as representative to the conference her Foreign Minister, Ismet Inonu Pasha, a personal friend and confidant of Kemal and a very stubborn and taciturn man. Ismet had a hearing problem and communication with him was difficult even with his personal interpreter sitting beside him. Taking advantage of his problem, he unfeelingly allowed the delegates to state the terms of the Treaty concerning Turkey again and again. His game was to make them weary and finally to give way to Turkey's claims in order to keep him quiet. He kept the delegates at the conference in a state of intolerable irritation for many days, repeating monotonously his answer that «Turkey insists on having absolute sovereignty over her nation». All the rulers of Turkey knew well the profit-seeking ambitions of the Allies for the exploitation of her lands from the abundant expressions of friendship and from the conspiracies between them for advantage and friendly preference.

On the other hand, the Allies recognised that they now had to deal with not a defeated Turkey but a proud and victorious nationalist Turkey, armed by them and ready - with the bluff which Kemal had mounted - to capture the region of Constantinople which he had already surrounded with his troops and to advance towards Greece and impose his terms when he reached Athens. The Turks knew that all the Allies had withdrawn their armies and that none of them wanted to open a war front with Turkey. For this reason the Allies, fed up with the endless delaying tactics of the Turks, gave way to their demands and softened their burdensome terms against them.

Britain, however, unyielding in her demands with her equally stubborn tactics and her equally stubborn Foreign Secretary Lord Curzon, succeeded in forcing Ismet to agree and to submit to the basic British demands with the term: Freedom to the Straits (Dardanelles) and an order for rights of suzerainty in Mesopotamia, on condition that the League of Nations would decide finally on the difference between them; the vote was in favour of Britain.

The Treaty of Lausanne finally included the decision on the exchange of populations between Greece and Turkey, the ceding of Eastern Thrace from Greece to Turkey and, in a mutual term, the exemption from this exchange of the Greeks in Constantinople and of the Turks in Western Thrace. The Treaty of Lausanne constituted a historic victory for Islamic Turkey against Christianity. But this victorious exchange was also the triumph of the shameful political and economic calculations and rich profit-seeking exchanges won by the Western Powers.

Although the State Department mobilised all the auxiliary means it had at its disposal and tried with stubborn energy and exertion to persuade the US Congress to approve and to vote for the necessary ratification of the participation in and responsibility of the USA for the terms of the Treaty of Lausanne, the majority of the American people felt a strong reaction and outrage and had formed the opinion that a real betrayal had taken place at the expense of the Christian minorities of Asia Minor; the US Congress finally prevailed and refused to vote for the ratification of the Treaty of Lausanne. Thus this treaty remained unratified and without validity for the USA.

May 1924

Dr Ralph S Harlow, Professor Emeritus of Religion at Smith College USA, lecturer until 7 September 1922 at the American College of Smyrna (in the suburb of Paradeisos) and one of the most intellectually reputable members of the teaching body; an eye witness and expert on the whole situation who, with uncontrolled and deep sadness, stated: «The American missionaries were a disgrace» with the hostile behaviour which they showed to Christianity in contrast to their friendship with the Turks and their tolerance of the crimes which they committed. «I remember» he writes «the mental ordeal I went through as the greatest disappointment of my life».

27 March 1924

Bristol Documents in the N.A.

Report by Bristol to the US Navy Department: «For two days, following the departure of the High Greek Commissioner and of the other officials from Smyrna, there was no government nor any form of disciplinary control. It was during that period that the robberies, the lootings and the murders began» *a plain outrageous lie.*

(With incredible unscrupulousness, *he shamelessly* rebufs other naval leaders and even his own trusted Lieutenant A.S. Merrill who, as has been mentioned above, stated with monumental gravity in the official reports which they submitted concerning those critical moments that, until the Turks entered the city, complete calm prevailed).

THE FOUNDATION ON WHICH
THE SUBJECT-MATTER OF DIPLOMACY IS BASED

THE ANATOMY OF A LIE

«In the size of the lie there is always contained a certain factor of credibility, since the great masses of the people will more easily fall victims to a great lie than to a small one».

ADOLF HITLER
Mein Kampf, 1937

Admiral Bristol was an enthusiastic supporter of Hitler's dogmatic principle and he put it into practice, as is proved by his above stated action and by his other actions which are exactly the same.

Man, in his strict biochemical makeup, is clearly a biologically complex biochemical group of cells, an almost perfect biological creation amongst the infinite number of other earthly creatures having material substance. Long observation of the phenomena of life confirms the fact that man has a rooted innate tendency unavoidably to manifest the devious peculiarity of almost always expressing a negative withholding or yet worst dissenting and contradictory opinion to the recorded version of an event, and this applies in the case of almost every given historical event; it is thus interesting and useful to briefly present the other side of the case with its opposing arguments.

Bristol Documents in the *US National Archives, File 867.00/1573.*

«The atrocities and brutality carried out by the Greek army against the Turks and Turkish population».

Lt Perry Report, October 24, 1922, in the *US National Archives, File 767, 68116/36.*

«The American opinion and description of the extent to which the Greeks carried out inhuman savagery and horrific barbarities against the Turks».

1924 Certain leaders of Near East Relief, the Board of Commissioners for Foreign Missions and the Armenian Atrocities Committee and prominent American leaders, in striking contrast, expressed their admiration for the Turks and made caustic comments about the Greeks. George A Plimpton (a member of the above A.A.C.) posed the following question with rhetorical pomposity: «We believe in the principle (the Monroe Doctrine) of America for the Americans; why not Turkey for the Turks?»

1924

Richard Washburn Child: *Compared Kemal's revolution against the Greeks to George Washington's against the British.*

6 December 1924

In another striking contrast, Edward Hale Bierstadt (former American executive secretary of the Emergency Legislative Committee of Congress) writes in his historical work *The Great Betrayal* that the foreign policy of the State Department under Secretary of State Charles Evans Hughes, former executive president of the Standard Oil Company, aimed at and worked on behalf of «Economic American Imperialism» in Turkey (at this dramatically critical turn of human history) and not on behalf of the human tragedies which were taking place at the time.

13 December 1924

The reputable publishing house known as the United British Press announced in writing to George Horton, former US General Consul in Smyrna, that his historical work *«The Blight of Asia»,* which refers to the catastrophes and which names the hand which destroyed towns and villages in Asia, could not be published because it was contrary to British interests.

29 December 1924

Horton, *Diary*

Eleftherios Venizelos who was appointed by the revolutionary government of Greece as Ambassador to Britain to deal with urgent Greek matters and who not long before had been Prime Minister of his country, wrote a letter to George Horton, former US General Consul in Smyrna, confirming the refusal of British publishing houses to publish his historical work *«The Blight of Asia»* and expressing his bitterness on the unusual virulence of official British circles and of the British public against Greece and on the opposition which he met in his every act concerning the crisis, so terrible from every point of view, in which Greece found herself after the catastrophe of Smyrna and the accumulation on her infertile land of the refugee of various races population, which exceeded one and a half million people.

It is amazing, he writes, that no one in Britain is now interested in Greece in spite of the fact that Britain was instrumental in getting Greece embroiled in the catastrophic for her Asia Minor's war, and for cruelly letting her defeated ignominously and whom most people have written off altogether. They have even wiped from their memories the fact that she was recently their ally. They do not even want to hear or to learn the truth about the unspeakable tragedy of Smyrna and its aftermath which are tragically incalculable for poor and bankrupt Greece. «The only burning question which is of interest today to Britain and to all her population is that of oil and of Mosul (a great station of oil-pumping facilities on which depend her battle fleet, her cocky title of Great Britain and her imposing prestige as a great naval power). Britain is now vehemently against everything which is likely to anger Turkey because the British Administration has now turned all its attention to and is first and foremost interested in safeguarding its privileges in Mosul oil. And any publication which contains a hostile shaft against Turkey or which might excite the anger of or simply displease the Turks is for Britain a undesirable work which is unsuitable at present». Horton tried to publish his deeply thought out historical work *The Blight of Asia* in Britain because with the strict and oppressive orders of the State Department and of its supervisory censoring bodies, no American publishing house would dare to undertake to publish the work and to make it available to the public.

December 1924 The epilogue to the drama of Smyrna was played out in London and in the High Court of Justice in the first week of December 1924. The American Tobacco Company had brought an action against the British insurance company Guardian Assurance Company Ltd, claiming a total of $600,000 for its tobacco merchandise which had been destroyed in the fire. The terms of the insurance policy were - in accordance with the company's Memorandum and Articles of Association - that there was a right to compensation only if the destruction of the merchandise arose from an accidental event and not as a result of a human act or negligence. The decision of the court for or against the insurance company would be very significant because, in the event of the assertion of the American Tobacco Company being accepted as proven following the bringing of evidence to the court, in other words that the fire was an accidental occurrence, claims for compensation would be made by other insured victims whereupon the total amount of compensation would rise to the huge amount of one hundred million dollars ($100,000,000); because of this possibility, Mr Justice Rowlatt of the High Court of Justice gave special attention to the evidence of witnesses.

The American Tobacco Company produced many witnesses who tried to prove that the fire of Smyrna was an accidental event and not deliberate arson by the Turks as the insurance company maintained, refusing to pay compensation for this reason.

During the bringing of evidence on behalf of the plaintiff, the American Tobacco Company, a whole series of well-known characters processed through the court as witnesses, some of whom caused hilarity in the courtroom with their clumsy and confused testimony; this caused some obvious embarrassment to Mr Wright, counsel for the plaintiff. Even the official report of Bristol to the State Department (a copy of which had been produced in court as unshakeable proof) which said: «The real picture of what is happening in Smyrna is obvious: the fire of Smyrna was an accidental event and was not started by the Turks» did not however weigh in the unprejudiced decision.

Serious eye witnesses testified in favour of the insurance company Guardian Assurance Company Ltd; these people produced entirely unshakeable evidence which was reinforced by incriminating documents and which showed that the fire of Smyrna was a premeditated act and was started in a studied plan of action by regular Turkish troops using flammable materials.

On 19 December 1924, Mr Justice Rowlatt announced his considered decision which he gave in favour of the defendant, the Guardian Assurance Company Ltd, throwing out the action of the plaintiff American Tobacco Company as not proven and as unfounded.

Melvin Johnson, *petty officer in the American Navy battle fleet, anchored in the Gulf of Smyrna at the time that the tragic developments of the horrific events of the catastrophe had been unfolding.*

He was one of the eye witnesses and the most substantial witness who, not being intimidated by the orders he had been given by the naval commanders of the American Naval squadron «not to say anything of what he had seen or heard», «to turn his head the other way and to pretend that he had not seen», had the nerve to reveal the brutal and horrid savageries which were perpetrated by the Turks and to inform humanity scrupulously and with the unadulterated harshness of reality about the pure truth.

At that very dramatic period of the terrifying savagery which broke out in Smyrna simultaneously with the invasion of the inhumanly wild Turkish army, Johnson had been given the job of supervisor at the naval security posts which protect American installations and interests. He had shouldered the responsibility at guardposts which were at key points in Smyrna and thus important for the Americans; responsibility for security at certain American institutes; responsibility for giving security cover and preventing crime as an official escort at the dangerous moments when VIPs had to pass through the masses of refugees in order to reach their destinations; and responsibility for other similar dangerous missions. Melvin Johnson spoke before a committee of writers who asked to learn the unadulterated truth about what had happened. The people on this committee managed with difficulty to find his home address; Johnson made time from his work and agreed to give them an interview. The committee found him simple and unassuming in his manners and behaviour. He related to them his personal experience of what had happened, saying to them in the following words: «Every day I saw people being killed before my very eyes - being knifed, bayonetted and butchered with a brutal savagery by wildly raging Turks, men, women and children. I could hardly take it. Do you see my hair? It's grey. I think that's what caused it. I think that these visions will haunt me to the end of my days».

1927

Bristol was officially acclaimed, as US representative in Turkey, for «his masterly!!! diplomatic activity» by the US Chamber of Commerce, by President Coolidge and by other important dignitaries in the political arena. And he was rewarded by being given the Admiralship of the US fleet in the Pacific. Up to 1932, when he retired on a big pension, he continued to talk disparagingly about the Greeks and Greece.

29 January 1971

Senator Walter F Mondale, who was later Presidential Candidate in the United States and who nearly won the election with the millions of votes cast for him, shaking the Electoral College, revealed to the American public in an official announcement on 29 January 1971 that the US gave free aid to Turkey from 1945 to 1970 (i.e. a period of over 25 years) of *five and a half billion dollars*. This was the cost to the American people, the mass one-way aid received by Turkey from the USA over that period of time. But, apart from this huge amount of aid, Turkey also received an abundant and additional inflow of many millions of dollars a year from American capital which American businessmen were continually pouring into Turkey to establish factories in order to industrialize this undeveloped country toward the end of deriving rapaciously plentiful gains.

Despite all this, Turkey did not cease officially undermining the health and the life of the American people with the thousands of tons of opium (hashish, as the Turks call it) which is smuggled into America to make a rich profit for Turkey, even though it had officially promised the United States that it would take drastic measures to stop the cultivation of the opium - poppy in Turkey. Unfortunately, the U.S.A. continues to subsidise Turkey with millions of dollars in aid every year, as well as dozens of other poor countries all over the world. But instead of the gratitude which should be due to America's generosity and an indication of their friendship, these countries maintain a hidden or even an obvious feeling of hostility and an envious reaction which manifests itself in every beneficial attempt by America to improve the standards of their deprived lives.

A great misfortune for the American people is that their political leaders who succeed each other have never learned and are not learning from their experiences that *«friendship cannot be bought with money»* (in whatever form and for whatever purpose it is given). It does not come easily to the pen to promote and to bring to historical light such a completely ungrateful reality but the writer mentions it, however sensationally darkly, as the conclusion to this work and as an unattractive fact which is difficult to believe.

Jennings of Smyrna, by William T Ellis, ed Scribner, August 1928. Also in the *USA National Archives*.

Jennings, the saviour of the wretched refugees of Smyrna, was the sensitive man who, being filled with emotion at the sudden outbreak of spontaneous and pure gratitude of the refugees, fell on his bed and wept with great sobs at not being able to take any more of the uncontrolled and ingenuous emotions of his fellow humans. The man who risked his life with the big and very dangerous trick which he played on the petulant royal government in Athens, a drastic trick which suddenly and unexpectedly resulted in his becoming the leader of the Greek fleet and was thus able, with all the available seaworthy Greek passenger ships, to transport and to save from death almost half a million refugees and, on top of this, to rescue them in a truly dramatic and very urgent situation just eight days before Kemal's ultimatum ran out. This devout and modest former cleric, whose spiritual pain had been aroused to such a degree by the unimaginable misery and the continuous violent deaths of the refugees who were being killed with such bloodthirsty savagery that he became decisive, audacious, unreflecting but under the circumstances truly a large-hearted saviour of the refugees, this Jennings, so wonderful for his spiritual virtues, did a U-turn and became progressively anti-Greek, an ending mournfully gloomy which no one could believe.

The worldwide renown which Jennings had acquired so suddenly made the infernal US Secret Service calculate that they could use his personality for their own purposes, with its glory and global fame, in the interests of their ambitions in Turkey; the US wanted to win back the sympathy of hostile American public opinion by putting into action its diabolic plan and using Jennings as its instrument on account of his good reputation.

On Bristol's suggestion, the State Department suddenly raised Jennings in an impressive promotion, making him President of an organisation which it created for this purpose - an «aid» programme. They loaded him with medals and official government documents showing the admiration, appreciation and gratitude of the American people and they turned him suddenly into a grandee with undreamed of riches and opulence.

At first Jennings resisted the temptation but as time passed and he became used to his new life of luxury, to the glory and the comfort, the large salaries, bonuses and extra perks and the free and luxurious government-provided transport placed at his disposal to go wherever he liked, his resistance to the government's suggestions lessened. In the end, Bristol's nefarious plan bore fruit: Jennings did a U-turn and flooded the State Department with letters which were favourable to the Turks, letters which were notified to all those who were opposed to the Turkophile policy maintained by the USA and this helped greatly to turn the wrathful spirits and to promote the actions and the profit-seeking ambitions of the scheming American businessmen and to increase the influence of the State Department over the rulers in Turkey. Thus Jennings progressively became hostile towards the Greeks and Greece. «Money, while never making true friendships, is doubtless *a great corrupter of consciences*».

«Fight with silver lances and you will always win» was the prophecy of the world famous in ancient Greece Oracle of Delphi to those sent by Alexandrer the Great who, following this prophecy, conquered Asia and reached a point outside the modern capital of India, New Delhi. *(Silver lances here means money)*.

«L'argent fait tout» say the French. «Money talks» say all the English-speaking peoples of the world. «If you don't» grease the wheel, it won't run» say modern Greeks. Almost every nation has a similar adage in its own language, ingrained in that immoral dogma of corruption by which you can buy off everyone and everything.

The human sense of sight (and that of hearing) is exceptionally sensitive and susceptible to external impressions and influences of the various phenomena and manifestations of life and causes humans to be easily influenced and to tend to react immediately and usually with uncontrolled haste. This imponderable and unthinking innate tendency is one of the most important human imperfections which usually leads to disheartening aftereffects with sad consequences. There are abundant examples and everyone at some point in his life feels this mental frustration.

It is possible for someone who is naturally gifted to use his charismatic and persuasive eloquence to deflect a person from the target which was his original direction and which he was aiming to achieve but which slips and gets away because of some pointless and damaging action which he later regrets bitterly. Alternatively a person may be dissuaded from his goal by gifted, skilful and diabolic acting on the part of the seducer, who weeps crocodile tears and who, by perpetrating an optical and acoustic illusion, moves the jury at the court to give their verdict in favor of him or her. Again, using more or less the same device, the seducer can influence his fellow men to support an enterprise the outcome of which is undesirable and which makes them bitter and brings them unexpected sorrow. The same thing happens in all professions and in all aspects of work and of leisure. Usually in such cases the disheartening disadvantages and vulnerable points appear unexpectedly after a while in the work they are doing or writing. In the field of intellectual pursuits, there are many badly researched historical works which are written without balanced and well-prepared groundwork. It is extremely detrimental for the credibility of the writer if his description of events is soft and imprecise owing to his being intensely influenced by his impressions at the time the incidents being depicted took place and to his being shocked by what he saw and what he heard.

Impartial critical observation and experience of life interprets war as a primitive and instinctive brutal human manifestation. In a war, excesses and savageries are committed by both opposing camps. Whoever is easily influenced by sympathies or antipathies of whatsoever form, by interests, by chauvinism or by momentary impressions is not a true historian. He shows, in his inconsistency and his shallow and easily changing spirit, a lack of profound research and crystallised conviction and he cannot give a true version of historical events. The old English historian, Arnold J Toynbee, can unfortunately be classifed in this category of historians. He is famous in Britain as the most experienced historian on Near East questions, yet who completely changed his conviction and his faith in what he had up to that time related in his historical works, being deeply influenced by the adroit propaganda of the «Red Crescent» (an organisation similar to the Christian Red Cross, *Smyrna Affair* p 62), and he rewrote the Asia Minor tragedy, completely reversing it this time.

Toynbee may be counted as a leading man of letters for the exceptionally charismatic style of his narration which distinguishes his writings and for which he became famous in Britain; but a historian - a credible, honest and irrefutable expert in research in the true and honest sense of the word - he shows, with the amazing and proven superficiality which characterises his narrations, that he is demonstrably not.

There is no room for «easy belief» in the impression created by a big famous name for the deep researcher into history, nor for all those who thirst to know the plain truth and the historical events as they actually happened. The only indicative element which is able to give the necessary genuine picture of the historical events which took place is a patient and painstaking comparison and cross-referencing with historical works which are concerned with the same historical topic but which are characterised by their profound seriousness in research and verification.

Hitler, in 1937 at a convention of his hand-picked Gauleiters (the local commanders of the Socialist Party, as Hitler called it), tried to make his men cold and unemotional in their crimes and exterminatory killings which were carried out ostensibly for the survival of the nation and the good of the party. Having in mind the planned extermination and genocide of the Jews, he referred with rhetorical eloquence, a sardonic laugh and a bitter smile to the so-called civilised human society of today in this irrefutable adage: «Who speaks today, after just half a century, of the more than half a million Armenians killed by the Turks in an extermination of their race? The world soon forgets. It remembers only the mighty ones who make History and whose name goes down for some momentous, strikingly impressive achievement». «Killing for the survival of the nation and the good of the party is not a crime but the greatest national service which can be asked of one».

It is fitting to put once again, with a suitable sardonic laugh and a wry smile, the same question to the so-called civilised human societies of today. Who still today, after seventy or more years, remembers the more than three million Christians whom the Turks exterminated? They were the final remains of the many millions of Christians who had lived in Asia Minor from the period of the Greco-Roman Empire and up to 1453. They were a Christianity which the Turks systematically destroyed from the fall of Constantinople and afterwards. Who still remembers the last vestiges who were, apart from a comparatively very few, slaughtered by the Turks?

FACT UNBELIEVABLE

NO ONE! «THEY HAVE BEEN FORGOTTEN FOR EVER»

SUPPLEMENT

IN LETTER FORM

EXTRAHISTORIC FACTS, ANCHORING
THE UNVEILED STARK EVENTS NARRATED
IN THE BOOK

«THE INFAMY OF A BETRAYAL»

WITH DOCUMENTARY PROOF OF THE REVEALING FACTS

INFORMATION, BASED STRICTLY ON SUBSTANTIATED

AUTHORITATIVE REFERENCES

EXTRA HISTORIC MOST REVEALING EVENTS

ORIGINAL AND UNRECORDED HISTORICAL FACTS
OF SPECIAL SIGNIFICANCE

PRESENTED

IN MINUTELY-EXPOUNDED DETAIL

BY THE AUTHOR

JOHN MURAT

(JEAN DE MURAT)

Jean de Murat
Miami, FL
From 7 December 1993 to 10 January 1994

MS «NANCY HORTON»
WASHINGTON D.C., 20016

Dear Ms N. Horton:

It is with great personal respect that I address myself to you, being filled with emotion. For although my desire to admit it is involuntary, yet the contents of this letter bring back to me memories of indelibly tragic moments.

I am one of the last few still living survivors of the century's greatest tragedy, of the most atrocious and brutal events of the catastrophe of Smyrna.

I am also one who witnessed for himself everything described herein or in my History books which have been published; one who at that momentous period constantly observed with his own eyes the horrible events which were occurring every single minute; one who unwillingly and with great abhorrence, was predestined to witness the unbroken continuity of the enormously frightening chain of inhumane, very ugly and sadly consequential events which were inevitable to their course and thenceforth those distressingly sudden and grave ramifications which crop up, and all those dramatic sequences which continually and spontaneously spring up after all hideous crimes.

I am now a nonagenarian but I am still keenwitted, mentally alert, and of sound mind and healthy body. Born and living in Smyrna with my parents, I went through untold suffering at the time and following the holocaust and deliberate conflagration of that great civic and metropolitan center of Asia Minor.

At this historically critical juncture I was a local, well- educated youth, seventeen years old, full of energy and living vivaciously of course.

That's why, being motivated by a keen curiosity, I was paying careful attention to what was taking place. Actually I'd actively been all around during and after the catastrophe, observing keenly the very apparent and easily distinguishable and recognisable, clearly manifested tragic occurrences which a keen eye should notice.

Namely what? «The indescribably horrible turkish brutalities». «The bloodcurdling incessant slaughtering of the refugees who were crowded into the streets». «The incredibility of the immunity from crime accorded to all the Turks by the then ultimate Turkish military source, Kemal. Total and complete immunity from punishment for the mass, ferocious tormenting of their killing at will. To their slaying any and all they wished to kill so long as the targets of their killings were their enemies, that is Asian-born Christians from the beginning of our era!» «The unimaginable asperity and pain of the tormenting torture which they inflicted on their victims with extreme pain and agony (with the utterly beastly cruelty which they inflicted upon the butchered bodies of persons who were still breathing and sensing everything» And the monstrosity of their final deed which horrified the world: «The deed, thoroughly achieved and fully realized, of completely annihilating and exterminating all the Christians of Asia Minor.» Indeed the ghastly achievement of the mass and utter extinction of Christianity on the continent of the Near East. The accomplishment of the barbarous Turks (the direct descendents of the historically noted bloody and destructive «HUNS») who from the beginning of time have aimed to finally arrive at this sorrowful end, so regretful for all Christianity.

The irrefutable documents show the real, genuinely- stated and unadulterated facts of History and have been distinguished by those few deeply knowlegeable historians who are recognized for their unbiased presentation of the actual ugly events and who do not decline to expose the bitter truth. Historians placed in the «Pantheon of History» for their *virtue of accuracy* have already substantiated the indescribable calamity before all the world, all those omissions and commissions consciously committed by the Western Powers which brought horror to the course of world events. They committed a whole series of very grave and upardonable blunders and erroneous judgments which brought about the inconceivably largest catastrophe of the century as far as *its tragic effects are concerned.*

Yet, worse than anything else, is this: The *immensely* distressing and *morally* revolting aspects of the colossal errors made by the «circles» then ruling the world - of those four great powers (France, England, Italy, and America) – which led to the shockingly loathsome carnage of all those millions of innocent Christian souls, and the ensuing tragic catastrophe of Smyrna– was knowingly and cruelly perpetrated as the *«ultimate end of human greed»*. Greed clearly expressed from their wanton haste to gain profits quickly and easily by the disgustingly used method of exploiting countries whose people were very backward people, as on this occasion was the vastly undeveloped and thus easily exploitable continent of the «Near East» (Asia), and the Turks, the majority of whom were so abysmally backward.

The intelligent and eagle-eyed Greeks and Armenians were obvious obstacles in the path of these great powers, a factor which greatly hindered their successfully achieving their long planned schemes; so they had to get them out of the way in a hurry, to dispose of them pretty-damn-quick. And so they did. How?

By supplying the initially insignificantly small band of rebels, as they were called in Constantinople by the Port (ie the only Turkish government recognised worldwide), with the essential means and methods of locking into the successful conclusion of a modern war at which they aimed, that is:

1. With an abundance of the necessary amunitions (badly needed by the rebels)
2. By initiating them into the strategic techniques of modern warfare.
3. By furnishing them with effective equipment indispensable to an up-to-date army.
4. By providing them covertly at first but later overtly with fatal secret intelligence on the intended Greek military maneuvers those officially being declared «Allies of Greece».
5. By the drastic final effect of pinpointing the entrenched Greek frontline fortifications with their airplanes.
6. By openly intervening themselves and by breaking the internationally respected and lawfully accepted regulations of the maintenance of neutrality if and when one of their supposed allies was fighting with an enemy who was friendly to them , they started bombarding the strategic nerve centres of the Greek frontline with their own planes (supposedly on loan to the Turks) and pilots.

(A French pilot's insignia had distinctly been recognized, and this fact was corroborated by Turkish captive pilots. Ninety years ago airplanes had no plastic cubicles which surrounded the pilots and protected them from sudden gusts of violent air disturbances and from the upper jet-streams. To drop a bomb accurately on the target, the pilot had to descend near to the ground at a sharp angle and almost vertical to the target. It was possible to distinguish the pilot's insignia, the type or make of the plane, and other details).

Confirming sources:

Nicolson, Harold, «History», p. 260. Lord Kinross, «Kemal's Biography», p. 235. Gibbons, H. Adams, «History», George Horton's documents in N.A. p. 452.

The shockingly criminal betrayal of Greece by her so deplorably called Allies has by now been recognised by history as a crystal-clear fact.

How was Greece caught up in this quagmire? Disheartening and disbelievable as it might seem, History was completely re-written concerning the events of the Asia Minor war.

The naked truth was badly distorted by deceitfully ridding it of all those most unethical and obnoxiousous outcomes that occurred in Asia Minor during this historically momentous two-year period. That is, those abhorrent and most repulsive events (repulsive for the duplicity, intrigue, chicanery, and betrayal which were obviously involved and easily detected) *had summarily been muzzled* by those who had the World Governing Nation's heads upper hand at the time and who therefore had the despotic power to do this.

From 1922 to about 1960, rivers of money were poured into the hands of talented, persuasive writers (who could express themselves with grace and who could affect charm) and of historians who skillfully and dexterously could change the facts of History and reconstruct it by altering all the facts which were detrimental and defamatory to the guilty persons by re-writing History the way they were told to do it. From that time on, the world book market was suddenly flooded with a profusion of books narrating the facts of the Asia Minor war with distortions and misleading events. Events were adroitly adulterated and doctored and the truth was presented with all the hideous yet real facts entirely reversed.

Yet there is a demanding and burning moral question which arises spontaneously and which must be answered: «Who were the plentiful suppliers of this unimanigable large amount of money»?

The answer is: «All those who were certain that all this *dreamt-up gold* could be had, and their dream could be realised only with *a totally independent and sovereign Turkey;*». «Not a Turkey ruled over by Greeks and Armenians».

«All those who were motivated by a very fond desire and the dreamed-of successful end towards which they were working with all the efforts and means at their disposal, both moral and immoral, in order finally to realise this dream».

«Ultimately by all those who became astronomically rich by willingly and consciously stepping on dead bodies, upon millions of corpses of innocent human beings inhumanely killed and immorally sacrificed on the altar of the Deity «gold» which they worshipped!!!».

The factual historical events are already well known. By refreshing the human memory, all still might not have been in vain.

When the First World War broke out in 1914, the great maritime powers mentioned above were entangled in a mortal struggle with the imperious Central European powers who had started the war and which in the beginning had been victorious in all the frontal battle zones, while the allied powers opposing them were badly beaten back, and in their retreat things had reached an ominous crisis.

The thus beaten back and fast retreating maritime allies all of a sudden found that they had fallen into a state of great exigency and they badly needed to find military aid as swiftly as humanly possible.

In order to hasten their efforts and to increase the possibilities of achieving the sought-after end of acquiring the urgently needed force to fight the war, they approached all those nations who were maintaining neutrality at the time and invoked them with a warm appeal. And in order to make them join their fighting alliance, they used the enticing and alluring technique of liberally promising them pie-in-the sky.

Thus Greece, being so allured, was brought out of her neutrality. She joined in and, with her mobilized army, aided the warring alliance in fighting a now common cause in many war-fronts.

However, Greece took this drastic step of abandoning her neutrality after a covenant of warranty had solemnly and irrefutably been drawn up whereby the allies promised and consented to fulfill one most justifiable and morally lawful wish of hers: «To the actual ethnic unification of Greece with the huge Greek population of Smyrna», to which the allies agreed.

From then on Greece contributed to the common cause of the alliance, that is to reach a victorious end to the war with plenty of blood and thousands of dead, maimed, and totally disabled soldiers. At that time, Greece, under a liberal administration presided over by that intelligent and charismatic politician Eleftherios Venizelos, was acclaimed as a trustworthy and faithful ally by the Powers who then needed her.

The actual events which followed are now History:

After the armistice was signed in 1918 with the defeated Central Powers and the signing of the subsequent PeaceTreaties of Sévres in 1918 and Lausanne in 1922, Greece, as was specified by certain articles in both treaties, was assigned the land of Smyrna with its surrounding area, its sovereignty to be transferred from Turkey to Greece. On February 6th 1919, Greece was authorized and even urged by Lloyd George, the Prime Minister of England, and Woodrow Wilson, the President of U.S.A. to send troops at once, to make a landing in Smyrna. This common agreement of all the allies, with the strict exclusion of Italy, (the consent of most of the allies thus to let Greece occupy Smyrna), was taken at a time when the alliance were being strongly pressed to preempt any occurrence which would be adverse to its sustained policy i.e. an imminent fait accompli plotted by and effected with sudden speed in an imperious act by a member of the alliance, Italy, who coveted and wished to grab the very same piece of Turkish territory. The occupation of Smyrna took place when the interests of the allies at that time concurred with those of Greece. Yet, very soon the picture was reversed. The fabulous gains to be acquired from profit-interests in Turkey by all the said allies, resulted in their arriving at the final conclusion that Greece had to evacuate this land and leave Turkish territory for good. And so very soon various obstacles which hindered the fighting of a successful war began to be put in the way of the Greek army, bringing it daily trouble and distress, even though it had successfully served the originally claimed ostensible vital interests of the alliance.

The harsh contrary factors and opposition tactics against the fighting Greek army (which was trying, in accordance with the instructions originally given to it, to fight the Turkish rebels and to push them out of the way) had gradually been increased to an impossible extent; to such a degree of magnitude which was no longer bearable and this brought on the collapse of the Greek army and the great catastrophe of the century.

The insensibility of all those four Governments was very callous and cruel and the high-up people in charge of those Nations lacked all moral quality. They had not even a grain of honesty to admit to being guilty of contributing with their inhumane policy to this clearly criminally-led mass human destruction of the entire extermination Asia's Christianity and this is a fact which is indeed unbelievable and deeply disheartening.

There was only one recorded striking exception; an open admission of the British Government's guilt by Lord Beaverbrook, on 8 September 1922.

At the said above date (Sept. 8, 1922, just a day before Smyrna fell to the Turks), the British Consulate in Constantinople (the Turkish capital at that time) was giving an elaborate lunch in honor of some distinguished personalities.

Among the honored guests was the U.S. High Commissioner who was stationed in the old capital city of Turkey, Admiral Mark L. Bristol, who represented the American Government in this part of the world and who pursued its policy with his foremost undertaking to influence the further-ance of avowed American interests in Turkey.

[Mark Bristol was openly characterized by the resident International Diplomatic Corps as a rabid-Turkophile. He had been in this post from the date that the Wilson Administration (with its rational views for settling world problems) was replaced by the Harding Administration in the 1919 elections, and this Administration viewed world affairs from a different perspective. The conception espoused by this Administration concerned the profitability of U.S. Foreign Affairs in this specific region: *Turkey*. The most important objective at the time, was to promote American busi-ness in Turkey and to enhance its profitability by all possible means. («The American Chamber of Commerce», and «The Council on Foreign Rela-tions» composed of leading Financiers and giant Corporations, with their great influence on the new Administration, succeeded in reversing and en-tirely revamping American Foreign Affairs on the lines of the *self-serving European «model»*. At the same time they never stopped advertising to and alluring businessmen by openly depicting Turkey as the land of limitless profits and of undreamed-of possibilities for quick gains and riches).

It therefore became crystal-clear to this Administration that American businessmen could achieve this only with a sovereign and independent Turkey which was not occupied by the Greeks. Of course this meant mak-ing an open decision against the success of the Greek war effort. And Bristol did everything possible within his power to see the Greeks de-feated].

An unexpected guest arrived at the British Consulate lunch (he was not on the official list of invited guests) and this displeased Bristol, for it thwarted his diplomatic plan to lure the British into supporting his viewpoints. (Lord Beaverbrook had been sent by the British Government to see «Kemal» and, if possible, to arrange peace terms with the Greeks).

During the lunch, there was a sudden sharp exchange of views on the critical situation of the mass and pitiful exterminating process of the Christian population from Asia Minor which was then taking place on account of the «Reign of Terror» which broke out with bloody violence by the advancing Turkish Army. Lord Beaverbrook was much angered by the evasive arguments of Mark Bristol, who was covertly supporting the Turkish side, to the point where he could take it no more and exploded, hurling at the Turkophile Bristol:

«The Greeks have had a rotten deal from us all». «They were supported by us, and we let them be wiped out by the Turks. Lloyd George backed Greece up in every way exept that he couldn't give money. And now they are left in the lurch» (it is noteworthy that Beaverbrook himself was, as he himself frankly admitted, a recognized Turkophile. But seeing the great injustice done to the Greeks, he said: *«My conscience is revolting and I am starting to go over to the other side»*). The unconscientiously callous Bristol couldn't understand this and he was puzzled by Beaverbrook's change of position.

Beaverbrook's mission came much too late and he never had a chance to act. For the very next day the great collapse of the Greek army was brought to its dramatic end. Three days after the dramatic conflagration of Smyran ensued with the inhuman crime of the mass slaughtering of the crowded thousands of unprotected refugees, lying on the streets like piles of potatoes, and the annihilation of millions of Near East Christians, something which was sought by the Turks as the final stage of their program of expunction.

It was in this way, this utterly mournful manner, that the Turks carried out the entire and complete extinction of the Christians of ancient Asia Minor, a devout people who were more than a millenium old and who were descended from the original Christian stock. Christianity was established there by Saint Paul himself and his Christian «brotherhood» and was greatly expanded by the Emperor Constantine the Great (and Saint Helen) of the Eastern Roman Empire from the year 330 A.D..

Human memory might be short-lived and may not retain even the most dreadful occurences of life for more than a brief period, but the loss of Christianity from Asia will linger for a long, long time, and the Christian religion *as a whole* will never forget the great loss.

Inconceivable and entirely incredible as it might seem, this incalculable loss took place with the tacit consent and encouragement of the all-mighty Christian Nations of the World. Anchored inside and close-by the harbor of Smyrna were twenty two (22) all powerful battleships which were dreadful to behold. The presence and threat of using this immense war-power could easily have prevented this horrible Christian annihilation and the savagely brutal catastrophe of Smyrna in a conjointly and simultaneous action. They could have nipped it in the bud simply by threatening to take severe reprisals if the Turks started to exercise any violence against the Christian populace.

Yet, instead of this, something incredible occurred. The admirals of the war-fleet, plus the commanding officers of the battleships, and the conjoined Diplomatic Corps of those most powerful Christian Nations (except for George Horton, the U.S. General Consul in Smyrna who, to his great honor and contrary to the orders he had received from Bristol, refused to submit himself and his Country to this outrageous humiliation by humbling himself to the point of offering respects to those who are devoid of any sense of respect), conjoined in a combined action went to the mansion which had been chosen as the Turkish Army command post by the arrogant and haughty-mannered Turkish generals colonels who had only just arrived, to offer the congratulations of themselves and of their Nations on the great and glorious defeat of the Greek army and to offer the friendly cooperation and help of their Nations. And also to state that they had been ordered by their Governments to remain neutral in this conflict, no matter what the situation might be. (All those Nations already had very profitable secret agreements with the now victorious Field-Marshal «Kemal», and they did not wish to jeopardise these by any act which might be offensive to him. . And the act of helping the tragically despairing Christian masses would definitely have been a repugnant action to him and would clearly have been antagonistic to his plan to eject and expunge all Christians from his land for ever. Meanwhile all the officers and the battleship-crews were standing by on board their ships watching with icy, cold and indifferent eyes the mass slaughter of the crowds on the quay which had already started; these people the masses of refugees were concentrated there because they hoped to be safe by being near to the Christian battleships; there were hundreds of thousands hardly pressed throngs of refugees, (jammed in like sardines in a can). But the men on the ships were totally deaf to the heart-rending voices which were entreating them for urgent help to save their lives from imminent death. Alas! Their sensibility, war-hardened by the vivid images of the cruel loss of their own shipmates who had been killed in action, and the innumerable enemies dispatched by the gunners of the ships' batteries, had all contributed to make them inhumanely apathetic to the century's greatest bloody carnage which was in progress.

The aforesaid joint and simultaneously declaration by the four Governments of the great Christian Powers to the victorious dictator «Mustafa Kemal» that they would not intervene in the internal affairs of his Country in whatever way he planned to shape it as an «Islamic» State, was of course a positive signal to the Turks to go ahead and start doing freely whatever they were planning to do.

Almost everybody now admits the fact that those Great Powers could easily have prevented this colossal catastrophe, but they did not do this because of the fabulous gains they hoped to realize on the consummation of this astronomically colossal «crime», so indescribable in its inhumanely effects.

The «Penal Codes» of the most highly developed and civilized Nations of the world distinctly characterize and judge a crime, not only by the one who personally commits the crime, but also by the one who could easily have prevented the execution of the crime and yet doesn't do this because he has much to gain personally from the consummation of the crime. The «Penal Code» describes him as an accomplice to the crime, accountable and equally responsible for the murder.

In accordance with this legal interpretation of the Penal Code (analytically expounded), the «criminal» *concurrence* and *equal share of responsibility* of all those Great (so called Christian?) Powers for this incalculable loss become crystal-clear. They were the principal accomplicers to blame for what actually happened by contributing with their deliberate criminal *failure,* planned for their own gain, to avert the tragic and colossal catastrophe.

Deeply disheartening as it may be to all morally honest and conscientious people, these Great Christian Powers were in dire need of war help when they were being badly beaten by the Germans in the 1914 war and were retreating on all war fronts. In order to attract the neutral countries to their alliance, (and of course their battle power), by hypocritically pretending to be utterly honest and serious, they spelled out their solemnly given promises to the world, as to what they intended to do if they were victorious. And what were their solemnly given promises? «To apply and adhere to the moral and noble tenets constituted by the globally agreed and signed Charter of the «League of Nations» What were those basic tenets to which they voluntarily and solemnly subscribed and to which they promised to adhere?

«Sovereignty for all the nations then under the Yoke of slavery». «Liberation of the ethnic minorities groaning in torment and grief». «Freedom from the bondage of oppression for all sufferers», etc. But did they ever keep and apply those promises? Never! Not one of them! Promises were quickly forgotten!!!

Greece was treated in exactly the same way. With «deceit», «chicanery», «duplicity», «treachery», «betrayal». In other words with the now widely employed by them means of getting quick success. In reality at the end of this century, these are the principles which prevail in the decadence of the permissive society and the contemporary generation. The high human values we were brought up with, those of honesty, integrity, respect, dignity, trust, truthfulness, etc., have been discarded and ridiculed by the great majority of our contemporaries. Sadly, the shallow human character is getting shallower every day.

The late Barnum, Phineas Taylor (1810-1891), intelligently and correctly diagnosed this utterly puzzling phenomenon, which he expressed in the popular vernacular peculiar to the language of his day. «A sucker is born every minute», meaning all gullible people, those human beings easily duped, those quickly persuaded by captivating slogans, with golden catchwords and phrases, enticing with mesmerizing oratory and false promises.

An anomalous fact. This proves to be a functional anomaly in the human brain. Man is expected to judge everything he is doing, to weigh up the pros and cons before he does anything; not to follow instictively like a flock of sheep or cows, nor to be influenced or affected by what the other does or says. Yet that's what is regularly observed in everyday life. Man is very susceptible to the example of others. This is a definite demonstration of the «anomaly» of his brain, as if he's devoid of intellect. This proves the surviving instict of the animal-like flocking trait of his premordial existence.

And this must be the cause of the mistakes and wrongs done by man, mistakes which he has continued to make from time immemorial.

Another anomaly of man's brain is his markedly subnormal and the functional lack of intelligence demonstrated by his ability rapidly to forget both the beneficial good he receives from his benefactor or the mortally detrimental bad he suffers at the hands of an inhuman foe. Adolf Hitler *based* his affirmation on this fact when addressing his Supreme Commanders and gauleiters in a great Nazi assembly on August 22, 1939. He tried to encourage them to forget the crimes they were committing by throwing at them the rhetorically impressive and persuasive *proverbial argument* with the question: «Who remembers today the annihilation of the half a million Armenians butchered by the Turks just a few decades ago?» (something which occurred at the end of the 19th century). And he added: «None! The world remembers only the bold and the powerful who creates «History» himself, not the weaklings!».

This anomaly and ability to forget rapidly is one of man's greatest moral deficiencies; it hurts badly and almost kills the kindness and benevolence of the people who are desirous of doing good to their fellow-men. That is why many consider this moral deficiency of «ingratitude» a crime which kills man's noblest sentiments.

To confine ourselves to facts, this is clearly manifested and proven in the case of Greece. Throughout its History, Greeks persecuted, maligned, and condemned all its great men. During this century they twice tried to assassinate Eleftherios Venizelos, one of her great men, who had succeeded in reviving the old forgotten name and who, for a short while, almost managed to bring back the erstwhile glory of Greece. Yet the ever ungrateful Greeks not only voted him out of the post of leader of Greece but also tried to assassinate him for a second time. Then Greece, defeated and thrown into abysmal poverty and misery, again remembered this great man and its people prayed him to represent Greece in London, England, as the ambassador of Greece (he was living at the time in self-imposed exile in England, to get away from the assassins). They wanted him to try his best, with his charismatic personality, to exert his influence upon his old political friends to do whatever good he could for the horribly defeated, greatly impoverished and bankrupt Greece. Yet the political climate had entirely changed by that time (1923), and the situation with the then governing Tory regime was openly anti-Greek. As Winston Churchill reveals in his papers («Memoirs» etc.), the British people had lost any sympathy for Greece. As he unceremoniously writes: «For the average Englishman, it came to be repulsive even to hear the word «Greece» being spelt». They'd already ungratefully forgotten that the Greek army had saved the British garrison in the «Chanack Affair» from being annihilated by the Turks of «Kemal's» army. They'd forgotten that the Greek army was almost pushed into its precipitous landing in Smyrna, because at that point the Briitish Empire wanted to keep intact its naval hegemony in the Mediterranean sea and to preclude any other power from usurping it.

Man's ingratitude is proverbial, epigrammatically so in regard to the extent of its truthfulness.

The then ambassador of his Country and former Prime Minister of Greece, Eleftherios Venizelos, knew George Horton personally and had great esteem and admiration for him as an exceptionally knowlegeable man, a person of high moral character, as well a worshipper of the classical intellectual works of the ancient Greeks. George Horton, on the other hand, nursed almost the same sentiments for this charismatic politician. In other words there existed between them a mutual respect, a genuine friendship and a true understanding.

Eleftherios Venizelos had read George Horton's very weighty, tremendously important and truly penetrating manuscript «The Blight of Asia». As a resident of London (on account of his Ambassadorship), he volunteered to make an effort to see his friend's book published in England. George Horton gratefully accepted the service so courteously offered to him by Eleftherios Venizelos, a courtesy much more welcome because his diplomatic duties deprived him of the necessary time to search for himself and to track down a well recognized and reliable publisher.

Eleftherios Venizelos tried his best both by himself and through his influential British friends in England, but with disheartening results. He finally addressed a letter to his friend (it is saved and kept in George Horton's historical papers), in which he reveals to him the following unknown facts:

«In Britain everybody right now is preoccupied with the on-going task of achieving the acquisition of petroleum and the *oil-wells* of Mesopotamia in a land presently under Turkish sovereignty - this is the most important thing for England's fleet («rule the waves»). «I find it very surprising that the general consideration prevailing in everybody's thought right now is to carefully avoid offending or provoking the ire of Turkey; England is now sparing no effort, overt or covert, to keep on good friendly terms with Turkey, with the aim and end view of obtaining an exclusive monopoly to exploit the oil-rich Turkish lands of the fields of Palestine (the three great allied powers of France, the USA and Italy also coveted this monopoly and they intrigued towards the same end). For this unique reason, one which was presently occupying every mind in England, no publisher in the entire United Kingdom of Britishers has agreed to publish your book «*The Blight of Asia*», for they consider its contents offensive to the Turks».

The absolute dominance of the world's petroleum sources had at that time become a «monomania» in England. Lord Curzon, the British Foreign Secretary in the former Lloyd George Administration, proclaimed characteristically in November 1918: «The Allies Floated to Victory On a Wave of Oil». Winston Churchill, then First Lord of Admiralty, sent an urgent memorandum to Lloyd George pressing upon his attention the immediate needs of the British Empire to gain control of the world's oil-fields.

This petroleum monomania then spread around the world to all the Great Powers. Henry Berenger, a very important Frenchman, sent a letter on December 12, 1919 to Clemenceau, the French Prime Minister, urging him to take prompt steps with this warning: «He Who Owns Petroleum Will Own the World».

In April 1923, when the Peace Conference assembled in Lausanne, Switzerland, and the debate started on the serious war-problems waiting to be solved, every other problem was quite unexpectedly set aside at the very start and the whole session was usurped with a sharp controversy and discord which arose from the various demands of the Great Powers to get a proportionally divided possession of the oil-yielding fields of the world.

The U.S. representatives at the Conference, with their insolence and display of quite undiplomatic behaviour which affronted the others with their rashly made demands (the most uncouth boorish among them was a certain R.W. Child), disrupted the whole session with disrespectful and vehement remarks accusing the British of trying to commandeer the world's petroleum! One of them (named above) hurled such barbarous insults against the British Foreign Secretary, Lord Curzon, that the refined old Diplomat to shed tears.

The U.S. Government demanded afterwards via an officially lodged request to the Council of the Assembly that the Secretariat of the Peace

Conference be ordered to erase from the detailed records being kept all the debate referring to oil with the shameful remarks which were in distinct bad taste hurled during the very argumentative discussion by the U.S. representatives. They also requested that the whole section of this debate be obliterated from the officially kept records of the Assembly, a U.S. demand to which the Council gracefully agreed and put into practice.

The same oil «monomania» reigned in America too, and especially so with the then prevailing mentality of the enterprising rapacious financially ultra-powerful sharks who had succeeded in occupying the State Department with the Secretary of the State Dept. C.E. Hughes, formerly an Executive Director of the Standard Oil Company and foreign affairs were accordingly formulated with regard to the policy concerning Turkey.

Nothing could be printed and circulated in the United States if it did not concur with the desires and the set policy of the State Dept. The printing press was literally terrorized by the secret service, which was assigned to enforce the demands at the discretion of the State Department, and not a single word which might offend or displease Turkey could be published. It was officially stated by high-up Officialdom and the notion was widely propagated that a nation is much more sensitive to offence and touchy to a greater degree than an average individual.

And for this incredibly absurd reason, George Horton's psychologically penetrating manuscript «The Blight of Asia», so very valuable for its intelligent diagnosis of the barbarous and brutal Turks, was not published in the U.S.A. before the year 1926, in spite of all the efforts and attempts of recognized literary agents to do so.

The Great Powers, the victors of World War I, were still ostensibly allied; they still superficially keep up a fallacious and misleading social intercourse, thus giving a false impression of unity, by their frequent participation in joint diplomatic courtesy meetings, yet they were distrustful and dishonestly polite. The real unity of the alliance had been broken since 1918 under the deceivingly calm surface, and an antagonistically merciless war was being waged, with each of these Great Powers trying to get the better part of the Victorious Spoils. Oil of course was the principal and most valuable part of the Spoils, and this is why it was coveted by all.

It's unbelievable to consider the dirty intrigues and the satanic methods used by the agents of each of these Powers, in their efforts to surreptitiously outplay and outmaneuver each other, in order to gain the advantage in the Turkish game. Never before had «morality» tumbled so precipitously, fallen so helplessly into the bottomless pit of Nadir.

Meanwhile «Kemal» with his cunning oriental mind, played the rapacious pursuits of each Power off against each other and eventually succeeded in gaining everything he wanted. This even included his foremost sharply audacious and blackmailed demand to accept the already planned by him and intended to completely obliterating and for ever extirpating Christianity from Asia Minor demand which they timidly and ignomously accepted, and for also making the victorious Great Powers do the disgraceful act of compelling Greece (their supposed ally) to empty East Thrace of all its Greek population and to return it to Turkey together with all its farm animals. The new refugees from Thrace, adding to those from Asia Minor and to those fleeing before and seeking asylum from the brutal Russian Communism, literally flooded the mountainous and mostly untillable small area left to Greece, reaching the numerically total of nearly 1.7 million. All those refugees were in a lamentable state, destitude, hungry, roofless, most of them sick and suffering physical and mental injury from being inhumanely victimized by the Turks and Bolsheviks, and being lightly clothed in the middle of a freezing cold winter of 1922-23.

Greece, although greatly impoverished, having being declared bankrupt by its creditors and infamously betrayed and abandoned by her allies, yet accepted every refugee who sought asylum on the little land still left to her, making no discrimination whatsoever between the refugees. Greece welcomed into her narrow space not only Greeks, but also Russian refugees, Armenians, Hebrews, and even Moslem Kurds (the last ones as allies of Greece, when a whole regiment of Kurds under their commander the colonel Etem Bey joined the Greek army and fought bravely with the Greeks against the Turks).

The «epitomy» of the Great Powers' disgraceful and infamy betrayal of an ally was made obvious with its inhumane completion in January 1923, when the U.S. State Department accepted the cruel and inhuman recommendation made by Admiral Mark L. Bristol and ordered the discontinuance of any further aid to Greek refugees by instructing the American Red Cross and the Near East Relief Organizations (which indirectly depended on the U.S. Government and in this instance on the prerogative guidance of the State Department's arbitrary chosen indications where to be given financial help), to cease and desist from offering any further substantial, yet badly needed, assistance to the destitute, sick, roofless, and greatly suffering refugees in Greece. On the «antipode» and in shocking contrast, the ineffable Turkophile Mark L. Bristol suggested to his friends in the State Department the Dulles brothers and of the same opinion friends, which gave its acquiecence to his advice, that the money involved and intended to relieve suffering, instead of being spent to give supposed help in Greece, should be spent on the suffering Turks left behind. This fact, incredible as it may seem, actually happened and the State Dept. acquiescenced.

To add further insult to injury, Mark L. Bristol had the callousness to openly declare and suggest to his friends in the State Department this inhumane phrase coined by him: *«Let Greece simmer in the frying pan in her own grease».*

(P.S. Not all those 1.7 million refugees stayed permanently in Greece, a hungry and impoverished country with no work for all of them to make a living. Between 200,000 to 400,000 of them left Greece; they moved out and dispersed to other countries around the globe, to states which accepted them on plain humanitarian or other grounds).

Going back for a moment to the time of the colossal catastrophe of Smyrna, the aforesaid rapaciously minded victorious Powers of the First World War, being possessed with this utterly iniquitous philosophy and clearly expressing this abysmally immoral behavior were destined, while exercising their mighty dominant allied authority in Smyrna in the chaotic situation which existed in the locality, to display a lack of any sensitivity by openly exibiting *a callouslack of any sensibility compassion* for the immeasurable magnitude of the misery surrounding the refugees.

For this reason, the horizon for their continued existence in this world looked pitch-black to the utterly despairing masses of refugees, mortally persecuted by the Turks and pitifully helpless.

We could compare this *figuratively* to an underground basement under a large mansion sheltering people from bombs, and yet the bombs of war fell upon that target and the huge edifice cascaded to ruins on top of this basement, inextricably entombing the sheltering people in its massive debris and pitch-black surroundings; so the horizon became similarly inexorably black for the entombed people, desperate for air.

Then somehow, miraculously, the mental attitude of all those entombed people, who were in a despairing state just a while before with no hope of salvation, changed all of a sudden. How did this come to be and what was this miraculous occurrence?

A very thin and almost imperceptible ray of sunshine somehow penetrated through a tiny crevasse of the debris of the ruins of the massive huge building which had entombed them. And yet this tiny spark of sunshine, peeping in through a tiny narrow opening, revived the hopes of those entombed in the shelter, those people who a little while before were despairing with lost hope, by raising the expectation that help would arrive through the unexpected crack of this tiny opening and that eventually they would be saved.

This metaphor of raising hopes, parallel to the above figurative example, happened to the hopeless masses of the refugees. A rumor, *though somehow exaggerated a bit,* had spread which raised the refugees' hopes; a rumour that a kindhearted man with a loving sympathetic concern was looking at the plight of the refugees. It was unknown in the beginning to the masses of refugees, who he was and what his name was; yet it was swiftly learned. The name of the man was George Horton, U.S. General Consul in Smyrna.

The spreading of this rumor made thousands of refugees move towards and encircle the American Consulate, thus blocking both its ingress and egress.

The two marine sentries who were guarding the access points of the Consulate, on the orders of Captain Arthur Japy Hepburn who had been delegated as Chief Commander in Smyrna by the US representativeHigh Admiral Mark. L. Bristol, were unable to repulse the masses of refugees and, afraid that the Consulate might be mobbed, telephoned to Captain Hepburn asking for reinforcements. Captain Hepburn had strict orders to remain neutral under all circumstances and to try by all possible means to avoid becoming embroiled in the critical local situation.

In accordance with his orders in this urgent case, he called the Chief of the Turkish gendarmery to send a detachment and to clear the place of the refugees. The Turks needed no better chance to eliminate Christians. Bellicosely arriving on the spot, and with their bayonets pushing and stabbing and their rifles detonating and discharging at the refugees indiscriminately, they menacingly dispersed the masses of refugees and freed the public square fronting the Consulate, clearing up the place of the dirty rayahs, giaours.

Those few of the crowd of refugees who managed to get through and to enter the Consulate were accepted by George Horton in his Office and heard in a nice and polite manner. He was sympathetic and considerate to their plight and, trying to offer some help to them, he supplied them with letters stating that they supposedly worked for the Consulate as cleaners. These letters had no value whatsoever for the Turks, for they were savage and abysmally illiterate, not even knowing how to read their own language. Every typed paper shown to them was grabbed, wrinkled up in their hands and thrown down and stepped on in disgust. Yet George Horton intelligently guessed that the pompously typed Consular letterhead and the impressive stamp underneath with the red ribbon adorning the letters might produce an impressive effect on some of them at least. And he was right in his judgment.

George Horton was ordered by Admiral Mark L. Bristol, and these orders included all other navy and army personnel, to remain strictly neutral and not to try in any circumstance to help the Christians who were being persecuted by the Turks, lest this act be interpreted by the Turks as American help or protection given to their enemies (and the Christian refugees were the most hated of all their enemies). This would, according to Mark. L. Bristol, displease or even inflame their anger against America and may act as a wedge against friendly relations with the Turks, a fervent policy which the U.S. was following, and it was eagerly trying at all costs to activate the furtherance of such amicability.

George Horton's intelligent perception was thirty (30) whole years ahead of the famous trial at Nuremberg of the crimes committed by Hitler's underlings. The world-renowned legal counsels defending the criminals at the trial, in the arguments they presented to support the justification of the actions committed by the accused, (rejecting entirely the object of the arraignment against the accused) introduced formally to the Court the following legal reasoning which they offered as proof vindicating the acts executed by the accused; the supposedly legally irrefutable argumentative statements were as follows:

The Army Code of «military principles» –and all the Army Codes in the world include this principle– lays down the rule that «discipline» has priority over all else. A military order is THE order! A soldier must blindly obey and immediately proceed to execute everything he is ordered to do with no question asked. A soldier has no right whatsoever to demand to know or to argue the purpose of the order, the why, who, or for what good reason such an order was given to him. The *«principle»* demands that the soldier is bound and has the duty to blindly proceed to follow throughout all he is ordered to do. If a soldier were ever granted such a privilege, from that very moment on there would be no Army. From that instant, and as a consequence, the Army would be riddled with dissentions, arguments, controversy, and open disobedience. No longer would there be the fundamentally needed adherence of a well diciplined and traditionally united mighty powerful army, capable of successfully fighting the outlined course of action, expertly planned by the Army Staff, in order to protect everything cherished and held dear by a Nation.

Such a right – if it is ever going to be granted as a privilege to soldiers – should be translated as an act tantamount to dissolving the indispensable military power needed for the Nation's protection. It would be the Army's *death-knell.*

NOT SO! declared the consonant decision of the Judges and the Jury in the now famous international trial held at Nuremberg, Germany, for the crimes committed by Hitler's underlings. The *celebrated decision of the Nuremberg trial* further elucidated the judicial consequences which would follow on a punishable crime. The soldier becomes personally responsible for committing a offence characterized by the Penal Code and can be condemned to a punishment related to the magnitude of the crime; that is a crime which is highly immoral, inhumane or so bad that it shocks everyone's deep consciousness. A soldier may get the order from an irrational head of government, a paranoiac commanding navy or army chief etc., officer, or egocentric and egomaniac dictator. Because he had in this way been ordered to commit a crime or crimes but he executed the order with his own concurring active volition, the order given doesn't absolve him from responsibility for his own actions, neither does it make him exempt for the crimes he committed, nor does it grant him immunity to responsibility for his crimes. He is endowed with the well-balanced sense to judge his actions and to distinguish those which are constructive and which tend to the success of his nation's morally justified objectives, from those which are criminally irrational or are inhumane orders.

The very strict orders George Horton had received from the rabid-Turkophile Admiral Mark L. Bristol were inhuman. They were orders to abolish or suppress his consciousness to such an extent so as to be acting as an hetero-movable inanimate object. This was something he would never do. He was acting intelligently in accordance with his conscience and disregarding orders to the contrary, no matter who was giving those orders.

Acting exactly on the other side of the unacceptable scales of justice was Mark. L. Bristol's commanding officer in Smyrna, Arthur J. Hepburn, who was blindly obeying such orders like Hitler's underlings. Fortunately for the refugees, Captain Halsey Powel, who later replaced Captain A. J. Hepburn as Commander of Smyrna, acted conscientiously as George Horton did.

George Horton was a personality with an inborn geniality. He was well known and respected across the entire Diplomatic Corps as a man who was endowed with a high-minded perceptiveness; he was extremely knowlegeable, kindhearted, noble, dignified, with high moral standards and an incorruptible integrity.

For nearly 35 years he had been serving his Country faithfully and with a genuine patriotic loyalty since the turn of the century, and in unbroken succession from 1893 as U.S. Consul in Athens, Greece, where he had greatly surprised the Diplomatic Corps with his knowledge of the classical language of ancient Greece by reciting verses from Homer's Odyssey and Iliad in their original form. Then from 1909 he was Consul in Salonica, Greece, and from 1911 until the catastrophe close to the end of the year 1922, he was the General Consul in Smyrna, Turkey, where there was a huge Greek population, spoors of the still surviving remnants of the former Greco-Roman «Eastern Roman Empire». The then Vatican Conclave in the «Vatican City» at Rome, after 476 A.D. when the Western Wing of the Empire was subdued by Germanic tribes, had ruled the area which had been colonized throughout its length on the whole Appenine Peninsula and which was greatly fragmented into catholic segments of racially divided small kingdoms. It was about that time when in the absense of one homogeneous and ethnically united nation had established themselves forming those little kingdoms in the lands of the Appenine Peninsula which had been invaded and inhabited by races of different origin, which being descended from the upper Northern Countries. Yet the plain heterogeneous fact as they were in origin, was also the cause of holding not any forbearance among themselves (those established different kingdoms). Moreover, the sense of their general belief to the same catholic religious concept was the only apparent element of a somewhat very weak semblance of uniformity.

Exploiting this favorable to it coincidence of their belief in the same religious faith from all those otherwise heterogeneous kingdoms, the Vatican authorities in the eternal city of Rome being recognized everywhere in the world as Head of the great Religeous Center of Catholicism, grabbed the thus presented to it chance to extend through its leader (the body of cardinals in their conclave) a strict dominent rule over and even beyond the whole of the population of the kingdoms which had been inhabiting the Italian Peninsula. Those various little kingdoms were unified firstly by the Italian patriot Giuseppe Garibaldi and then and especially by the great statesman Conte di Cavour in the 19th century; all those racially different segments of population (which in small independent localities had divided the Appenine Peninsula) were united and the newly unified Country was given the name of «Italy», from the dialect of *Tuscan,* called «Italian» which was then the predominent one spoken in the southern portion of the Peninsula.

The Eastern Roman Empire officially bore this name from 328 A.D. when it was incorporated into the Great Roman Empire, until 1453 A.D. when it fell to the Turks. Yet, after the Fall in 1453 A.D., conspirators at the Vatican Conclave who wished to erase the word *«Roman»* from the «Eastern Wing» (which *no longer existed)* of the former Roman Empire, concocted a falsehood by inventing and giving the pseudonym «Byzantine» in place of the word «Roman»; it was an utterly feigned name, and so the segment of the former Roman Empire which was no longer in existence was Christened the «B y z a n t i n e   E m p i r e», by borrowing the name from the ancient city of Byzantium, which was named after Captain «Byzas» who established it in around *600 B.C.* In 330 A.D. this old almost dilapidated city had been totally demolished on the orders of Constantine the Great, who built his glorious city in its place and gave it the name of *«New Rome»;* from then on it became the new capital city of the «Roman Empire». At the same time Constantine ordered all the Government offices and services to be transferred from the old Rome to his «New Rome». A little later, to boost their master's ego, the sycophants at the Court of NEW Rome gave it *an added* name, calling it «Constantinople» and thus honoring its founder «Constantine the Great». The new resplendent capital city (which was from then on called «Capital of the World»), bore the name of the Eastern Roman Empire until 1453 A.D.. And so its last king, Constantine Paleologos, was officially named as the Roman Emperor.

Historians in the Middle Ages led by the orders of the then almighty

Vatican Conclave, by being most of them catholics, blindly obeyed and followed, continued this concocted falsehood of a not existed ever «Byzantine Empire» in the habitually arbitrary practiced way and by their writings.

The so feigned pseudonym was thus spread through the then historically semi-illiterate world. Later historians who at the time lacked any other official historical sources, copied the falsehood contained in the old ones into their own books and by doing so left behind to succeeding generations and thus perpetuated the spurious pseudonym of the «Byzantine Empire», which has remained up to the present time.

At this point it is expedient to make a noteworthy remark. No historian until now has ever tried to refute this pseudonym so spuriously made by the Vatican Conclave, and to restore the true facts of History. Yet what is stated herein is genuine and irrefutable historical fact. It's high time to expose and lay open the cunningly concocted wicked «myth» which has been served to the world; it should be cast out and the historical truth should be restored].

* * *

I have never had the opportunity nor the honor to meet George Horton in person nor to receive any help or favorable benefit from him. I emphasize this point even though after the conflagration of Smyrna we were for a short while staying in two dwellings which were by chance close to each other and which had not been burned down; it was a casual occurence just before he had left. Yet because, after our ordeal in the cemetery, I circulated among the masses of those refugees who were most pressed along the quay (a piece of land which was very near to the falsely hoped-for protection of the European and American war-fleets), I heard and saw with my own ears and eyes over a dozen men among the mass of refugees narrating how they had been saved (for a while at least, for Kemal's orders were that no refugee male aged 16 to 45 would be permitted to leave the country), by showing those fanciful letters George Horton had supplied them with. One of them declared, with tears in his eyes: «May God bless and keep George Horton safe always»; With this letter which he gave to me (and he showed us the letter) I have been saved up to four times now from the clutches of those blood-thirsty Turks (who were inspecting the masses of refugees and who were catching men huddled up among the females, and sending them into concentration camps for «deportation» (meaning death from hardship in exile). Then the man looked up to the heavens and made the sign of the cross, eulogizing George Horton. On another occasion I saw a man running like a hare, being chased as if by a hunting dog by an enraged Turk who was running after him and discharging his gun at the refugees in the direction and at the spot where this man had disappeared by slipping in; it wounded two women and a child who started screaming with pain. It so happened that a little later my steps led me very close to that man who was crouched in a corner with the crowd of refugees pressing all around him. He was trembling with fear. I was so moved that I asked him if I could be of help in some way. He looked at me and took some encouragement on seeing a friendly face and not an enemy. Then he showed me and the others a wrinkled up and trampled dirty little ball of paper which he was holding. «Look at this», he said to us all, sobbing. «It's a letter which this great philanthrope George Horton gave to me. Through this letter I have been saved up to now from being caught by showing it. It has been a life-saver to me. Now that beastly Turk has destroyed it. He grabbed it, crumpled it up in his hands, threw it to the ground and stepped upon it. I managed to stoop down and pick it up before I slipped away from his clutches. But who will now ever take this dirty mess of a letter seriously?» And he continued sobbing. The case was dramatically pitiful. I said a few comforting words to him for I could offer nothing more than that. I actually started all of a sudden to see how vulnerable my own safety was. I was skinny, thinly-built and pale, wearing shorts, so I looked like a child rather than a grown up young man. But for how long could I escape those barbarous men who were searching among the refugees just to catch men between 16 to 45? I had actually seen a few days before a small squad of young men like myself, guarded on both sides of the squad by four Turks with bloody bayonets fixed into their guns and ready to skewer any of those young men who might try to escape. My blood turned cold with fright when among them I perceived one of my class-mates of small stature, age fifteen, blond, baby faced, wearing shorts and yet being captured, who had seen me standing among the crowd of the refugees and in a state of agony called out my name loudly; with great anxiety he was looking me straight in eye with his green shiny eyes as if asking for help. I was frozen to the spot. I might have been in the same squad by now! There was nothing I could do to help. Smyrna now was in a state of blackened horrible ruins with no more addresses to help you to search for anyone. Furthermore, if I'd made any movement toward him, this might've betrayed to them my presence by revealing the point where I was standing among the refugee-mass, and a point which wasn't yet obvious to those blood-thirsty and beastly guards, on account of their attention being entirely absorbed at the time upon the task of watching the squad they had caught. And so –if I did– I would've given them the chance of perceiving me by revealing to them the spot where I was and simultaneously there would have been the virtual probability of their grabbing me and placing me in the same condemned group with the others, hardly any of whom had any chance of being saved.

Later on, with the enrichment of the fruitfully gained experience which comes with old age, I spent a long time philosophizing on the matter by marvelling about the tendency of young people to belittle danger even when it gapes openly in front of them, as it does in most perilous situations; and the inclination or propensity to disregard the dire risks implicit in those often clearly perceptible perils -that is, the easily discernible hazards which are usually present in any dangerous and yet thoughtless youthful venture.

Logically reasoning, I started to wonder how and why I had been saved up to that moment and why I hadn't been caught by those ferocious and brutal Turks. Maybe – I guessed – because the divine supreme intelligence of the eternal universe kept me alive because I hadn't yet finished performing what destiny had ordained and assigned to me in this woefully wretched world in which we live. Or maybe – I presumed conjecturing – because the divine mind of the supreme intelligence of the «cosmos» had designed for me to do something constructive or helpful to others before I go.

Before our family's greatly eventful and most dramatic final departure from the awfully blackened and terrifying ruins of Smyrna, I had seen and heard directly from grateful refugees who had in some way been helped, or from men greatly suffering ill-treatment, similar acknowledgments about certain touching and most heartwarming actions of the spontaneously offered philanthropic kindnesses and loving help of the for ever unforgettable George Horton.

A characteristic case which unfolded in my presence and before my own eyes was this: Some human buzzards, (which are always present and can be seen hovering above the carcasses of deadly circumstances) pretending to be mindful of others as genuine Americans, offered their help and free labour to the Consulate personnel, who badly needed assistance; by means of this crafty pretence they managed to penetrate into the building which housed us and which it was chock full with other refugees too. By exploiting the presumed weight of their position because of their American identity, intruded in pretending that «they were shipping agents of a boat about to depart from Smyrna, and as in a great detail is being divulged further down in the narration, succeeded to carry out a great fraud against the lamentably pitiful wretched refugges, and take away of the women. every gold item they had succeeded to save in hiding about their garments. To extract and get those articles of gold, they had artfully set the following trap.

They pompously produced a trunk of fake boat–tickets for a non-existent steamship which, as they disgracefully insisted, was scheduled on its itinerary to make calls at Greek ports. Then with great impudence, they stated that only those passengers holding one of these tickets would be accepted aboard this ship which was shortly to leave Smyrna. Furthermore, they shamelessly stressed the point that on philanthropic grounds they would accept articles of jewelry and gold instead of dollars in exchange for the tickets; their price was specified in American currency but nobody had any of this under the circumstances.

At once some anxiety could be seen among those refugees who were massed into this building. Some of the women moved quickly into the darker corners of the dwelling in order to bring out their well-hidden gold medallions or other articles of gold. Finally the gold collected was carried at once by some of the young and gullible refugees (who bona-fide acted for the ravenous buzzards) to the American Consulate; they entered by showing their identity cards but an official, seeing unusual actions and suspecting that something fishy was going on, brought the case to the attention of George Horton. He was being kept profoundly busy with serious cases which were unexpectedly arising all the time from the very anomalous state of affairs and was unaware of the presence of the buzzards and of their secret operation under his official roof. As the gullible persons who brought the gold to the buzzards later narrated, George Horton became so enraged with this infamy (as he called it) that against his normally gentle nature and always refined manners he grabbed the buzzards by the hair and, knocking their heads together, gave a mighty strong kick to each one and threw them out of the open Consular door. Then, giving back the bundle of gold to one of the gullible refugees who had brought it to the buzzards and accompanied them, he ordered one of his trusted personnel to go along with him to the building I was staying in and to return all the items of gold to their owners.

This was a remarkable and extraordinary act on the part of George Horton and it shows what a jewel his character was.

Endowed with a bright, intelligent mind, George Horton was also a self-disiplined man who always observed the priorities of established moral principles and the dignified methods of conducting himself properly while aiming at the goals of his occupational pursuits. He strongly resented and inwardly detested arrogance; he never in any way exhibited any showmanship neither did he display a disgusting presumptiousness and self-importance.

George Horton never disavowed his humane insticts nor the acutely working sense of his conscience and he never agreed just for his own advancement, as others do, to comply with any order (no matter who was ordering him), to suppress the standards of his inner conscience and to degrade this to such a low level that he would become a slave without any will who was bound to execute the wishes of somebody else who stood a little higher in the commanding authority of public service and who had a grandiose title.

Another of George Horton's precious moral possessions was his impressively unsuppressed truthfulness, an attribute conventionally highly valued. However, paradoxically strange as this may be, this attribute which greatly affected the sensibility of an intellectual man like him, weighed with exeeding heaviness against him in the balance of appraisal with regard to the extent of his Consular usefulness with the Civil Servants who were then temporarily occupying the State Department and who were pompously marked with impressively distinguished titles.

It is worth divulging to the general public that great pressure had time and time again been exerted upon George Horton by those higher-up in the echelons of the Public Service to make him offer the mighty help of his historic hand as a weighty witness, and join the Department in the then agonizing effort to re-write the horrible History of the Asia Minor History by reversing completely the true facts about all those bloody years, in favor of the Turks and against the Greeks and Armenians (Christians). This task had been undertaken by all those who had great profit-interests in Turkey and who were vested with authority and had the upper hand in the State Department in formulating the Foreign policy of the U.S. Government. He was also psychologically pressed to amend the contents of his book «The Blight of Asia» by reversing all those segments of the book which were derogatory for the Turks.

George Horton did not agree to this and he vehemently rejected their unethical request. Yet from then on, he fell into disfavor in the entire State Department. From then on he met only adversity, as was clearly revealed with the refusal of the U.S. Printing Press to publish his book; the publishers were terrorized by the special Secret Service detached to the State Department which had threatened to confiscate or suspend their printing-licenses if they did not obey the orders given to them not to print any of the contents of George Horton's manuscript «The Blight of Asia», a truly remarkable and very informative book. At this point and time it is advisable to throw light on this important subject and throw it wide-open so that the public can clearly see it, by exposing the facts which have long been kept in obscurity. The reason why these facts were impeded from being brought to common knowledge was the reluctance of the printing-press, under orders, not to publish anything against or unfavorable to persons in high executive positions appointed by the Government to implement U.S. foreign policy.

It is indeed very queer and shocking to the sensibilities to consider the greatly dissimilar, unjust, and monstrously contrasting procedures employed by U.S. Officialdom in its duty to judge its distinguished functionaries who stand on the upper steps of the Government Service ladder in order to award recognition to them for their purported beneficial contributions to the Nation during the attributed loyal service of their careers. The chicanery involved in this is clear and deeply disheartening. The most inequitable treatment which results from two utterly contrasting and divergent sets of recognition awards is strikingly unjust; these are clearly politically-influenced and arbitrary judgments which speak for themselves.

To elaborate the case with an example which is clear and suitable to the subject, we bring forward for this purpose two well-explained biographical profiles:

1. The U.S. Consul General George Horton and 2. The U.S. High Commissioner in Constantinople, Admiral Mark L. Bristol.

George Horton was a refined, straightforward man who had high moral standards. He was an intellectual of high caliber, endowed with a brilliant mind. He excelled in the classics in his early thirties and won distinction as a literary critic and for his clear-cut expression of thought in the Chicago Herald, where he worked as a journalist. When in 1893 the newly-elected President of the U.S.A. Grover Cleveland (who admired his writings, and especially a constructive criticism which he had written about him in the said State's newspaper where he was working as one of the editors) appointed George Horton in an appreciative gesture as Consul in Berlin, Germany (at the time the most coveted Post after London), George Horton declined to accept it and rejected the offer. As he said, he hadn't the talent to enter into a career in Diplomatic officialdom. In his judgment there was not even a minute amount of compatibility between the two scentific human endeavors of intellectualism, and politics.

In his opinion, the Classics constitute studious research-work, by which one digs deep into ancient literary works in order to find out, bring the findings to the surface and expose to the light of contemporary literature the remarkable technique and beauty of the renowned literary works of the addition ancient Greek's classics.

Politics is a charismatic capability to manipulate circumstances adroitly and to exploit anything perceived to be in your favor, to take the chance to grab it swiftly in order to achieve your aimed-at goal of climbing high and often reaching the top.

President Grove Cleveland admired the qualities of the young intellectual and, wanting to satisfy his thirst for classicism, subsequently appointed George Horton to be Consul in Athens, Greece; this time, George Horton accepted. Thus in 1893 George Horton was wrested from the midwest at the age of 34 and went to take charge of his Post in Athens, where classicism was born, originated and glorified.

George Horton was, as has been said, an «anomaly» in the Foreign Service. At a time when almost all the Foreign Service Officials appointed by their Governments spoke no foreign languages, not even the tongue of the country they were appointed to, George Horton spoke fluent French, German, Italian, Turkish and Greek (he mastered both ancient and modern Greek). He was renowned for his acknowledged excellence in ancient Greek literature and for his profoundity in the literary classics.

In almost 35 years of Consular Service, he spent 30 years serving in countries located in geographical regions which were under Turkish domination. He was thoroughly familiar with Turkish History and wholly aware of the prevailing tendencies, customs, disposition, morals and bias of the Turks and of the Turkish character in general.

George Horton served his country for nearly three and a half *decades* with loyalty, honor and distinction. However, and despite his remarkable lifetime contribution to the glory of his country, he fell into great disfavor and disrepute because he refused to agree and thereafter proceed to commit a grave dishonesty to re-write the horrid crimes committed by the Turks during the Turko-Greek war which ended in the entire annihilation of Christianity in Asia, with the tragic presented events upside-down in favor of the Kemal's nationalistic islamic new Turkey, and this in order to gain the exclusive monopoly of exploitation of Mesopotamia's oil promised by Kemal to America, for which great pressure had been exerted upon him by his superiors in the State Department. From then on he incurred their open enmity with obviously detrimental effects on his career. Moreover several hurtful deeds of animosity and clear opposition took place, as has already been stated. These facts embittered his sensibility, wounded his feelings and left him broken-hearted and greatly disenchanted for the rest of his days, although his profound self-respect and dignity never allowed him to express his wounded feelings publicly.

We now bring forward the abysmally contrasting profile of Mark L. Bristol, the most suitable case study. He is the archetypal character in portraying the common «cliché» of the typical American young man of today who wants to climb up the ladder of success as quickly as possible, but by contributing and employing as little hard work, elbow-grease and conscientious effort as possible. This, of course, cannot possibly be achieved by anyone unless he has recourse to ways which deviate from the standard norms; that is, he must resort to astute, wily, and shrewd devices, aptly employed in order to achieve as soon as possible the goal he has aimed at.

Mark L. Bristol was a very authoritative personality, extremely presumptuous, boastful, self-important and deliberately unconscious to tragic victims. Worst still, he was self-consciously cruel and he used inhumane methods to gain his ends; that is, the procedures he used in his pursuit were utterly merciless as long as he achieved his goal. In exact opposition or «antipode» ie contrary to what George Horton refused with disdain and disgust to do, Mark L. Bristol conscientiously committed the great moral crime of being the foremost and forcefully implemental agent in the effort undertaken to re-write History by reversing and presenting the facts the wrong way round. He took the lead in the strenuously agonizing effort of the State Department to reverse the true events of the bloody catastrophe of Asia Minor and to forge History by fabricating non-existent events, exeeding and surpassing Turkish propaganda by his intelligent manipulation of words and by forwarding this concoction of falsehood to the State Department. All this greatly assisted it in its effort (via the venal arrangement of richly paying experts to dexterously and masterfully wield the pen) to reverse the indescribably tragic History of Asia Minor History in the Nineteen Twenties by holding the Greeks and Armenians responsible and blameworthy for everything which then occurred in Turkey and by declaring shamelessly that the Turks were innocent victims of the Armenian and Greek crimes and brutalities.

He used the trick of showmanship to his advantage and to the utmost extent. To his superiors in rank he was dexterously flatterering, blindly following their orders regardless of whether or not they were moral or immoral, cruel and inhuman or whether brutality and crimes were involved in order to implement them. He adroitly employed crafty and wily ways, and aptly so, to wring praises from his superiors for his, forsooth, *splendidly carried out* performances and diplomacy, in greatly persuading the Turks and the Turkish people of the warm friendliness felt towards them by the Americans and of U.S. support for Kemal's nationalistic movement for the independence of the Turkish nation. He was widely applauded and praised by the financially mighty powerful and most distinguished dignitaries of the land; by the U.S. Congress, by the next U.S. President Herbert Hoover and especially by the mighty Financial Circle of the country's commercial, industrial, and enterprise interests for greatly ingratiating the Turks and thus smoothing their scheme of action to rapaciously exploit the presumed riches of the Turkish territory.

For all those astutely executed theatrical performances, he was promoted to Admiral General over the entire American possessions in the Pacific Ocean and over their administration and trusteeship; as a reward for his «masterful diplomacy», the then President of the U.S.A. Calvin Coolidge also awarded him with a Commission to China. He finally became historically famous and a rich man, with a top pension when he retired in 1932.

M. L. Bristol was actually the genuine portrait of a very cunning «yesman», who fiendishly schemed and always looked after his own advantage and good fortunes.

Former U.S. Senator Walter F. Mondale, who was a Presidential candidate a few years ago and who had just lost the presidency for few thousand less votes he had received in the then executed general elections to the antagonizing him and also a candidate for the Presidency Ronald Reagan who was declared by the Electorate the winner, and in accordance with the U.S. Constitutionally defined process was installed U.S.A. President, made it known on January 29, 1971 by an official notification to Congress, that from the year 1945 until the year 1970 (that is for a period of 25 years) the U.S.A. had donated to Turkey in aid only, *five and a half billion dollars*. From 1970 to 1999, that is until now, the number of billions has not yet been officially given to the public, but there is no doubt about it that the donated billions, if not far above the previous number, are with certainty no less. And this kind of said unbrokenly continues to pour in, in addition to the many billions of dollars being brought into Turkey every year by private concerns. There are the billions which the ventures of our industry and enterprise are up to the present time pouring into Turkey in order to build factories for petrochemicals and all other imaginable and hard-to-enumerate manufacturing ventures.

Why so? Because the Turks with their cunning and for ever unreliable oriental mind (with the instinct of their progenitors, the beastly «Huns») had always done it like this through the centuries, and they are doing it all over again right now. Their age-old familiar gainful *pursuit is:* «Suck the West Dry». They offer our industry land and territory free of charge to build their factories or other ventures, they grant them the privilege of paying no taxes, they supply them with water, electricity, and other conveniences at absurdly low rates and they also offer them their low *labor costs,* which are advertised all over the world; there are no greedy Labor Unions always demanding higher pay by threatening to close their factories down by strikes unless they agree to pay their usually illogical demands for ever higher pay increases, which make their manufacturing products unprofitable. The managers of both our individual business concerns or various Corporations, Consolidated Combines, or the giant Conglamorates have been deluded and duped with all these very attractive offers, exactly as happened long ago, with the same technique to the then named Ottoman Empire, and they have started to fall into these diabolically covered invisible traps and to pour into them billions and billions of dollars, having been entirely assured that the very expertly constructed legal arrangements of binding guaranties, pledges, land mortgages, etc. will supposedly offer them ample assurance of safety and protection.

Man Never Learns. He is ever greedy and longs for easy ventures with rich returns. This makes him forget that this sort of scene has already been played out many a time in the History of mankind, the latest one in living memory being Turkey's «Kemal's» despicable and provocative act of arbitrarily abolishing all Turkey's old financial obligations, by brazenly declaring as null and void all such similar securities contracted by the previous Turkish regime, the Ottoman Empire. With this dictatorial action of Kemal, all the European creditors lost innumerable millions of English gold sovereigns, a currency prevalent at that time and considered as the safest money unit by the lenders. France alone lost 60% fact being substanciated with documents refered before of all loans contracted in gold by its Financial Circles, which the Ottoman Empire had borrowed but which «Kemal» dictatorially abolished and never recognized. This is a fact that has been Substanciated with documents refered before. For the European creditors the only way they could impose their demands and insist on Turkey's repaying its debts was by declaring war on Turkey, a drastic step which no European country wanted to take. Instead of this, countries and Financial Concerns started once again to proceed along the same old lines, by their cutting off and forgetting the sustained losses which had previously suffered, and they are striving now to lure and entice the new Turkish regime into awarding them monopolies and granting them permits for various kinds of land exploitation. The Governments of the new Nationalistic Turkey have accepted and still accept to operate on exactly the *same* pattern of that done by the old Ottoman Empire. The bitter lesson of the past has not taught them anything. As the old adage states: *«Man Never Learns»!* The experience man gains by long scientific observation of the world's cycles of repeated historical events which return again and again (in slightly different surroundings, methods and shapes) lets us foresee that all those occurrences of which man in his foolishness is oblivious of are going with certainty to be repeated, perhaps even before the end of the twentieth century.

The profession of the science of behavioral research wishes to discover the indisputable truth as to whether or not the inborn behavior of a wild animal can be changed by the influential effects of its surroundings (this is the presently prevailing theory which is accepted by a majority of judges, lawyers, and a large segment of our society). Scientists have proceeded to carry out the following practical experiment. They have found three newly- born baby wolves, taken them away from their mother, brought them into their homes and tried to raise them in loving surroundings like three baby doggies. In the beginning, these wolvies were fed with cow's milk and later on with a variety of ordinary dog-food. The experimenters were very careful to bestow on the little wolvies extraordinary care and loving attention, even giving them pet-names.

In the beginning everything went smoothly, with the little wolvies behaving almost like three young puppies, obedient, understanding their names and almost thankful to their masters. Yet very soon after they were fully grown, their behavior changed entirely; they disregarded the orders given to them by their masters, howled angrily at them and finally they reached the point where they attacked and even bit their masters badly when forced to obey their orders. One day they just jumped over the fence they were kept in and disappeared into the open space yonder, instinctively following their senses to find out some woody place. They never returned in spite of the calls of their masters, who followed the tracks they left. What happened?

The wild instinct with which they were endowed by Mother Nature had never changed and this ever unchanging instinct led them to find the way of escape and to reach some semi-natural habitat.

Exactly the same ever unchanging instinct has been endowed by Mother Nature to all creatures, *including man*. However, in man's case, the instinct is dormant (in suspended animation) most of the time, as long as he can find the needed staples for life's elementary sustenance. Yet, many a time when circumstances are suitable, when there is no food to satisfy his voracious appetite, man's dormant wild instinct wakes up and emerges, revealing its beastly nature. Then man behaves as does the premordial wild beast, led by the beastly instinct of the brute he previously was.

The properties which constitute the instinct never change, despite the surroundings or any other influential fact, including pseudo civilization - the supposed genuine and true acquirement at which deluded man professes he has finally arrived.

This concrete truth has been proven time and time again with the

Turks. The beastly and savagely brutal instinct of their progenitors, the Huns, or to express the point more scientifically the constituent element of the ever-unchanging D.N.A. with which they are born, has never changed nor is it ever going to change (in spite of and contrary to a theory to the contrary, a theory in which some deluded and gullible persons believe).

If we resort to events which occurred recently - just a few decades back - we can observe these facts. During President Einsehower's administration, U.S. foreign policy was directed by the Turcophile Foster Dulles. He was the younger brother of Allen Dulles who left hard-to-forget bitter memories. As the U.S. Intelligence Service eye in the State Department, he was (through secretly- acquired information on the intentions of other countries which he had gained with the help of spies) the true instrumental factor in guiding the process of the formulation of U.S. foreign policy. He promoted the granting of maximum U.S. support to Kemal's nationalistic military forces - this was greatly favorable to the aims of the Turks but, in sharp contrast it was against Greek aims (the supposed Greek's Allies that had pushed out Greece to get embroiled into a war with Turkey, in order to materialize their own national pursuit and perspectives at that very moment). With vividly-expressed animosity, he exerted upon the Greeks rabid opposition to the target they were aiming at; this was and still is U.S. policy, a fact which has deprived the Greek army of the skillful achievement of successfuly beating the Turkish forces, which were unwarlike and disorganized in the beginning.

He (Foster Dulles) persuaded the Congressional Appropriation Commitee to appropriate billions upon billions of dollars for Turkish defence. Then the justification for this was the fear that Communism would spread all over the globe and the unfounded belief that «islamic» Turkey would be a bulwark against this. President Eisenhower was a military man who did not need to be persuaded because he had the same fear of Communism. (At this point it is worth stating that the Tory Government in England was completely terrified by the same fear, of the eventuallity of losing the oil wells of Mosul to the prevalance of Communism. And, as Winston Churchill admits in his memoirs, all the English military were Turkophile!)

The billions then pouring in were spent on very expensive «listening posts», and hundreds of American personnel were spread all over Turkey to occupy and man the Posts which were equipped with the latest scientific methods in order to organize and teach the very backward Turkish army the use of new or much improved weapons and armaments, to supervise fortifications forged along the northern borders of Turkey toward the U.S.S.R., to supply Turkey with tanks, airplanes, communications and various warfare equipment and machinery, etc., and to provide the greatly needed money to sustain this gigantic undertaking.

Foster Dulles was openly Antigreek and against the growing military strength of Greece, and so were all the Governmental regimes which followed the Eisenhower Administration. Furthermore, and for obvious reasons of expediency, they turned their eyes away and overlooked (being unwilling to effectively proceed into action and stop it) the shipping to the U.S.A. of tons upon tons of opium (the basis of heroin production) which was cultivated in great amounts by farmers in Turkey from opium-poppies and sold for a profit in America to the great detriment of its citizens. The same line of conduct was followed by all administrations afterwards until the Johnson Administration, when the U.S.A. agreed to spend billions of dollars on compensating the Turkish farmers who cultivated the opium-poppies in order to allow them to turn to the cultivation of other agricultural products and to stop producing opium.

The Turkish Goverment collected the money given for this particular reason, which was appropriated by the U.S. Congress in order to stop the dreadful menace to its citizens of the opium traffic, but the money given hardly ever reached the farmers and was disposed of instead for various other purposes. Meanwhile, secretly and with the tacit consent of the Turkish Government, opium had continued to be cultivated and was sent just the same to America, via artfully disguised traffic methods. Again the U.S.A. administration looked the other way, both on account of the billions of dollars spent to gain Turkey's friendship, and because of the theoretically needed the Islamic bulwark against Communism.

The Turkish Government then, contemptuously and with open effrontery, exploiting the tolerance of the U.S.A., went much farther and reached the point of going against the openly declared U.S. policy with respect to the status quo. Belligerently and without any serious reasons, it invaded the island of Cyprus, an equal member-state of the United Nations Organization, and proceeded by wildly murdering unarmed and peaceful Greek agricultural peasants to occupy half of the island, turning it into a part of Turkey. Again the U.S.A. tolerated and condoned this hostile act done against a member-nation, this brutal challenge by Turkey and breach of International Law. The U.S. war-fleet, which was at the time patrolling the southern waters of Asia Minor and just above the island of Cyprus, did nothing to stop the invasion, on orders given by the Johnson Administration; again for reasons of expediency the Americans did not wish to break and lose the valuable friendship of Turkey. And the provocative, audacious and contemptuous manner exhibited by the Turks (the offsprings of their brutish Hunnish progenitors) against the U.S.A. (their benefactor) has gradually increased and has continued long after and is still vividly continuing up to the present day, as the brutal massacre in Constantinople (Istambul) and expulsion of the most part of the Greek inhabitants there, in 1955, in open and flagrand disregard of the terms of the Peace OF MUDANIA which provided with a status quo to be observed reciprocally by Turkey and Greece concerning Greek inhabitants in Istambul (Constantinople) and Turks inhabitants in Western Thrace. Again America manifested its Turko-phil policy by openly protecting the Islamic Albans in Western Macedonia who criminally and cruelly kill the old domiciliary Christians (Greeks and Serbs)

It is also well known that Turkey is trying to extirpate the Kurds, who are in their country for 25 centuries. Historical references state that Alexander the Great fought against the Kurds. The U.S.A. claim that Sadam is trying to extripate the Kurds. The Turks are doing now exactly the same old exterminating attempt, trying to annihilate the race of Kurds. Again the double-faced American policy's doing nothing just not to anger its cherished valuable friends, the brutish Islamic Turks.

It is notworthy at this point, to be made internationally known that the Kurds are people who traditionally value and holding in high esteem to the correct interpretation of the meaning «independence»; there are extremely fond of and holding the highest esteem of this concept for which from ancient time were persistently and unyieldingly trying to preserve it with all means. During the Turco-Greek war, they volontarily allied with the Greeks and fought hardly the turkish army together and in great harmony with the greeks. In their mutual defeat with the Greek army, many of them sought asylum in Greece, which welcomed them as told already. The then military government which had replaced the politically repugnant royal one, in recognition of the Kurds alliance and struggle to fight the Turks, together with the Greek army, and although Greece was bankrupt and betrayed by the great Nations pleges for help, yet it alloted to the Kurds general Etem who had come to greece as refugee, a pension to live along in a friendly surrounding with Greeks. As the writer remembers him walking along in the streets of Athens (shortly after the debacle of the Greek army), Etem was a slender and lean man, with blue eyes and deep-blond hair and mustache, this characteristic disclosed that he belonged to the Indo-European family and not to the Altaic-Mongolic one of Turkish family.

[The previously offered interpretation of the islamic Turkish character proves plentifully the opportunistic, impertinent, and never credulous and trust-worthy oriental mind, a greatly detested barbaric inheritance of their rapacious and treacherous and murderous Hunnish progenitors which is still clearly manifested by today's Turks].

Mark. L. Bristol was bestowed by U.S.A. Government the most gratifying treatment. He was awarded the highest authorities of the land with such rich display and with such absurd pomposity, has also been bestowed upon those high U.S. officials who either issued or blindly applied those inhumane orders, the implementation of which resulted in the saddest conclusion of an indescridably horrible and colossal catastrophe. Plus the religion of Christianity from Asia which has been expunged for ever, from this continent, a heinous dastardly deed, very profound in its depth, and exceedingly large in its extensiveness.

* * *

WHO, WHY, WHERE, and What effect Has «The» Order?

All those inhumanely cruel «ORDERS» issued by those perpetrators standing on the higher steps of governmental authority. The most irrefutably true historical facts reveal that the perpetrators were the so-called Great Allies of World War. I.

A. For having been morally and factually responsible for the colossal catastrophe by betraying their Greek ally with shamelessly employed duplicity in their loathsome policy which followed.: I. By deceiving Greece, and 2. By energetically and effectively bestowing ample military and diplomatic help on the Turks –with whom Greece was fighting.

B. For being morally for ever guilty of grave and stark culpability in the Court of Eternal Justice, for their unpardonable crime of the ineffably extensive slaughter of hundreds of thousands of innocent people (even infants and little children) by infamously assisting the ferocious hordes of Turks (by their conscious acts and omissions) to bring about one of the greatest holocausts and colossal catastrophes in the chronicles of History.

C. For positive and irrefutably substantiated fact of the rich assistance with which they furnished the barbarian hordes of Turks in order to achieve their long-sought ultimate goal of ridding from their midst all-non islamic people; they thus contributed to the conclusion of the Turkish goal - the thorough and complete annihilation of the last few millions of Christians who had been residing on the mainland of Asia Minor for hundreds of years, the indisputable remnants of a body of millions of Christian inhabitants of the former Eastern Greco-Roman Empire – a geographical segment of the Empire which was solidly populated by Christianity.

Jean de Murat
Miami Fla. 33127
April 4, 1994 To May 30, 1994

MS «NANCY HORTON»
WASHINGTON D.C. 20016

IMPORTANT FACTS REVEALED IN LETTER FORM

Dear Ms N. Horton

I greatly appreciated your nice letter of March 26, 1994. It was most welcome and I thank you from the bottom of my heart for it. I do understand the situation you faced on your return home; that is over and above the jet-lag, the various annoying expected or unexpected jobs which one always has to do. We (my brother and myself) experience this every time we come back home from a trip abroad. As for your explanation about the long time it took you under the circumstances to read my writings, this was very understandable; I considered the fact that you wrote to me about it a very graceful action on your part. I state honestly to you that you have all the time you need or wish, and I will never misunderstand you on account of this; I actually never expected you to make any unreasonable criticisms, whether favorable, logically questionable or unfavorable.

I do understand that there are parts of my writings of which you are not aware or with which you are not acquainted; this is quite plausible and easily explained as I doubt whether you had even been born at that time, so long ago. Yet even if you had seen it at that remote date, you would in all probability have been a tiny tot or a little girl and thus unable to judge for yourself the very tragic state of those horrible occurrences which were taking place by the minute at that eventful time. Even if you had been sojourning with your late father and mother in Smyrna long before these terribly tragic events occurred, you would have been sent home by your parents as a precaution for your protection and safety.

I shall now try to elucidate some points which may be intriguing your curiosity; We (my paternal family and myself) were very lucky indeed after the terror of the mass slaughter by the Turks who were persecuting us and the heinous act of the conflagration. We endured an indescribable ordeal in the cemetery where we managed to find temporary refuge and safety from the brutal killing by the Turks who were chasing after us, inside the grave of a mausoleum. It was a covered tomb which smelled awful and emanated an asphyxiating sickening odor of ptomaine which was coming from the buried and decomposed cadaver below us. We were in conjuction to this very lucky at this tragic juncture to have the chance of finding ourselves under the horrid cirumstances a tolerable shelter under a roof –while millions of wretched Christians all over Asia Minor were roofless and exposed to the Turkish cruelty, rain, cold etc. As I say, we finally did attain a tolerable shelter –thanks to the Divine Grace–, inside the crowded former Greek administration building where Stergiades – the former Greek governor –had had his post, that is his office and residence.

This edifice was a huge building which belonged to the rich widow Pantazopoulou who had donated its free possession to the Greek Government as a token of her love for Greece. It was situated on the Quay on which was its main entrance, its egress being at the back and in the parallel so-called street, just two or three small blocks NW of the building which at that time housed the U.S. Consulate where your late father, the Honorable U.S. Consul General, had his Office and residence.

I hereby now divulge «and repeat» the occurrence of the rapaciously fraudulent collection of the very few articles of gold which the deeply desperate and pitiful refugees had hidden in their attires. This was done in our own presence in the crowded building which was then sheltering us, by sinister and evil - minded rapacious sharks. These ravenous buzzards (which always thrive by hovering above dead bodies or dying creatures) had somehow craftily managed to creep into the American Consulate and there after to machinate this fraudulent plot. For a very short time they exploited a usurped orderliness but very shortly they were kicked out unceremoniously when they were detected, as has been narrated elsewhere. Pretending to be shipping agents, these two characters entered the now crowded former Greek administration building (one of the pitifully few buildings which was spared from the voracious fire and from being burned down), and after identifying themselves as coming directly from the American Consulate, addressed the crowd of refugees sheltering inside, conveying to them this message (approximately worded): «We have come here from the American Consulate. In a couple of hours from now a steamship will leave the harbour of Smyrna and is scheduled to call at some Greek ports. It might be important to many of you to know that the steamship company will allow the embarkation aboard ship, in accordance with the ship's regulations, of a limited number of passengers who hold tickets ; they may travel and disembark in Greece if so they wish. However, because the tickets are sold in dollars and because hardly any of you have any dollars under the circumstances, we have been instructed and ordered, as the representatives of this Steamship Company, to sell those few tickets, instead of for dollars, for any items of gold which you may have saved and may still have in your possession. The Company is willing to accept this loss because of its sympathy with your plight, and it wishes to demonstrate that to a certain extent it shares the misery and pain you are going through.»

This message had an immediate effect on the greatly tormented refugees, who were being threatened at every moment by the Turks, the prolonged famine, the contagious diseases which had struck, the complete absence of any basic sanitation, etc., and who were longing to save their lives at any cost. An immediate stir could be seen. Many older women (the building was sheltering mostly women; most of the men had been captured by the Turks and were either imprisoned in concentration camps or were facing something immensely worse than that), stepped into the darkest corners of the rooms of the building and took out from hiding places inside their dresses gold items which they were keeping as a last means of survival and salvation.

The swindling buzzards produced a perforated pad which was divided into two pages, (it was printed with some regulations which could have been common to the paper of any company) and whose pages were numbered, although it said nothing at all about being tickets for a steamship, and they started tearing off one of the parts of the two perforated pages on the main body of the pad every time a woman tendered something. In exchange they collected the proffered articles of gold (such as solid gold brooches, valuable gold pendants, diamond rings made of gold, gold medallions, various gold coins, wedding rings and so on and so forth), and threw them all into a money-pouch and placed this inside a tiny case. Then they started to go on their way. However there were two young men who were sheltering in the crowd of women and who were able to understand and to converse in English and who served on the occasion to give a more explicit interpretation of the broken Greek being spoken or mumbled by one of the two impostors. These young men were urged by several of the refugees who had given up their articles of gold, to go with them and to find out if all those articles of gold were really going directly to the American Consulate as was hinted. For the impostors had by word of mouth given the crowd of refugees the clear impression that this collection was for the purchase of embarkation tickets. and the refugees wanted to see if giving their articles of gold instead of money to these two who claimed to be lawful agents of the said steamship Company was indeed a project under the auspices of the American Consul, or not.

Arriving in the American Consulate, these two buzzards dashed hastily in with shameless audacity, flashing their identity cards with photographs in them at the young and probably inexperienced sailor guard who was standing in front of the Consulate door. One of the two witness refugees who spoke English accompanied them and they advanced into a little auxiliary study nearby. They turned and looked haughtily at the sole witness who had accompanied them and tried to allay his anxiety by addressing him «Do you see? We are in the U.S.A. Consulate». However, an attentive official of the Consulate, on seeing strangers hastily entering the little auxiliary room, went after them to investigate who they were and what their purpose was in the Consulate. Upon learning the truth by questioning the witness, he tried to grasp the little case with the pouch containing the articles of gold . The two imposters strove to prevent him from doing this, and this fact strengthened the suspicions of the serviceman in charge and caused him to call for help. The Counsul was notified at once of the cause of the altercation, the little case with the pouch inside was confiscated, and the final outcome is already well known to you from my former written narration. A member of the Consulate Staff later said that this was the only time they had seen their Master, who was always so gentle and self-restrained, acting in an indignant and unrestrained manner on account of this infamous matter.

This occurrence took place during the few last and very dramatic days shortly before the departure from Smyrna of your late father. Soon afterwards the Consulate Building was encircled in flames and was burned to ashes.

I try to be as brief as possible in my historical references yet I do this being very mindful not to keep out of the text the most significant of the factual events referred to. For if I was to expand the content to minute details, then I would have written another book in which only those very few of the old generation who are still around would have been interested. The new materialistic generation isn' t interested (even if some of them pretend with pseudo-courtesy to be so) in occurrences that happened almost a century before this it was even born.

If you still have any other doubts or questions which interest you, please make them plain to me so that I can elucidate them to you before I am gone for ever. Right now I am in bad shape after a tortured bout I recently had with a fungus, for the cure of which my physician prescribed me a very drastic drug which I took and which poisoned my system to such a degree that I couldn't eat anything and this has left me emaciated and badly run-down. I am still able with effort to pound the keys of my typewriter but I don' t really know for how long. I am 91 years old (at the time this account was written three years before that is in 1994) and while my brain and intelligence have not yet left me, nobody knows the final issue.

I do hope and pray to live a little longer because I still have to settle the case of my real estate, known as the Villa Atlanta, the place of my wife's birth in Georgia, U.S.A. (the name of the historic capital of the State of Georgia).

I wish to add herewith some necessary and essential explanation about my book «Anatoy of a Disaster». The voluminous appearance of the book (which I have sent to you) makes some people reluctant or disinclined to read it, because its bulky appearance gives the false impression that its print is tiresome to the eyes. Yet the real truth is that this volume is not one book but two books. The first book, which is divided into two Sections, deals with the very tragic catastrophe of Smyrna and its unimagainably great consequences; the real causes of the Greek army' s collapse; the sad extinction of all Christianity from Asia Minor; and finally the question of the real origin of the present day inhabitants who comprise the population of Greece - the various races who have invaded and occuped the land through the passage of centuries, of which they are the descendants or at least their real and recent ancestors.

The second book is an autobiography representing a silhouette of my personality.

This case (the biographer's) is strongly illustrative of the agonizing, swift process of the extremely dramatic developments which jut out at every moment and which emerge as if in a cinematographic sequence. It refers to abhorrent facts which spring out clearly and which are obviously the consequences of the ever shameless and infamous betrayal committed in 1920 by the victorious Great Powers of the First World War. It was a betrayal because they flagrantly despised their solemn pledges and signatures to the Articles of the 1918 Peace Treaty of the First World War which was signed at Sevres, France at the conclusion of the bloody war and because they faithlessly deserted those little nations who were allied to them (and the solemn pledges which they proffered to the world to restore justice, to liberate nations which were under the yoke of bondage and slavery etc, etc.). These promises were given under duress when they were in dire straits during the war and sought to allure the then neutral small nations into joining their war alliance providing to them supplies and manpower, in an effort to defeat the all-powerful enemy who was up to that point winning all the critical battles. In order to persuade the neutral nations to come out of their neutrality and join their war effort, they were not stingy in giving solemn pledges and in proffering false promises. Yet instead of keeping all those solemn promises mentioned above, they proceeded unconsciously to bring to their great nations the indelible stigma of infamy by their 100% reversal of the former Wilsonian Foreign Policy in shamelessly adopting instead a rabidly strong Turkophile Policy and making dirty profitable ventures in Turkey. And this was just in the interests of their foul, dishonest, morally greatly offensive and nauseating greedy gainful interests in Turkey. Namely: *Great Britain* on account of its Mosul oil, in Baghdad, the Pakistan oil-wells which she was exploiting but which until then were under Turkish sovereignty; and also in the interests of her hegemony in the Mediterranean Sea and of her other open sea possessions. *France* in the interests of its complex and wide network of railroads and other businesses in Turkey, and, more than any other consideration, because Turkey owed a solid 60% of its National Debt from loans contracted long before to the Ottoman State as Turkey was named before by the French Treasury and other important French Financial Institutions. In cold reality *a colossal financial capital* was in danger of being lost unless a regenerated and financially healthy and invigorated New Turkey came out of the war, when France hoped to regain this colossal sum when the Turkish debtor was able to pay off its debt.

Italy, to which its other allied partners had promised by Treaty Smyrna and its terrritorial land, before Greece was later promised exactly the same piece of land. This was land which Italy had coveted long before, rich Turkish land, especially Andalia and Smyrna with its fertile interior, in which she could disperse and re-distribute the already bulging and hungry citizenry which was overpopulating her metropolitan areas. Because of this open betrayal by her war allies, she was so bitter against her other allies when Smyrna was ceded by the Treaty of Sevres to Greece instead of to Italy, that she started to counteract each and every decision taken by the Council of the Treaty in regard to helping Greece defeat the then disorganized band of Turkish insurgents. And furthermore, she started divulging to the Turks every secret decision which was taken by the Council behind closed doors regarding the partitioning of Turkish land and the distribution of the same among the victorious Allies, as had been provided by the articles of the Treaty of Sevres. Furthermore, Italy started helping the rebel with guns and amunition, and intriguing in every possible way, setting the Turks against the Greeks, and striving with every means in her power to see the Greek army defeated. *America*, the great U.S.A. World Nation , with the State Department now having been successfully taken over and solidly grasped by the Republican Party (the unavoidable result of the recent US General Election), under the absolute control of the American Chamber of Commerce and the very great Financial Circles of the country who were so eager to make profits. And wielding authoritative power and command in the new course of Foreign Affairs, the newly appointed and eminent Secretary of State of the U.S.A was the hitherto President of the American Standard Oil Company of N.J., the most gigantic petroleum company of all the gigantic petroleum companies, who, so shockingly for most of the world, had temporarily resigned his S.O.C. post for this purpose. In his powers of broad and wide jurisdiction, the new Secretary of State named C.E. Hughes, changed overnight the policy which had until that point been followed in the Foreign Affairs of the Nation and ushered in the new and openly stated policy which was strictly advantageous and plainly exploitative for the ventures of American businessmen in order to make them realize quick profits from their projects. The American Chamber of Commerce, through its affiliate members and via the media of the press, announced an open promotion drive by claiming that there was now in Turkey a field of unlimited opportunities for American businessmen to gain from their entering –almost securely– into business transactions for profit. At the same time the State Department, with its now ample jurisdiction, ordered all U.S. agents in Turkey to exercise from then on an openly strong Turkophile policy and a new line of approach to make friends with them (i.e. the Turks). The worst part of this new policy was the issuing of strict directives to turn inimical strong and full opposition to the Greek expedition, and its agents were ordered to do everything possible and to use all means at their disposal to see that the Greek army –which was then victoriously advancing into the interior of Asia Minor – was stopped and ultimately defeated and kicked out of Turkey. *Biographer's Note:* All the facts stated above are corroborated and proven by indisputable historical sources, diligently cited in my book, yet the result was painstakingly traced, investigated, and brought forward very carefully so as to dig out the plain and bitter truth.

The biographer' s life has been eventful to the highest degree, greatly frustrating and at times throwing him shockingly out of balance. Twice he reached the upper levels of the –so called– important personalities in society, attaining success and public recognition, and almost reaching the borders of the ultimate point . And twice also he has tumbled, falling mercilessly and precipitously down, in his awful fall reaching almost the frightful borders of the pitch-black bottom point of the hopelessly dreadful and depressing darkness of Hell.

The unfolding hellish events of the catastrophe, one of the greatest of the century, involve many important points which interconnect like the links in a chain. Likewise these particular parts of the frightful disaster which has unfolded succeed each other by connecting and interlocking the gradually unfolding sequence of events of this tragic human History. That is, each one of those metaphorical links of a chain rolls outward from the reel of History, revealing a certain portion of its length, just as each one of those parts of the sequence of events reveals each time by itself, and in a much more completely analytical way, certain dramatic historic occurrences of the great catastrophe of the century, possibly the greatest of all on account of the utmost severity and bestiality involved in it: the bloody annihilation and the complete extinction of the entire Christian faith from the geographical territory of Asia Minor, its basic cradle for the thousand years of rule of the Roman Empire. It also stands out for the equally severe and inhuman deeds of bestiality, unique in the annals of human History, which were committed by the instinctively by their Nature savage and destructive Turks, the direct descendants –as has now been historically established – of the cruel and wantonly destructive Asiatic barbarous hordes HUNS who invaded Europe in the fifth century under their brutal leader Attila and who turned it into a wasteland, a shambles and a bloody ruin The success of their ghastly plan, something against which the conscience revolts, was the fact of attaining their long-sought goal of completely, radically and mercilessly wiping out from Asia Minor (and from their old national domain) *two* ancient and historical races which had inhabited this land for innumerable centuries - the Greeks and the Armenians.

The master plan for this hideous crime of the mass extinction of these two races, had been astutely calculated to succeed in its criminally conceived and exterminating purpose. It was the brainchild of the Islamic religious fanaticism of its original founder, which the heads of almost all Turkish governments have since inherited, and naturally showed up in the nationalistic spirit of Turkey's leaders during the Greco - Turkish war of 1919-1922. The then Commander-in-Chief of the nationalist government named Kemal Mustafa, also being strongly possessed with the Muslim spirit of a country which was wholly impregnated with that spirit , was the first to envisage that the time had come to form a purely Islamic Turkish State by exploiting the unexpected and extremely favorable conditions which would enable him to act quickly towards fulfilling this goal. These conditions were now entirely feasible with the rapidly rolling turn of events, a unique opportunity presented to them all like a sudden gift from the almighty ALLAH!

Islamism is a fanatical faith doctrine of the moslem religion and for its factful believers «there is no other god but ALLAH» *(webstes Dictionary)*.

Muhammad (or Mehmet the conqueror) was and still is considered by Muhammedanism «The Prophet» and the founder of Islam. He has established the «Muslim» religion with its extensively wide although with somehow loose concept of «Islamism», the sole religious faith of all the faithful Muhammedans. Muhammad – a fanatical muslim – was a very astute man; And he had early conceived the factual notion that in order to cope with and successfully surmount the grave problem, he had to face, by being obligated, to deal with a large multiplicity of non-islamic people of various other religions faiths; People long being inhabiting and throughout the then having been conquered nations in the vast amounted territorial expansion of lands now on his supervision; He actually thought of taking recourse to the only remaining to him way of solving that crabbedly hard problem, by subjugating and by ruling out all non-islamic religious faiths, thus effacing them all and entirely from his domain and, by so doing, clearly unite this nation with the one and only muslim faith. At the same time, and in order to set on a firm basis his nation's unique faith, he officiated with a great religious ceremony installed and established the supreme Head and the top faith-leader of Islamism the Authority and Dignity of the venerable SHEIHUL ISLAM, the sole infallible, wholly incorruptive faithful who was treated with religious adoration, worshiped, revered and recognized world-over as the muslim leader and religious Head, ruling and reigning above all Sultans and or the various other chiefs of Islamic faith, being considered throughout Muhammedanism as having been ordained by ALLAH himself thus blessed with a halo to execute ALLAH's instructed dicta of HIS critical sacred judgement to men. It was arbitrarily considered by Muhammedanism as ALLAH's pivotal point of HIS WILL that all the non-islamic-faith persons are dirty infidels, and as much had to be completely eliminated and as quickly as feasible.

The supreme religious power invested in SHEIHUL ISLAM and extended above all world's Sultans, had brought forth an uncontrollable envy to the then occupying the Ottoman Empire's throne, the rapacious cruel, and ever machinating Sultan Abdul Hamid (1876-1909), who couldn't stand any longer this overpowering him feeling of envy, which was tormenting him and devouring his heart's colossal ego. Being propelled by this overwhelming feeling of envy, in his rage overextended his given political power in the government, and dared to go above the over him invested authority of SHEIHUL ISLAM by abolishing his divine status with a Sultanic decree. Yet considering the stormy reaction for this of the whirlwind would be raised by the crowds of Islamic faithfulness, proceeded to finalize his intentions with the lasting action of a brutal assassination. By killing the Dignity of Islamism this Sultan, had openly committed a palpable transgression of the divine orders of the Ten Commandments and of the Muslims' sacred «Coran» (the Holy Gospel of Islam). The dead body of SHEIHUL ISLAM was found floating over the sea-waters of the then notorious «Dulma-Backsé» palatial sea, where the assassinated undesirables to the Sultans customarily were thrown into, and which sea was across and facing the various Sultanic palaces where the favored dignitaries of the Sultans were lodged. The dead body of the SHEIHUL IS-LAM had by the Sultanic clique been cunningly and with adroit slyness explained to the arisen upon the death learning crowds of the islamic faithfuls – with a gross lie that as purported, he had been drowned while he was swimming in the Dulma-Backsé sea wrestling the turbulent at the time sea-waves. The treacherous Sultan Abdul Hamid having thereafter a joyous satisfaction by seeing his villainous design successful to the end, had appropriated for himself the functional authority and the worldwide religious dignity of the assassinated divine for the Muslims Head and sacred leader.

For the Turks, the favorable development which allowed them to grasp this unique opportunity was the fact that the great majority of the Greek and Armenian populations of Asia Minor were terrified and fleeing with the collapsed and panicking Greek army, which was being instinctively driven westward toward the littoral large and important Mediterranean ports and civic centers, in the hope and expectation of obtaining the needed transportation vessels for its withdrawal and final removal from Asia Minor; along with them, also swept away and panicking, were millions of Christians. These were nearly all the Greeks and the Armenians who were capable of walking or who were willing in their advanced age to leave behind for ever and to abandon all they had succeeded in achieving and gaining with great struggle, untold efforts and the sweat and toil of a whole life. They were streaming swiftly forward all along the road, crushing into the city of Smyrna and to other littoral towns and villages in great throngs, overcrowded and compressed in their masses (numbering over two million souls, by the computations of Ankara in 1922 in regard to the number of giaours (giaours = dirty infidels) expelled from the Islamic Turkey's nation). These millions, through lack of space, were dispersed in every street and open space which was close and adjacent to the great port of Smyrna. The harbor at that time contained the increased and displayed war-strength of the combined fleet of battle-ships of a considerable number of the Great Powers; ostensibly alas, giving out the false intention of their plan to jointly protect the civic mostly christian population of the unusually crowded city and port of Smyrna from the advancing Turks. The refugees who had poured out from the mainland had been attracted by this supposed protection, and the contributing factor of this pseudo-safety was the reason why they had been induced to drive toward and to prefer Smyrna, which gradually had been flooded and inundated to asphyxiation point with the great masses of the displaced, panicking and stricken refugees.

The local people of Smyrna sympathized greatly with these unfortunate and tragic refugees who had left their homes in such a hurry, leaving behind them their fortunes and everything but those very few things which they had been able to carry, mostly by themselves, through their weary long trail down the beaten track toward Smyrna; they reciprocated truly for their suffering by opening up their houses, by receiving them with love and compassion and by demonstrating in the most practical way that they were sharing their plight. Yet the great masses of the refugees which were squeezing in continually from the mainland, had also flooded all of Smyrna's streets, both large and small, sinking down exhausted somewhere alongside the few heaped-up belongings which they were carrying.

This was the awfully tragic picture of Smyrna at that point and time. The great masses of the gathered refugees were in a pitch-black Hellish condition of suffering and distress on September 9, 1922, just when the regular army of the dreaded enemy entered the city. The indescribably amorphous impression given by this picture of the refugees, with the untidy piled masses on the streets of a compressed crowd of people who were greatly varied in their dress appearance and who were coming from everywhere, avoided any attempt to give an accurate description. It is important to note that almost all of the compressed masses of terrified people who were piled up in the streets in deadly silence and who were expecting nothing but the worst were Greeks and Armenians. The foreign nationals had been instructed by their Consulates to get out of the city because they anticipated trouble, and had left already. And the Turkish quarters were out of the city boundaries, separated from the giaour (infidels) by a very small distance and situated up a hill.

The victorious Turkish army entered the city at about 10 o' clock on 9 September 1922, triumphantly and with fanfares, its cavalry preceding it and performing a showy parade through the promenade Quay with its mounted riders proudly holding up their scimitars (curved sabers), and with brutal insensibility trampling down all those refugees who weren't able to or who couldn't move away in time by pressing themselves towards the already very crowded sidewalks.

So appalling was the hopelessly bad and black condition of the displaced Christians, so hurriedly displaced by terror. This was the unimaginably miserable situation and state of affairs of the great mass of approximately two million despondent refugees. But on the contrary for someone else, this situation presented a hellishly unique and extremely favorable opportunity, under the circumstances a most profitable opportunity to exterminate those masses of giaours, a radiant perspective. This for someone else was the devilishly fierce, scheming, and mercilessly cruel, heartless and brutishly hardheaded leader of the Turkish Government , the dictatorial Chief of Army and State, and then beloved nationalist Turkish Leader. At that point and time, this Turkish leader and Chief of Staff Mustaffa Kemal discovered that the long sought for critical moment had come for him to exterminate those two races most hated by Turkey –the Armenian and Greek races. And he had already decided to proceed quickly and dexterously with a determined and well-calculated program of drastic action, to annihilate both at the same time in a simultaneously executed action, a plotted and infernally deadly violent blow struck against both races. This blow was struck against the Armenians and Greeks, the two races which he deeply hated and profoundly abhorred among all others, and which numbered at this particular time over two million in Smyrna (in accordance with the calculations and the computed statistical data produced by Ankara Staff). Two million Christians who, as good luck would have it for Turkey, had been squeezed into the boundaries of Smyrna, a peripheral area quite manageable on this occasion for the calculated success of the scheme of extinction plotted by the Turks.

It is worth while noting that this densely compressed number of approximately two million Greeks and Armenians presented a unique, unexpected and favorable chance for the Turks. A hard pressed multitude found to be condensed into the comparatively confined area of the limited boundaries of Smyrna had greatly impressed the cruel and dictatorial Turkish Leader, Kemal, to the point of urging and propelling him on to grasp at the opportunity so happily given to him to annihilate these two races, a goal which none of his predecessors could successfully achieve by the defective methods which had been applied time and time again; their piecemeal extirpation was a mode of procedure which had started from the fifth century onwards and since the time of Mohammed (Mehmed the second), the conqueror in 1453 of Constantinople, the former capital of the Hellenic-Roman Empire.

This devilishly shrewd scheme for the annihilation of the two races had initially been the inspiration of its originator, who had diligently worked out all of its detailed points i.e. the authoritative and inhumanly pitiless dictatorial Leader of Turkey, Kemal Mustafa.

This predetermined scheme for an abhorrent action had been studied, organized, and improved to a strategically perfect point by the Turkish Army's Staff Council which consisted of absolutely reliable friends of the Leader's entourage who were appointed by him and who were of the same ideology i.e. they envisaged the formation of a pure Islamic Turkish State. The Turkish Staff's Council named this «master plan».

This infernal and satanically inspired action anticipated the simultaneous causing of a violent and sudden fiery explosion by a conflagration all around the area; an intense fire of very high saturation, girdling and engulfing the city of Smyrna, making it entirely impenetrable to access or exit by the violently combustible agitation. The wild fire had to be kept incessantly ablaze by continually rekindling it.

Keeping the fire going without cessation was (for the inhuman perpetrators of this criminal plan) a comparatively easy task on account of the plentiful and varied combustible material which was found to have been left by the collapsed Greek army, which had departed in panic. This was left and stored in huge warehouses nearby on the outskirts of Smyrna; they were filled with plenty of flammable substances (huge tanks full of benzine, kerosene, naphtha, and other combustible hydrocarbons, as well as a variety of flammable dry material, powders, boxes of dynamite, handgrenades and a variety of other matter useful to the army for road-making and for many other of its war purposes).

The tragic thing is that it had been an almost impossible task for these extremely useful materials and plenty of war ammunition and explosives besides, to be forwarded to the Greek front lines where they were urgently required– on account of the lamentably worrisome and stark lack of operational lorries to provide the necessary transportation.

The skillful handling of the entrapping of the giaours with an impenetrable fire, the most important and critical task for the success of the master-plan being the decisive factor of keeping the huge fire furiously ablaze at all times, was to be given (as it was reckoned to be the one momentous and most critical responsibility) to designated squads of fanatical Turks well known for their rabid hatred of Armenians and Greeks, who were chosen on this occasion from among hundreds and hundreds of volunteers. Paradoxically and contrary to all expectations, their task was greatly –but unsuspectingly– facilitated by their being able to use the city's fire-engines and conduits into which they poured flammable matter instead of water. It must be admitted that, even though it was a ghastly and macabre scheme, nonetheless it was, as the Turks said, a strategically elaborated masterpiece, intelligently carried out to martial art perfection.

But if it had been implemented exactly as strictly and as strategically as was prescribed by the Turkish Army Staff, it would have succeeded in incinerating in its entirety the Greek and Armenian population of the city, now innumerable with the crowded refugees, by viciously trapping them inside the encircling inferno of raging flames. This inferno would have transformed both human beings and the structures housing them into an ugly calcinated mass of incinerated human bodies and the burned down black skeletons of the city's buildings as the fury of the raging fire sprang forth from the extreme boundaries of the city limits and advanced into the center.

All but for two very important but elusive elements - two paramount prerequisites for the sound success of the plan which were grossly missing. The two factors were omitted from the outline of the plan and drastically influenced its outcome. Because the missing components escaped the planners' notice, their plan did not contain two of the fundamental essentials for a thorough success. One of these weighty elements, it is true, had not been or could not possibly have been foreseen by the planners, and so this otherwise perfect plan failed to be a triumphant success and to achieve the desired outcome.

Because of these unforeseen deficiencies, the Turkish plan was to a great extent abortive and partially unsuccessful, a fact which gave time to and helped to a great extent considerable numbers of the refugees to escape the deadly danger of being incinerated alive.

However, the great consequential inherent urge of the refugee masses to save themselves with a panicky rush resulted in a huge and extremely precipitous stampede away from the furiously blazing city, through the pitifully very few still accessible main thoroughfares which had been purposely left unblocked by the rapacious-minded and undisciplined Turks. The highways and streets through which the stream of refugees were trying to squeeze in panic led to the interior of the country and to the very dangerous open fields.

In stark reality, the greatly frightened masses of refugees who were running blindly were actually nothing but a panicking stampeding and terror-stricken crowd of people who, in their inordinate rush, injuriously trampled on and crushed against each other.

Worse was still to come because the Turks became fiercely enraged when they saw that their plan had been aborted to a great extent, and that those whom they hated were escaping the hoped-for extinction by holocaust which had been ingenuously contrived by their adored master, a scheme which planned to wipe them out from the face of the earth.

Possessed by a blind Islamic fanaticism, and taking a sort of revenge for the unexpected and repugnant turn of «giaours» events, they had increased their unquenchable hatred of the Greeks and the Armenians and multiplied the intensity of their mass and indiscriminate killing –ghastly crimes against helpless people, actions accompanied by firstly robbing the victims and then perpetrating all sorts of grisly bestialities.

The burning question which arose internationally was: «What were those two missing fundamental prerequisites for the Turkish «master plan» to its achieving success?» The two essentials which had eluded the planners' foresight, and yet had been so tremendously important for the success of the outcome, essentials whose non-incorporation in the plan and non-implementation had so enormously upset and overthrown the otherwise perfect Turkish plan?

In analyzing the first of the two missing elements which were so tremendously important it is necessary to point out the following.

The planners conceived their «master plan» and laboriously worked on it, hoping for a grand and shining success. They thought that their plan was perfect, and they were with certainty expecting a triumphant success; the success which they dreamed of was to clean-sweep Turkey and once and for all, wiping out Greeks and Armenians, many centuries-old Christian races who, the Turks considered in their Islamic fanaticism, had inflicted a double scourge on Turkey. Yet, «Astonishingly missing, and very conspicuously apparent, was an indispensable and tremendously important component in the mechanism (or arrangement of the absolutely needed essentials). The component which was thoroughly absent was a completely non-existent adaptation to an integrated stark conformity; the complete absence and non-existence of a harsh, severely unsparing, very strict and uncompromising «discipline» on all those responsible to apply coordinated action and to keep a vigorous «control» and a sharp eye upon all the accountable squads, to see that the timetable of the plan was relentlessly enforced to the letter.

Even the orderly and necessary disciplinary control was deplorably lacking and this determined and affected the conduct of action which every single one of the performers in a subordinate position was responsible for doing.

This grave prerequisite was flagrantly missing. The question «Why?» might be asked. This becomes partially intelligible with the following psychological explanation of the Turkish character.

As a race of roaming nomads in the Kirghiz Steppe, where their direct ancestors, the Huns, lived, they were instinctively a typical aggregated flock race, similar by nature to the vegetarian type of animals who herd together. But each member of the race had to find food and feed himself or herself individually. The pattern of human society in the present day whereby most people share did not exist; instead each fed himself by his own effort. as still clearly done by cows, goats, sheep, and most vegetarian and even some carnivorous animals. «Discipline» was unknown to them, and usually they had nobody to obey. In other words they were a race of an inherently self-centered and disobedient people who grouped together for protection from other flocks who were wilder than them.

The Turkish soldiers and civilians who were involved in this project lacked the «discipline» to obey and to follow strict instructions. And by their own spontaneous initiatives, they clearly disobeyed and deviated from their instructions, individually straying from and in their subordination frustrating the planned and intended simultaneous outburst of a fire which would encircle the city.

Then there were many obvious delays and irregularities with regard to the all too important synchronization of the planned integrated action in the creation of an unbroken chain of fire around the periphery which would engulf the whole city, a prerequisite which was mighty essential and enormously indispensable to the brilliant success of the Turkish plan.

Then those responsible and appointed to man the various warehouse depots where the flammable materials were kept were eager neither to instantly distribute the urgently needed stuff nor to be energetically active and quick in their part of the whole scheme. The hundreds of squads carrying out the obligatory and very essential job of supplying the necessary combustibles which would be hurled into the fire in order to keep it ablaze incessantly, slothfully waited for hours at times for the sluggard keepers to dispense the firematerials to them and to fill up the receptacles in the vehicles.

On the other hand, most of those responsible for keeping the combustibles had not been supplied urgently needed buckets or with the proper flexible tubing conduits or the absolutely necessary artificial channels of rubber pipelines for conveying the fuels. Also apparent and very obvious was the absence of the essential means of communication with their superior officers and lay-functionaries whom they could ask to smooth over their many difficulties and the problems which arose.

Finally, because under the circumstances they had been providently given varied instructions to carry out, depending on the still unknown developments of the situation, these multipurpose orders threw them into a state of true bewilderment and filled their minds with confusion and indecision. They were told to act intelligently and in conformity with the conditions which existed at the time and to carry out the order which the moment most urgently demanded.

They were very uncertain about these dubious orders which involved multipurpose occurrences – and especially considering that they were illiterate people. (They are grammatically used at that time, to make a doubtful yet and undeveloped in the present point and time event, yet which is expected to be coming hereafter usually with a preposition distinguished with the preceding words «if», «maybe», «perhaps», «as maybe the case», «with God's wish», etc.). Most Turks, who had a low acumen and who were a very backward race of long-living bestial nomadic hordes on the Kirghiz Steppe, came south-west with the name HUN-YU in around 3.000 B.C. Then they spread all over Asia under the name of Hunni or Huns, the butchers and destroyers of all Europe when they invaded it in around 450 A.D. and they brought unimaginably great death and destruction. They, the Turks, are now positively affirmed as the direct descendants of the Huns, or Hunni as the contemporary Byzantine historian Procopius calls them (those people today known as Turks).

They were familiar with a plain and very simple way of life, following a routine and an uncomplicated pattern of work and abyssmally backward at that time. This meant – and it becomes obvious – that the Turkish plan openly failed to be carried out to the letter and thus to accomplish its planned scope.

It was pointed out that this was the first of the two most indispensable elements for the expected triumphant success of the Turkish «master plan», one which had eluded the attention of the planners and which they had erroneously omitted to seriously consider and completely scrutinize. Yet it wasn't done and thus one factor of paramount importance, which was a fundamental prerequisite necessary on the occasion for the successful conclusion of the plan, was missing. On the contrary, the grave omission of this factor helped greatly in the adverse derailment of the plan and led to the failure to materialise of the desired outcome.

The second of these two very weighty elements, which was also a prerequisite for a successful accomplishment of the Turkish «master plan» and which couldn't possibly have been foreseen with the imperfect meteorological instruments in use at that time, and yet was a prerequisite which was perceptibly missing, was the benevolent support of favorable weather conditions.

At the beginning of the implementation of the plan, everything seemed to be greatly assisting its success. At that very point and time the wind was blowing very forcibly in a north-east to north-south direction; this greatly helped the Turkish plan by strongly enlivening the circular course of the blaze and actively quickening the speed of the fire which had been so fervidly kindled, aiming for a wholesale incineration of the entire Christian population which was caught inside the city limits, trapped by the huge encircling fire which had been so satanically started.

From an elevated point on the roof top of our semi-three-storey family house, we could clearly see the indescribably huge conflagration, its voracious fire of death steadily advancing towards the area of the city where we ourselves were standing. This was in harsh reality a gigantic and awful inferno extensively spreading out, engulfing and tending to encircle the city in the shape of an colossal two-edged pincer. The central point of the pincer of this immensely wild blaze (and probably its original starting point) seemed on the dark horizon which we could see from our high observation post to have started in the far away south-west part of the city; it was coming fast and taking in the very area where we were standing (the great heat was already brushing our bodies).

The fire had a distinctly semi-circular shape, with the pincer points of its utmost extremities advancing clearly ahead as if at a galloping speed, and luminously indicating with the progression of its circular course the calculated and intended aim of encircling the whole city. This in turn revealed a-plenty the ultimate intent of the Turkish «master plan» final aim ie of entrapping all of a sudden the very crowded population, which at that time was extremely compressed within the space of the city of Smyrna, and of abruptly incinerating all of it, together with the «giaour» city of Smyrna which they hoped to burn to ashes and thus to calcinate for ever the once large, thriving and beautiful Greek Metropolis in Asia Minor. (I can pinpoint here the exact time of the descriptions given just above: it was on the evening of September 13, 1922, between 6.30 and 7 pm, Smyrna Greenwich Meantime).

Unfortunately for the Turkish plan, one of the two most important factors which were prerequisities necessary for accomplishing the desired success , which was so urgently required on this occasion, and which initially concurred so favorably with the plan, was unexpectedly and all of a sudden lost. A little after midnight the strong north-easterly wind which had been fiercely blowing until then shifted to the north-west, blowing hard in the harbour of Smyrna against the almost two dozen battleships of the victorious World War I Great Powers, a most powerful fleet of warships which was then anchored very close to the city's piers. This was a serious, unfavorable and countermanding drawback which also helped (with its counterbalancing inherent power) to derail the Turkish «master plan».

Yet the most inexplicable and intriguing thing to be observed from the high altitude of the roof-top observation post of our family semi-three-story house was something really baffling; although a clear picture could be inferred and drawn from attentively observing the unobstructed horizon of the periphery of the city, a certain conclusion was judiciously being formed. It was a picture which depicted the visibly clear horizon engulfing the whole area of the city of Smyrna. From this fact we could deduce and see the clear picture of a peripheral encirclement of a deliberately circular fire. The picture outlined the direction of the blaze with a persuasive certainty and of the destructive fire which was already raging furiously to the south-east. A clear picture was unquestionably being drawn there and then. And yet, at that point and time, there was a total absence of any significant fire to be seen in the area opposite that which was already in the throes of a furiously blazing fire, the whole of the south-eastern. area of the city which was engulfed with fire. But none was to be seen in the far away north-western area of the city, although the route of the fire was undoubtedly circular, coming directly and speedily towards our area (I can again pinpoint the exact time of this description: it was 6.30 to 7 p.m. Smyrna Greenwich Meantime, on September 13, 1922). It will remain forever an execrable date for the utter infamy of the so-called Christian Nations which actively helped ISLAM to wipe out Christianity from Asia Minor.

At this point and time it is worth noting and we should consider the very interesting question of Who?, When?, Where?, and Why? the final decision to annihilate this human mass, so unimaginably and innumerably great in the annals of History (a human sacrifice to the deity of Islam «Allah») was taken and who ordered that Turkish «master plan» to be implemented, to start with.

Late in the evening of September 12, 1922, and at about 11 p.m, the Italian Consul in Smyrna had visited his colleague, the English Consul, (both of the Smyrna Diplomatic Corps) and had entrusted to him this first-hand secret information which he had acquired, adding: At this moment the Turkish Leader is having discussions with his trusted friends (he had hurriedly called a special meeting in the nearby Smyrnean suburb of Baldjova); he wants their consent to his decision to put into effect at once and without any delay, the plan for the extermination of the Armenians and Greeks «giaours» which is ready to be carried out.

He thought, he said, that the moment they were waiting for had arrived. They (the giaours) were now crowded in crushing compactness inside Smyrna, a fact which gave them the unique opportunity to start at once to implement their «master plan». (Italy had helped Turkey quite a lot in its struggle to defeat the Greek army, and this had endeared them to the Turkish Leader to the point where he trusted the Italian Consul). The very next day, 13, September 1922, this Turkish plan was put into effect. The entire Diplomatic Corps became aware of what the Italian Consul knew.

Who was this revolutionary Leader of Turkey who had established for the first time in Turkish History a so-called Democratic Government in the post-World War I modern Turkish nation? Who did away entirely with the effects of the terms of the World War Treaty which were so onerously oppressive against Turkey? Who had single-handedly abrogated all the terms of the decisions takne in 1918 in the articles of the First World War Peace Agreement imposed by the victorious Great Powers with the «Treaty of Sevres». Terms which imposed the complete dismemberment of the Turkish Empire, and the assigning and sharing out of the territorial areas among themselves? Who had the temerity and the nerve to abolish the great «Sultanic Regime» of the Ottoman Empire, established by Mohammed II, the Conquror, so long before (and so sacred among the Moslems)?

His real name was Mustafa Kemal. The word «Ataturk» added later to his actual name was a plain flattery. It was given to him by his close friends and the sycophants in his entourage, mainly to gratify his enormous ego, and then to help aggrandize his name-prestige among his countrymen, by glorifying his otherwise very common peasant name of Mustafa. The word «Ataturk» was translated from the amply bastardized «Hunnish» language which the Turks speak today, it is explanained in the English language by the meaning: «Father of the Turks» (that is «savior of the Turks»).

(Flattery and flatterers are an age-old tradition throughout History. Flattery is given to greatly imposing personalities and there are innumerable examples of it).

The flatterers of Constantine the Great in 330 A.D added to the name «New Rome» which Constantine had triumphantly given to his new Capital of the Empire; the name «Constantinople» just to flatter his ego and to gratify his greatly imposing personality. King Richard I of England was given in 1180 by his flatterers the grandiose title of the «Lionheart». King Louis XIV of France was flatterered by the title of the «Le Soleil» (The Sun). The King of the Germanic Frankish Empire Charles the Great, was flatterered with the title of «Charlemagne» (The Great Charles) and so on and so forth).

Mustafa Kemal was the victorious Commander in Chief at the time of the Greco-Turkish war of 1919-1922, the absolute Leader of the Turkish revolution against the terms of the Treaty decided upon by the Great Powers for its subjugation, and the first President of the Democracy of Turkey from 1923 to 1938. He was born in 1881 in Thessaloniki, (Salonica), a northern Greek city of a land which now belongs to the Greek Nation but which at that time was a territorial extension of the land which was under the jurisdiction and sovereignty of the Ottoman (Turkish) Empire.

He was by no means a blue-blooded Turk; far from it. He was actually a half-caste, the offspring of a mixed marriage. The matrimony of a «Turk» father and a «Jewish» mother. A «donmé» in their local turkish - albanian dialect.

He inherited the ferociously inhuman cruelty and the bestiality and utter brutality of his father's «Kirghiz - Steppe» Hun forefathers on the one hand, and on the other hand a discerning character with opportunistic flexibility, an acute astuteness and wily shrewdness from his «Jewish» mother.

He was a tall young man, thin, with quick-moving blue eyes, athirst with a burning ambitious innermost anxiety and possessed with the eagerness to become somebody. At about that time had started to be implemented a well calculated Germany's plan.

It foresaw the gratifying effects of turning the mentality of all those well-treated and highly educated young men in Germany's highly specialized educational Institutions, Schools and Universities –free of any charge– to form that way, and from then on to possess and display a clear-cut pro-German mentality of a mutually accommodating concern and friendship for the future. This program was initiated in the last part of the 19th century. It was officially approved and actively promoted by the leaders of the German Government, the «Reichskanzer», and highly sanctioned by Kaiser Wilhelm II Hohenzollern.

The ulterior motives which strongly influenced the inauguration of this German plan were pretty obvious. For almost four centuries the Ottoman Empire, under the dictatorship of the almighty Sultan, had been letting Anglo-French concerns have the monopoly of exploiting Turkey's various resources, while being adverse to those in Germany. With their plan they astutely and correctly foresaw that their learned and now friendly young Turkish friends would soon find a chance, favorable to them, to grab, seize and usurp the power of the Sultan, who was favoring Anglo-French interests in Turkey, in opposition to and to the detriment of German interests.

Kemal somehow managed to attract the attention of the German recruiters who were then dispersed all over Turkey's territorial lands and who had been assigned to implement a German program then in progress, which had been officially adopted and at the time was being actively promoted by the German Government which aimed at recruiting intelligent or ambitiously alert young Turks. This program was a shrewdly devised plan for its longer-term anticipated effects.

The German recruiters had correctly seen that Mustafa Kemal possessed the rudimentary essentials to be developed into a military high officer or even a leader. They sent him to Germany where he was enrolled in military schools. He gradually progressed and finally managed to get into the Imperial Military Academy of Germany. He was conferred enticingly with the then famous German iron cross and with several other military decorations.

(Source: «Germany's Official Records», Lord Kinross, «Kemal's Biography», which is nevertheless very biased in favor of Kemal's achievements and who soft-pedals on or omits altogether the totality of his very grave and barbarous drawbacks).

To return to our main narrative. We were the last family in our entire street to vacate and abandon our house and only did so when the hot flames of the colossal and voracious fire started by the Turks in the conflagration of Smyrna had already come very near, giving us the signal to depart. We had delayed evacuating our house for three reasons: 1. Sentimental - we did not want to abandon our beloved home of a lifetime 2. On account of my father being weak after an operation and 3. On account of the terrifying prospect of the unknown but certain traps which awaited us and which had been set by the Turks who were now lurking all around us, ready to grab anything precious you were holding and then to kill or bestially torture you.

We finally departed. We came out on to the empty street under a rain of red ash and little pieces of matter which were still burning which the heat-blowing power of the razing fire was constantly shooting forward in the strong hot wind.

Our uncertain steps led us to a rivulet of human beings who were streaming out. Little by little and with the tardy rhythm of a gradually increasing volume and development, this finally turned into the impetuous and wild human river of a mass exodus of refugees. This panic was actually a blind following of the sole arterial way which the Turks had left still open and which was therefore the only one remaining for the exodus of the refugees. Yet the terror-stricken and instinctive urge to run and run via this arterial way was a presage and a clear omen of the great danger lurking ahead. Because it was leading into the deep and very dangerous interior of the country, far away from the sea port of Smyrna, and the international war fleet which was anchored there and which, it was thought at the time (futilely as it turned out) would give some protection to the Christian population.

The sequence of our successful escape from the danger of being incinerated by the fire was destined to be tragically eventful for the entire family. It was as if we were all of a sudden snatched up and violently swallowed into the wild human sea, which was being impelled on and on in panic like an unrestrainable invincible force, a psychological terror-dominated streaming torrent, which was sweeping away everything in its path. We were each one of us lamentably snatched up - for ever as we frightfully thought – and we disappeared into the indescribable chaos of a moving compact mass of people, in the midnight darkness of insane surroundings. We remember having had the definite impression that it was an entirely unexpected miracle when those of us who were lost in that wild human sea were reunited with the family. This was owing to the cool-head of some of the young members of our family who had not yet begun to panic and who waited for a long time with their backs to a wall, trying all the time to repel the human bodies which were falling upon them, until the happy moment when they saw through the reddish light which was falling upon them (a reddish light which the cloudy sky was reflecting back to earth, the bloody red light of the blazing city), the silhouettes of the two older members of the family with their ill and weak father, moving with great difficulty helped by my brother and actually being pushed toward them, walking near the wall on the right sidewalk where they were standing.

Yet, even in the very early stages of our extreme anguish, when we were trying to flee the fire which was chasing us, we had a harrowing experience and a brutally painful, jolting blow in a very dramatic episode which took place even before the occurrence of the heart-rending event described above.

In the swiftness of the passing time, a certain moment arrived when the mad rush of refugees who were pushing us from behind had forcibly pressed us against a point which was greatly alarming and fateful, but unavoidable; it was the confluence, where all of the several rivulets made up of smaller refugee groups and which were flowing onward, were to join up by rushing into the wildly boiling and terrifying stream of the torrent of the main body of the mass exodus of the refugees.

When we had reached that very perilous point, having slipped along with and joined the human maelstrom which was swinging and bubbling with vibration, the above mentioned piercing dramatic experience happened. It was discovered, hardly a minute after it had happened, that the two little girls of the family were missing. They were nowhere close-by and had just disappeared all of a sudden. When our mother, who had kept them close to her at all times, finally succeeded in freeing herself from the dense mob surrounding her, which was pressing her and making it hard for her to move, she then perceived that the two girls were missing and were not close to her any longer. She was mightily stirred-up with great anxiety and jumped at once into action with agonizing force.

Mother was a highly cultured woman who had had a broad education in the classics, languages and fine arts and she was a well-known and distinguished member of Smyrna's intellectual society. These inherent qualities must have helped her to keep her cool at that agitating and very serious moment. She did not panic but instead immediately started to calculate how far the speedy mob was moving every second in its onward rush, and on which side of that main road the two little girls who had been swept away might be by then. And she figured out that the girls could not have been more than 30 to 50 feet away. Then, without a moment's delay, she darted into the mob like a wild enraged tiger, pushing and shoving hard with all her remaining strength, and gradually gaining on the moving mob in speed and going ahead.

Although she did not delude herself, knowing pretty well that she was searching in the chaos of a bubbling human multitude and in the darkness of midnight and that it was probable that she would fail to find the girls, yet she never lost hope, neither did she ever think of giving up her difficult attempt.

They were —as she figured out afterwards— 150 to 170 feet away from the point where she had started the search, when all of a sudden she heard the word.«mother»; She looked ahead and downwards and there was one of the little girls hard pressed inside the bulk of the mob. She made a sudden movement and snatched the little girl by her clothes. She immediately asked her where they had been separated and where the other one had gone and when the girl pointed in a certain direction, she darted on, pulling the little girl whom she had found with her. They were no more than 20 to 30 feet from the starting point of her desperately pushing and shoving search when she suddenly caught sight of the other girl, pressed into the mass of the mob (she recognized her on account of the bright color of her clothes). At once, using her last strength, she jumped violently, thrusting into the mob, and when she finally found her, she grabbed the little girl hard by her clothes and was now holding both girls. Panting hard, her heart beating fast and bathed in a heavy perspiration from head to foot, she started pulling the two girls at a slow snail's pace, pushing towards the right sidewalk. When she reached it, she turned her back and those of the girls to the wall, and waited until she had regained her composure. Then she laboriously started the toilsome task , step by step, of going back to find the rest of the family. She first met the two boys who were waiting with their backs stuck hard to the wall. She stopped, and after thinking quickly, she decided to leave the girls under the protection of the two boys ; she went back to find her sick husband and her elder son and this undertaking also ended succesfully. Retracing their steps they again moved with agony and close to the wall which somehow kept their right side protected from the hard pushing and the thoroughly terrified and almost insanely running and bursting onward just behind them people, until the three of them met the waiting boys and girls and so the family was once again reunited.

We were all physically and mentally tired-out to the point of extreme fatigue, and the idea of continuing to go along with the terror-stricken mob, in the middle of the night and to an unknown destination, was problematic. It was almost certain that the moment of complete exhaustion would arrive when one by one, no longer having the strength to go on, we would drop to the ground and be trampled upon, becoming a rug for the mob to step on; this had already happened to hundreds of the sick, old, weak or entirely exhausted refugees and they had already met that horrible fate.

We wanted to avoid this terrible fate, as well as the many lurking traps the Turks had set on the way to the terrifying unknown along the main road which led to the extremely dangerous faraway open country of the interior. As we were proceeding along the path, we entered the city's large cemetery, which was conveniently close by, on the wise advice and insistence of my elder brother that we should spend the night there. In order to hide ourselves from the Turks who were following close behind the running refugees, killing and torturing them, we concealed ourselves inside the upper chamber of a mausoleum which had been left pried-open.

Unfortunately for us, a member of the family who owned the mausoleum had recently been buried in the lower chamber and the decomposed and rotten body emitted a sickening, choking and suffocatingly awful odor of ptomaine.

That putrid and stinkingly rotten, hellish odor of ptomain emanated through to the upper chamber through the marble plaque which was very poorly and clumsily adapted to the square opening below. For the two nights we hid there, we suffered indescribably abhorrence and this greatly surpassed the wish to live on under such inhuman conditions and even the fear of being killed and of dying.

Early in the morning of the second night so horribly spent (and the second day from the start of the fire), we left the cemetery, and just in the nick of time, because a lone Turkish guard was placed in front of the three-fold iron gate, which was, luckily for us, very clumsily chained yet unlocked. Exactly the very next day the gate was securely locked - as learned-and all the inside people were shut in. My brother, with an imperious manner and entirely disregarding the presence of the Turkish guard, unchained it and opened it up thus letting the family go through and leave the cemetery. From then on the sequence of the tragic story is already known to you, as a summary has been written and dispatched to your Washington address.

So far I have given details which expose some of the very dramatic and noteworthy episodes which are of weighty historical value, which reveal some of our own excruciating physical and mental suffering and which give a clear eyewitness picture of the torments and travails which the wretched and unfortunate refugees went through right up to the end. In order to conclude the description of this excerpt from the great drama, I will now condense the ensuing sequel of some very frantic and hair-raising moments in order to arrive at the final historical events of the drama which it is worth divulging for their concrete and unshakable indisputability.

The end of the sharp ultimatum was now approaching; the Leader of the Turkish Government and victorious Military Commander had delivered it to the Great Powers (with their large yet inactive war fleet of menacing battle-ships still anchored in the harbor of Smyrna), telling them that they must either take all the refugees away from Turkey within two weeks or they would all be deported deep into the interior of Anatolia (i.e. they would perish).

During those two weeks after the ultimatum had been delivered, or from the much more accurate date indicated by the 1922 calendar ie the chronologically correct date of 13 September 1922 Greewich Meantime, when the Turks started the great conflagration and the catastrophe of Smyrna, we went through untold suffering which is literally indescribable - it was truly monstrously strong and unimaginable to anyone reading this written description of the distress which we endured.

Namely: Two weeks of the atrocious and tormenting anguish of the pains of starvation (a complete deprivation of any form of food); drinking heavily contaminated water full of pathogenic bacteria and germs; the complete absence of indispensable sanitation facilities; our susceptibility to scores of communally transmitted diseases which had been hatched in those most unhealthy and miasmatic surroundings; the fatal non-existence of direly needed medical experience and practical nursing skill and assistance; staying for a long time in unhealthy conditions and sleeping for days in the open in unfavorable and extremely inclement weather conditions of intermittent rain, cold, damp, a bone-chilling north wind, the heat of the sun, etc. And over and above all those calamitous evils, the daily Turkish torture, rape, robbery of everything dear to the refugees, killing, grabbing young and beautiful girls, abducting and taking away boys and men with the heart-breaking pitiful consequence of hearing the despairing cries and sobs of the wives, children, mothers, sisters, etc - a long, heart rending, vehement and loud lamentation because they all knew only too well that there was hardly any chance of seeing them again. And lastly there was the ever-present and harrowing question of what was going to be their end.

On the bright and sunny morning of September 26, 1922, and a short time before the two week «Kemal's» ultimatum ended, seven small Greek ships, which were not flying the Greek flag, appeared at the entrance to the port of Smyrna with a Turkish tug-boat leading the way, and heading toward the deepest point of the harbor where the commercial wharves were, and where the merchant marine ships were loaded. It was evident that some arrangement must have preceded this unexpected event (they were flagless except for the leading ship, on the bridge of which was Jennings who had raised a small American flag).

Later on it became known that the frail, shrunken, unimpressive little man of about 45 years old, who however proved to have a big heart, was named Asa Jennings. He was serving at the time as an auxiliary employee at the Y.M.C.A. in Smyrna and he had become consciously bitter and very critical of the inhuman and cruelly apathetic inaction of the Great Powers to do something to save this tragic situation in which the mass of those innumerable Christian refugees found themselves. (At that very time the Great Powers were mighty afraid of offending the sensibilities of the victorious Turkish leader by helping his most hated enemies, the Greek and Armenian refugees; they were afraid that by so doing they would lose his favorable influence which was very necessary for the success of their calculated schemes of profitable investment, interests, and future ventures in Turkey. And so they were the inhumanly inactive and merciless on-lookers at the greatest human drama in the annals of History).

Jennings finally revolted against this inaction and, being propelled by an inner urge, started acting energetically on his own volition and initiative, obeying none of the orders given by the higher-up officials of the U.S. Government. The new Commander of Smyrna, Captain Halsey Powell, was less strict and authoritatian than his predecessor Captain Japy Arthur Hepburn. On the contrary he was humanly sensible to the great suffering of the refugees, and disregarded Jennings' infractions of the orders. In the beginning Captain Powell showed a tacit tolerance to Jennings' repeated infringements of the various commands, but very soon and as the misery around him multiplied, he even encouraged Jennings' efforts, and approved his doings.

Jennings was daring in his efforts to obtain help and when he succeeded in doing so, he sailed to the island of Mytilini to take there some very minute number of the refugees initially under his protection and to leave them in the island governor's care; he had with difficulty found and paid for a little ship to transport them. When he saw 26 small passenger ships empty and idle inside the harbour of Mytilini, which had just transported the defeated Greek army from Turkey to Greece, and while there was such a tremendously urgent need of ships to evacuate the suffering and dying refugees of Asia Minor, he became greatly excited, reaching the point where he became foolhardy. He immediately sent a coded radio message from the Greek battleship Kilkis, the captain of which was willing to help Jennings and his effort to rescuing the badly needing transportation suffering retched refugees, and which was lying idle in the harbor of Mytilini, to the reactionary and recalcitrant royalist regime of the then Greek Government, and perpetrated a gross bluff on it. Claiming to be the Chairman of the American Relief Committee in Mytilini (which he wasn't), he told them in sharp and demanding language that «if he did not receive a favorable reply by six o' clock that evening, he would wire openly and without code, so that the message could be picked up by any wireless station, that although the Turkish authorities had given their permission and that although the American Navy had guaranteed protection (which was not true), yet the recalcitrant Greek Government would not permit Greek ships to be sent to save Greek and Armenian refugees who were awaiting certain death or something worse at any moment».

The Greek Cabinet (which four days later was overthrown by a massive revolution of the army and of the Greek people, who were enraged by the disgraceful defeat in Asia Minor and the indescribably awful catastrophe of Smyrna) acting even before the clock showed 6 o' clock, alarmed by his threat, replied to Jennings «All ships in Aegean sea are placed under your command to remove refugees from Smyrna». In other words, Jennings was made Admiral of the entire Greek fleet.

In this way, Jennings obtained the Greek ships and, as we have seen, began the evacuation of refugees from Smyrna and elsewhere.

A virtual sea of eyes, a sea of thousands of anxious eyes was glued on those 7 ships which sailed in that morning; they were the eyes of the great mass of refugees who were crushed and sunk depressed down upon the cold, damp flat pavement of the Quay. They had amassed upon the paved surface of this wide and picturesque Smyrnean promenade Boulevard in the hope of protection. Seeing this unusual convoy of seven small ships heading toward the commercial wharves, they intuitively apprehended that, these were just the first ships coming to take them away from the true hell in which they found themselves. And at once a multitude of this populace darted toward the road which led to those wharves.

This great urge to be saved as soon as possible had influenced our family too; in the excitement of the moment we had (quite prematurely and inopportunely as was proved by the unfortunate ill-effects of this haste) left the shelter of the roof we were under which was protecting us from all the inclement elements of the weather and from the great danger of the indiscriminate mass killing by the bloody mad Turks.

For the family it had been a very painful and extremely eventful odyssey on account of their rush to be saved. After great efforts to overcome many torturing obstacles which they met on their way, they reached the square where an iron fence surrounded the wharves. The wharves, which were closed-in with a circular iron rail, comprised a tripartite complex with separate platforms and berths, so that several ships could be accommodated at the same time. In every spot both inside and outside the wharf complex a mass of the most fanatical and bloodthirsty Turkish elements were gathered. They were mad with an insane hatred and incited by an Islamic madness which had now been increased and made strongly bitter by the sight of their «giaour» enemies being saved from the fire they had started and who were now escaping from their grasp. In their furious frenzy they started killing madly, employing for this end not only guns but also every murderous device which could inflict pain and agony on their tortured victims. The constant crackling of machine-guns and rifle shots was deafening. The crushed crowd which was preceding us turned precipitously back in terror in a huge and wholly unrestrained wave, falling upon us and entombing us under its bulk. My poor father was asphyxiated and he stopped breathing after having being nearly suffocated under the refugees who crushed on top of him and it took the desperate and extreme efforts of my elder brother and mother to rescue him and bring him near to the sea, where they restored his breathing with cold water and artificial respiration .

This hellish situation persisted with uninterrupted continuity, propelled by a rabid and insane Islamic fanaticism and bitter revenge for the Greek occupation; it seemed not to have slackened even after five hours of spending their energy with no respite by 2 o' clock in the afternoon. Yet the excessively great energy so morbidly consumed by the Turks for about five hours on end was bound to affect their strength and reduce it gradually so that it declined to almost nothing with most of them falling down on the ground and for the moment rendered them inactive. It was at one of such moments that one platform of the three wharves was seen to be empty of people with one of the ships permitted to be moored to one of the wharves. Exploiting this advantageous moment, some daring refugees proceeded speedily and boarded the ship, the only one which was berthed; the other six out of the seven were coasting in the surrounding waters because the Turks, disobeying orders, were shooting at them and would not allow them to berth.

The family stood still as if it were petrified on the spot which it had initially reached, terrified from seeing around them refugees cruelly murdered, moving neither forwards nor backwards.

Grasping the favorable moment of this opportunity, so unexpectedly given, the mother of the family run over towards us, the younger members of the family, and told us: «Don't wait, proceed at once and board that ship» and she pointed out the only one which was yet berthed. And we did so, but only after she had first with foresight delegated to me the responsibility and put me in charge of taking all necessary steps , as the elder one of the four, for keeping the group healthy. Although we disliked being separated, we proceeded speedily and we almost threw ourselves into the ship by almost jumping over the gang-plank. Yet, instead of taking it for granted that we were saved but to be left on our own, we waited in expectation for the others next to the gang-plank. At lightning speed, my mother run across the platform and came to see us again, telling us what had happened to our father and adding that as soon as our father's health was restored, they would come along to join the family with one of the next ships to leave. She stressed the point that the family's reunion was to be held in her sister's house in Athens, where she was residing, and that we had to strive to reach her as our destination. Her emotion was apparent at this point - it was reflected in her face and in the sound of her voice. It was obvious that hanging over her like a shadow was the question of whether she would ever have the chance to see her children again. She embraced and kissed all of us, and wishing us good luck, she said good-bye and left us, running back and disappearing like lightning, returning to her seriously injured husband and her elder son who was attending him in her absence. Her sudden departure made the little ones start weeping and crying, not wanting to be separated from her, and they tried to jump out of the ship to follow her. This presented to me –the supposed head of the group– a momentous problem of unwanted anxiety, and I tried hard with all my might to persuade the rebelling ones to stay in the ship, for this was her wish and order.

The success of the few daring ones who managed so boldly to reach and board the berthed ship had served as an inviting example to be imitated by the crowd of refugees who had retreated far back and who were watching and waiting for a favorable chance; they swiftly copied us. The mob rushed furiously toward the loading vessel, trying to catch up with and overtake the others and to get into that little ship before it became overloaded and departed.

It came like a human cataclysm, with the mob darting with a mad fury just to find any space in the ship which was still left. In a few minutes the ship was loaded over and above its specificied capacity to danger point, making the captain scream to the boatswain to pull the ropes off their moorings and go by saying «We are much above the vessel's tolerant weight's capacity; We are going to go down and all be drown». The sea was far above its water-line, and just a foot only away from the ship's deck. When the gang-plank was pulled up and the ship got away, the cranky sound of the turbines could be heard down in the vessel's engine-room, clear evidence of the fact that they were struggling to propel an overloaded ship. The crowds of refugees aboardship were heaped-up like a huge pile of old potatoes that no one wanted to take. It was a lucky coincidence for this hapless human cargo that the sea was calm, greatly helping the navigation of the voyage of a perilously overloaded vessel.

The short sea journey to the nearest Greek island of Mytilini (Lesvos its actual name) was extremely eventful and very dramatic. In spite of the captain's attention and prudence in navigating near to the land, our ship struck on a deep undersea reef. Thanks to the diminished speed, the overloaded ship did not sink or overturn with any human loss. It was however an acutely distressing experience for the hapless human cargo. We waited on board ship for the ebb tide which came after twelve hours. The captain then tried the only remaining way of shaking the ship off the reef by ordering his mechanic to set the turbines at full speed. The turbines and the whole of the ship's engines were ominously heard clanking and groaning but, thank God, we were shaken off the reef and in a little while the ship moved with a great vibration and a convulsive stir and started to go forward slowly with a vibrating motion, letting out a dragging, grating noise similar to something heavy being drawn along a rocky surface. This was acute and very evident to the senses of everybody on board . From then on the voyage was uneventful and in a couple of hours we arrived at the nearby island of Mytilini. Our captain approached a landing point for the refugees, probably indicated to him by the island's Authorities. It was the small sandy bay of a little fishing village, named Calloni where all the refugees on board ship were ordered to disembark. The fishermen's little village was inland, about a 25 to 30 minutes walk , and no house could be seen on the coast from the viewpoint of the place where the ship was anchored.

My responsibility for the health and well-being of the younger ones of our group was greatly bothering me, and especially so when I went out in a rowboat with the three other of us being ordered to go and inspected the conditions prevailing locally which we had to encounter and cope with.

The wide sandy circular beach of this little bay was densely occupied by many thousands of refugees who had arrived beforehand by other ships and other floating means from seashore ports and coastal villages of Asia Minor. There was no apparent roof, and no buildings or weather protected enclosures to shelter the refugees; no Greek government representative was present to provide care and assistance; there was no refugee or relief organization or society to take care of the sick or those in dire need of help; worse still no food had been delivered anywhere. The thousands of refugees had to sleep on the damp sandy beach under the stars, totally uncovered and in a painfully starving condition. This repugnantly dark picture was terrifying.

We returned to the ship after most of the refugees on board had already disembarked under the captain's strict orders and, after climbing up the ladder with some difficulty because of the strong and cruel resistance to letting me on which I encountered on the part of the sailors, I went straight to see the captain and found him busy in the tiny rudder room.

It so happened that, before we reached the island of Mytilini, I had accidentally overheard the instructions given to a group of sailors by the boatswain (they had been standing next to where I was lying down). Among other things the boatswain had told them the information he had been given by the captain: that they were going to sail to Pireaus because the damage sustained by the ship when it had collided with the reef had to be inspected. In this way, I happened to know the ship's next destination.

The captain had been ordered by the Governmental Naval Authority via the Chief of the Fleet to turn back immediately after dumping the refugees off at a nearby island, and to return to the port of Smyrna to continue the evacuation of the refugees. Yet, because of the probable damage which the ship had sustained when it had collided against the dangerous sea-reef, he decided for safety reasons to go back to Pireaus for the necessary inspection.

This unexpected change in the ship's sailing route presented me with a uniquely favorable opportunity for all my group to go to Pireaus and Athens; and when I approached and addressed the captain, I used the most persuasive words in order to make him inclined to accept my plea and to let us four young ones stay on board ship until Pireaus. I explained to him that in Athens we had my mother's sister to take care of us, while in the inhospitable locality of this seashore port we had nobody. At first he was sceptical and somewhat reluctant to yield to and to accept my plea, but when he saw all the others in the group waiting for me in the rowboat down nearby and perceived that they were little ones needing special care and attention, he agreed to our staying a few hours longer on board ship, but warned me not to say anything to any of the other refugees. I understood that he was liable and responsible for his actions and that he was under certain orders which it was distasteful to him to disobey , but that he was vested with some initiative and a free hand to judge the situation and to make his own decisions. We were lucky indeed that the captain was a kindhearted and considerate man; he might have imagined his own children caught up in a predicament of such magnitude.

The journey to Pireaus was uneventful and we arrived at the port next day at about noon. From then on we started taking the bitter pill of insult.

We were constantly scorned, belittled and minimised contemptuously and we were outrageously treated, in the way which was practised in that far-off time, as if we were second or third class primitive citizens. And why were we discriminated against? Just because we were characterized as «refugees»!

For anyone now reading the description of these revealing historical facts, this distinct and starkly clear account of the recollections of the undersigned author who analyses in detail with the stark detailed references which relate the hellish events he and his family went through, for someone who has never had the experience of having to live by himself during tragic moments which so shatter the consciousness , those historical events which occurred nearly a century before; whoever, I repeat, now reads this revealing presentation of the awfully grave and weighty historical facts disclosed here, would probably be sceptical as to whether, after such terribly tormenting and inhuman treatment which the narrator suffered, he is still a useful member of soceity by disclosing historically unknown facts and whether he still possesses a healthy mind with a mentally clear view of things which are almost a century old.

In my previously published second book «ANATOMY OF A DISASTER», where there is also my autobiography, I give an outline of my personality. This reveals how a miserable, very emaciated, and seriously ill refugee, who had been subjected for two weeks to the effects of untold suffering, of the tormenting physical pain caused by the natural process of starvation, and of prolonged of thirst and cruel treatment, who had been in a state of constant terror and extremely exposed to contagious diseases, maladies which bred fast in those miasmatic surrounding, arrived in Athens a seriously ill person and had to enter a sanatorium. It then describes the intriguing sequence of events which followed, how the narrator succeeded with his iron will and unyielding determination to regain his health and to become wholly recuperated and to enter a multifaceted and busy society once more healthy and sound as a useful, creative, and income-generating member of the community. It tells how he started from zero but made maximum efforts, how, without any political pull or other beneficial help but only by struggling throughout his whole life with untold hard work and determination, the narrator succeeded in rising to the lofty heights of society firstly as a respected attorney-at-law and later on as a judge; how the outbreak of the Second World War and the catastrophe which it brought to Europe contributed to his precipitous and awful downfall and to his reaching zero-point once again; how he started all over again almost from the beginning; how he managed to rise again from the bottom by making great efforts and exerting his unyielding will-power and determination, never avoiding the hardest work or problems, and struggling strenuously to overcome the seemingly insurmountable obstacles which stood in his way. How? By regaining his health, by practising law again, by accepting the status of Assistant State Attorney thus climbing further up. How for the last 30 to 40 years he has turned his whole attention to human History, delving and digging deep into the forgotten past and unearthing various proofs of events which occurred at certain points of human History not yet traced; how he has officialy been recognized as an internationally known historian with books in the Library of the U.S. Congress and many other Libraries in the world.

Finally I stress that in my autobiography I do not seek or intend to aggrandise my ephemeral personality – in most unmerited cases this is just a vainglorious manifestation of a foolish human desire–, but I wish to achieve a most merited and deserving purpose: to give an example of how will-power can bring results. I spend time and energy in writing this narration in order to show those of the new generation who are always grumbling that they are having no luck in their lives, that they have never been given a break or a good chance to get started on the way up, but who are unwilling to put in the hard work and effort needed, and to give a honest good struggle and effort to climb and reach their goal. Instead of doing this they morosely think that they are entitled to have high-up governmental posts or other important positions in the arena of the greatly sophisticated society of today - an entity working now with the complex and precisely regulated methods of any well organized human assembly. And they are accustomed to look at (and depend on to) the «Spoil System» of Politics. (Whereby a certain powerful political figure can give you a position by abusing his power) to gain a position for which they have neither the knowledge nor the experience nor the dexterity to handle the work involved. (This today is the customary way of easily getting a job). Yet without the indispensable honest-to-goodness effort and personal merit, it is surely impossible ever to arrive at the high plateau of international distinction and fame.

I genuinely wish and I do actually aim at this by projecting and giving my example in the biography of the aforementioned book (which is over and above the main historical work as a secondary and simply informative aspect of the work contained in that book), to instil in the brain of today's lazy youngsters the only true way and the sole real agent which leads one to success, fame, and a recognized name; ie through strenuous work, the hard, honest, and conscientious work needed in order to arrive at the top or somewhere up near it.

It is definitely not via the other fallacious and misleading way, illusory as is and unreal with its most deceptive semblance of success, which many youngsters absurdly think and foolishly believe they have achieved by riding under the patronage and care of the «Spoil System» of Politics. This is a preposterous belief which has been proven time and time again to have a sorry end and to die when the scene changes ie as soon as the patronizing powerful politician departs from the scene.

In my book I also in retrospect, by closely interlocking the historical text, deal with the very important and burning question regarding the origin of the contemporary population of Greece. Who are their actual and direct ancestors, the progenitors of which are they now the descendants?

Through the long, unchecked and arduous unrolling of the innumerable millenia of the ages through which our planet Earth has passed, the pace of progress and the unhindered evolution of mankind has also steadily and obviously increased in proportion. This development has taken place through the process of mankind's inevitable sexual intrinsic mixing and via the blending of the different primitive races. This almost unchangeable natural process has continued unbroken up to the present time. In stark and naked reality, there is no race in the entire world which remains unmixed and «blue - blood» as it originally appeared on this planet. This is in other words to say that contemporary Greeks are definitely and positively no longer the descendants of the classical Greeks, just as the contemporary inhabitants of Rome -the Italians– are no longer the descendants of the ancient Romans. Present-day Greeks (and I substantiate this statement and to a certain extent prove it amply in my book) are the descendants of the races or hordes of several invaders of this land; it is an indisputable fact that this occurred time and time again during the infinite millenia when many heterogenous races invaded or conquered this geographic corner of the planet, and established themselves by settling their race in this land, hoping that it would be their permanent domiciliary abode.

Lastly and in conclusion, near the end of my autobiography, I present very explicitly and in an open revelation, the great complexity of the intriguing question concerning the Greek language. I presented the research work I was seriously involved in and in which I tried to resolve a really puzzling matter which needed to be inquired into - a problematic question which I tried to clear up. I have proved and followed up its long process and brought to the fore (in detail) and explained the intriguing point with regard to the question: Where, When, and How the Greek language originated, the stages it passed through, the innumerable times during the passage of ages it underwent changes from its archetypal original form, the extent of assimilation of syllables, phrases, words, expressions, and vocabulary in general which were gradually adopted from various other previously existing languages or even from the contemporary ones spoken now. And – if this can glossologically be discovered – how much borrowed foreign linguistic phraseology has been incorporated into the today's Greek language? This is a gradual process which still continues to happen to all the world's spoken languages up to the present day.

This is the true original classical pattern of all of the world's languages and the unaltered old prototype through which the various articulate sounds that form a spoken language have gradually been developed. Actually all languages which have developed and reached their present form are nothing other but conglomerate languages. Every language spoken in the entire world of today is a clear conglomeration of parts and figures of speech which have been collected from various previously used and spoken languages. Words, phrases, expressions or linguistic forms have been borrowed, usurped or appropriated from pre-existing or even contemporary languages.

In conclusion, I wish once again to extend to you my deepest thanks and my honest appreciation of your noble gesture in sending me the most important and greatly elucidating book of your Late Great father, «The Blight of Asia», the book of our beloved and ever unforgettable and eminent U.S. Consul General of Smyrna.

From the deeply penetrating expressions in all of your letters, I perceive that you possess the mentality and the high caliber of your distinguished father's acumen and that you are a real grand lady, and I feel proud that you have had the friendly kindness to place me within the special circle of your few real friends.

As you might have observed, I have shortened my signature from Jean de Murat to John Murat, omitting the old-established practice of using the fief's mark of distinction which the old generation kept to and used up to the middle of this century but which has now fallen into oblivion and become a discontinued habit. For here in America for a long time, all such former marks of the distinctions of fiefdom have been discarded and ridiculed for ever by the democratic ideals and principles which now prevail. Only mental superiority – and justly so– is still highly recognized, respected and widely honored here - after.

Please forgive me for taking such a long time to finish this letter which I am now addressing to you. This has been only on account of the slow movements and the now limited and semi-corroded bodily strength which old age always brings with it, which fortunately had not touched my intellect.

I extend to you my kindest regards and best wishes for your health and well being.

I am most respectfully and thankfully yours,
John Murat
(Jean de Murat)

WEIGHTY NOTES OF THE AUTHOR

ELUCIDATION OF CERTAIN POINTS IN THE TEXT OF THE HISTORICAL WORK «ANATOMY OF A DISASTER» WHICH ARE IN NEED OF AN EXPOUNDED OBSERVATION

A. From an historical standpoint (and in that sense alone), it has proved to be an historically useful coincidence that Mark L. Bristol happened to be an intensively egocentric, self-important person who thought himself to be endowed with the gift of high intelligence which enabled him to master everything or to handle dexterously any situation in which he was involved (he was actually a wily feigner and a person who cunningly schemed and constantly calculated his own advantage). His vainglorious self-illusions were greatly boosted by the fact that he was chosen (with the vigorous support of his Turkophile friends in the State Department) as a suitable individual to take up the mighty important post of the U.S. High Commissioner in Constantinople, that is governor at large, the capital of the vanquished Ottoman Empire which was then occupied by the victorious Allies which were represented there by their High Commissioners, that is Governors.

Mark L. Bristol (a naval officer who had been promoted to the rank of Admiral a little before his appointment, was effectively boosted by the high praises of some important and influential business friends in Washington D.C., and even by Congressmen; these friendly Senators supposed and claimed that he had handled U.S. policy in the region of Turkey with brilliant mastery!!! They congratulated him on his success to such an exemplary extent in making the Turks prefer the warm friendship of the Americans to that of all other nationalities and accept with confidence – of course with financial assistance – American businessmen and their profiteering ventures in Turkey.

The way he was glorified with constant praises by some high-standing personalities in the U.S. may explain why Mark L. Bristol conceived the idea of immortalising himself in History by keeping detailed copies of all the papers he was signing (no matter to whom or where they were addressed) ie orders issued, reports submitted, ideas suggested to important friends, advice offered, details of his controversial debates, etc.

The result of his vainglorious decision was that we historians today have *access to the copies of Mark L. Bristol's papers,* which are classified in bulky files and kept in our National Archives and in the Library of Congress, each file having a specific number under its general title. These files are a treasure-house of information for the historian who digs deeply to detect and bring out through these papers, which state in detail everything said or done by Mark L. Bristol , *all those historical events which were so gravely destructive for Greece and Christianity,* with the sinister role played by Mark. L. Bristol in the tragedy of Asia Minor.

B. Towards the end of August and beginning of September 1922, the then Republican-dominated U.S. Congress governed according to the concern of their constituents who were possessed with the fear of losing profitable business ventures in Turkey if America angered the Turks i.e. if the Congress had ever even thought of adopting laws which favoured *Armenians and Greeks,* who, for the Turks, were the worst of all their enemies. This is why the U.S. Congress passed *the most stringent Immigration Law in the History of the United States!* regarding the entrance into the U.S.A. refugees of these two races.

C. On September 15 1922, Admiral Pepe of the Italian navy which was anchored in Smyrna, with his inside track on Turkish policy, was alarmed enough to call a conference of Allied and American officials. He disclosed to them some very ominous news which he had learned and the warning from the Turkish Quarters could not have been more explicit: *«If the refugees were not removed by October 1st, they would be deported into the interior and killed».* If you want to save them bring ships and take them away!

D. On Saturday September 16, *an official proclamation of Kemal's ultimatum* was issued and widely circulated. It declared that Greek and Armenian men between the *ages of 18 and 45 were prisoners of war, and would not leave; «All the others had to leave before October 1st, or deported»* .

E. (Again in the Bristol papers): The Commander of Smyrna, Commander Halsey Powell, who was also the authorized Captain of the cruiser Edsall, *reported to Bristol* the communication he had had with high Turkish Officials: *«The Turks say that if the refugees are sent in exile into the country, they will be killed». «If you want to do something about the refugees, get ships and take them out».*

F. On Sunday September 17 1922, Commander H. Powell called Bristol from Smyrna and reported to him «Italian admiral Pepe confered with Kemal who said that he would NOT take any responsibility to allow Greek ships to enter into Smyrna's harbor». (In other words he refused by denying protection to the indispensable ships needed for the evacuation of the refugees, a fact which was tantamount to refusing to let the masses of the sick, who were in great misery, and the dying Christian refugees depart from Asia Minor!!!)

G. Meanwhile the silhouettes of all the great American, British, French, and Italian battleships were hovering idly upon the waves of the harbor of Smyrna, *their admirals cruelly refusing to save the Christians from extinction although they could and should have done this!* (the great irony in this tragedy was the fact that they were supposed to be Christians themselves). Their ridiculously incongruous and inhuman justification was ostensibly the fact that they were obediently observing their Nations' orders by maintining a strict neutrality!!!

H. How large and powerful was the Allied Fleet of awesome battleships gathered in the Harbor of Smyrna? How many warships were there? What was numerically the flag count of each nationality? What wartype were they? For an elementary understanding of this somewhat confusing matter, it should be explained that the ships of all the battle-fleets represented were divided into recognised different clear distinctions or Classes. In general there were three Classes:

Class «A» was recognised by fearsome battleships with their heavily armed and armored impenetrable steel-plates - they could inflict the worst damage and *those were the so called «dreadnoughts».*

Class «B» was recognised by smaller and less armored ships but which were much speedier and which had the quality of nimble flexibility, that is they were adaptable and could quickly turn and change course; *those were the «destroyers» and «cruisers» .*

Class «C» was recognised by war-luggers, torpedo-boats (submarines), and similar war-vessels.

The Nation's flags and *the numerical presence of each Ally at the time:*

ITALY: *«A»* super-dreadnaught «Duillio»; with its leading naval officer Admiral Pepe.

«B» destroyers and cruisers: «Cavour», «Garibaldi», «Sardeg-
na», «Dante Alighieri»

«C» torpedo-boat and war-luggers.

FRANCE: *«A» fearful to look at* «Democracie», Admiral Levavaseur and
later on «Jean Bart» Admiral Dumesnil. *Two dreadnaughts.*

«B» «Ernest Renan», «Victor Hugo». *Destroyers and cruisers.*

«C» torpedo-boat and war-luggers.

BRITAIN:*«A»* «Iron Duke»*;* leading naval officer Admiral Osmond Brock.
(Dreadnaught)

«B» «Adventure», «Renown», «Interpid». *Destroyers and cruisers.*

«C» «Dixon», *war-luggers, torpedo-boat.*

U.S.A.   *«A» colossal* «Arizona», leading naval officer Admiral Dayton.
(Dreadnaught)

«B» destroyers and cruisers: «Litchfield» with Captain Arthur
Hepburn, Commander in Smyrna appointed by Bristol, «Simpson», «Edstall», «Lawrence».

«C» war-luggers.

Note: *During the «seventy nine»* years that have elapsed since that
far-off time of 1919, the technique of building battleships has been tremendously improved and perfected, and the above stated classifications
have changed too and are no longer the same. Most of the names of the
warships referred were written down by the then young and curious man
(today's historian), in a tiny little note-book which was unexpectedly
saved.

The lighter of the above-described warships, and especially the cruisers and destroyers, were not at anchor in a stationary condition but were
moving at all times in and out again, transporting military and naval heads
who needed to confer and consult on important matters with their Allied
High Commissioners in Constantinople.

IRREFUTABLE OFFICIAL SOURCES

I. Bristol's conversation with Lord Beaverbrook and his observations
thereon in detail is in his diary of 8 September 1922; it is now consolidated and on file in the National Archives under the title: «Bristol Papers». *Details of Beaverbrooke's mission in his book ,»The Decline and
fall of Lloyd George», p. 158.*

J. *Kemal's proclamation* (about men of a certain age being prisoners of war) *in Captain's Arthur Hepburn diary, dated September 9 1922*, in Navy Records - now *consolidated in the N.A. files 767.68/407, and 867.00/1522-81.*

K. Murder of Archbishop Chrysostomos described *in Puaux René: «Les Dernier Jours de Smyrne»*, Société Général d'Imprimerie, Paris, 1923. *Extracts in Bierstat, «The Great Betrayal» pp 24-25.*

L. *Correspondence Horton-Venizelos* regarding the latter's efforts in England to get Horton's book *«The Blight of Asia»* printed. Forwarding letter of well-known British publisher acquainting Horton and Venizelos that the book could not be published in Britain «because the British public was now (at the time) greatly concerned in to the Mosul oil-interests, that they did not wish anything circulated that might offend the turks who still are in domain of the oil-wells of Mosul». Venizelos in a letter to Horton confirmed this opposition as a «decisive» factor. *In «Horton Papers»* .

M.*Admiral H.S. Knapp, Commander of U.S., Forces in European Waters,* suggested to Bristol, who in turn advised the Authorities in the State Department, that it *was imperative that steps be taken to rebuke by refuting and disproving as inaccurate the many reports in European newspapers which gave information regarding facts of the brutality of the Turks and their inhuman actions against the refugees in the tragedy of Asia Minor.* Bristol in turn advised strongly his friends and heads in *the State Department, who assented warmly to the suggestion* and started to hire tested writers and essayists and to engage them *to cleverly reverse the true facts published in the European newspapers and periodicals* by distorting the facts in a sinister way in their own publications , *reversing the truth and re-writing History.* (Bristol Papers).

N. *State Department busy enlisting writers to re-write History regarding the tragic events and historical facts in favor of Turkey and against Greece,* by adroitly reversing the occurrences which brought on the disaster of Asia Minor. *N.A. 767.68/114.*

O. *Bristol absolved the Nationalist Turks of responsibility of the occurrences which led to the disaster of Asia Minor. In his diary, 1922 N.A. 867.00/1493.*

P. *The United States through the State Department was emphatically discouraging all private loans to Greece. FRUS (Foreign Relations of the United States) in National Archives.*

Q. *Dr. Lovejoy Esther P.* (who stayed in Smyrna up to the last minute, tending the sick, wounded and suffering among the masses of refugees, also delivering babies of pregnant women who were giving birth), *in her book,»Certain Smaritans», N.Y. 1927:* «I deemed it my duty to record my own observations and experience in details, *because my confidence in History has been so shaken by the misinformation circulated regarding the concluded finish of the Christian minorities in turkey».* «I found the human language insufficient to the task of description:* pain, anguish, despair and that dumb endurance beyond despair cannot be expressed in words»; and again : «The Turks proceeded under my eyes, of brutality, of robbery, of badly harming and killing refugees». A group of American women were the unsung heroines after the evacuation – among them Dr. Esther Lovejoy– *who constituted the* physicians and nurses of *the American Women's Hospital in Athens, Greece.* The AWH facilities were run entirely by women doctors. *It carried the entire burden of their care, and fed a flood of sick refugees.*

R. *Commander of Smyrna* (during that short interregnum) *(Captain Halsey Powell reported to Bristol:* «Flagrant robberies took place just before the first gate* (at the point where the refugees - most of them women and children-were supposed to board and depart into the transportation ships), *and again between the first and second gates* «Systematic robberies by soldiers on and off duty»* . Posting my enlisted men at the gates had no effect in stopping the robberies or the brutality. Putting an officer at the gates had dubious little more effect. I called it to the attention of the liaison officer, and the captain of the Port under whom were the Harbor Police, and finally as a final recourse I called Smyrna's governor Nouredin Pasha and reported it to him. It did not seem to interest him to any great degree». «Brutality and robbery at the gates and the railroad yard, was rather the rull than the exception».
*On the morning of September 20, 1922 –*and just ten days before Kemal's ulimatum expired– *Smyrna's Commander Captain H. Powell informed Asa Jennings,*who at the time was leaving Smyrna for Mytilini (a nearby island) with a chartered ship – which he had paid for– of refugees, that he had to unload them there and stay under the aegis of the Red Cross and *that the Italian admiral Pepe had finally obtained permission from Kemal for Greek ships to enter the harbor of Smyrna unmolested for the removal and departure of all the Christian refugees from Asia Minor.*

S. Mark L. Bristol and Allen Dulles *of the Near East Desk of the State Department, were ordered, on official orders which emanated from the Head of the State Dept, the then under State Secretary Evans Hughes (formerly and afterwards too highest Executive of the Standard Oil Company), to discourage the persistent notion that the conquering Turks had deliberately burned Smyrna;* (a fact amply exposed in the decision of a British Court which denied the claimant's false assertions, as well *the Court's records kept during the procedure of the legal arguments,* of a lawsuit brought by the American Tobaco Co. (which claimed that the conflagration of Smyrna was an accident and caused by no one whatsoever), against the Assurance Co. Ltd of London which claimed that the fire was a set-up affair. *A fact indisputably substantiated* by the many trustworthy witnesses who *were called to testify on the subject.* The Court in Chancery's decision issued by Justice Rowlatt was against the plaintiff, the American Tobacco Co.; it was judicially *persuaded that the fire was a set-up action, and in its decision it rejected the lawsuit of the plaintiff. Under the openly Turkophile policy* of the then Republican administration, the State Dept. was trying hard *not to anger the Turks for any reason, but instead to keep them in a state of friendly relations with the U.S.A., so that in return it would favourably accept all American business ventures in Turkey.* With its agents working through all the States, *the State Dept. encouraged businessmen to start business ventures in Turkey, claiming that there were unlimited opportunities in an unexploited land.*

T. *On September 22, 1922, Bristol cabled to the Deputy Secretary of State stressing to him his emphatic suggestion that the Greek Government be made responsible «to handle all relief work in her own country, and that our relief organisations not be drawn into operations in Greece». «The State Department was inclined to agree». At the same time Bristol recommended that the money for relief to Greece be spent instead for «relief for the Turks left behind», this, advice was accepted too. In FRUS 1922, VOL. II, p. 431 –and FRUS 1922, VOL. II, p. 444.*

U. *In the Autumn of 1923, when Greece had been inundated with one and a half million refugees with people from all races being terrified and fleeing from Turkey and was in desperate need of assistance, the American Red Cross, on the cruel and entirely inhumane orders of the State Dept., refused any further financial assistance to Greece* (it gave notice on March, 1923). *For Greece this pitiful situation was worsened tremendously with the flood of new refugees, the lamentable refugees arriving despondent from Eastern Thrace.* Bristol, with his characteristically inhuman and cruel disposition against Greece and in addition to the factual result of the second in sequence betrayal and infamous act on the part of the so-called Christian Nations and which were officially, bonded Allies of Greece, for whom she fought in the World War I which bled her both in war fatalities with bloodshed and financially with the protracted war struggle which had ensued by and for them. This ended up to become for Greece unable to pay part-due installments of her war-loans, and for this was declared by her own greedy allies bankrupt, an additional hostile disposition against Greece. Bristol had chosen this woeful moment to make a merciless comment which was full of enmity. *It was in December, 1923 when he cabled to Allen Dulles, his friend and collaborator in the State Dept. who handled matters on the Near East Desk, and made the horrible suggestion to him: «Let Greece on the frying pan simmer in her own grease».* The Turkophile Allen Dulles, *as the records indicate, consented. The State Dept. in fact, followed this policy exactly.*

V. Allen Dulles, in handling the Near East Desk at the State Dept. and the cases arising therefrom, ignored Greece's request for help in a humane effort to allow the return of prisoners of war who were being kept in Turkey in inhumane conditions *and who were progressively dying of hardship, malnutrition, sickness, and incessant killing. FRUSS 1922, VOL. II, pp 940-941, 942.*

W. *Bristol noted in his diary of May 18, 1919 the content of a letter he addressed and mailed to his naval colleague, Admiral Sims, in which he made more explicit his feelings of antipathy and hate for the Greeks by telling him this: «To me it is a calamity to let the Greeks have anything to do in this part of the world. The Greek is about the worse race in the Near East». Consolidated in the N.A.*

Y. *A true observation* by the most hateful personality *of the twentieth century* by the name of ADOLF HITLER: *«In the size of a lie, there is always contained a certain factor of credibility, since the great masses of people will more easily fall victim to a great lie than to a small one». ADOLF HITLER in his «Mein Kampf», 1937.*

Same source: Adolf Hitler encouraging his Gauleiters (territorial military governors) to become unconscious and psychologically detached from crimes indispensably committed in the name of and *for the glory of the German National Socialist Party ,and for the good of the whole of Germany; «Who after all, remembers today after having elapsed only fifty years since, the half a million Armenians, victims that the Turks murdered for their cause? They are forgotten; man's memory's short-lived. «Please keep in mind that only the almighty, potent and influential ones who make history are remembered». In «Mein kampf» too, translated in English.*

Z. ENLINGHTENING SOURCES

Assa Jennings wrote in his diary: «I have seen men, women and children whipped, robbed, shot, stabbed and drawned in the sea».
Consolidated in N.A.
Dr. Lovejoy Esther P., in «Good Samaritans», p. 220: «4.000 refugees with NO WATER at all»..
Ladas, Stephen P., in «The Exchange of Minorities»: pp 415, 429, 497 =«The Turkish defiance encouraged by the Allies», p. 498. «Turks violated all terms of the Treaty of Lausanne» with the treasonable forbearance of the supposed Allies of Greece».
Churchill, Winston, in «The Chanack Affair», p. 160; «The pro-turkish inclination of the British military». .
«Deautchland Uber Ales = Germany Above All', was the fundamental principle for all Germans; they were taught it in school and brought up with this haughtiness. When Kemal was in Germany as a military student, he was inspired to do something similar for his country «Turkey (above all) for Turks», and he was encouraged by his German teachers to do so.
Plimpton, George A., one of the chartered members of the Armenian Atrocities Committee and later Director of the Near East Relief Organization, rhetorically asked the assembled people in his lectures: «We believe in the motto «America for Americans», why not «Turkey for the Turks?»
Morgentbau Henry, Sr., in his work pp 365-367: «The Germans suggested to the Turks the so called «DEPORTATIONS», a sinister method to get rid of their undesired people.
«Beat down the cross», in Liber, p. 46
Frangulis, A.F.»La Grece et la Crise Mondial» , Vol II, Paris, 1926.

Oeconomos, Lysimachus, «The Martyrdom of Smyrna and eastern Christiandom», London, 1922.

Palis, A.A. «Greece Anatolian Venture - and After», London, 1937.

(Papers of Mark L. Bristol; they are consolidated and can be found in the Library of the U.S. Congress, and the Files of consolidated historical events regarding the Near East Affairs; and the two-faced, hypocritical stand, and the betrayal of the Allies committed shamelessly against the world's small Nations, which had helped them in their dire need to be victorious in the First World War by vanquishing the Allied enemy of the Central Powers), are found in many files in the *National Archives,* and especially under the Files numbers: *763.72, 767, 68, 867.00, 868.48, cited in the text kept in the N.A.* Also the *Naval Records Collection* under the initial *N.R. consolidated in the National Archives in subject File WT, Record Group #45.*

APPENDIX

At this particular point, it is essential to mention some of the most important historical events that took place throughout Asia Minor and its interior starting from ancient times.

The inner land named those years Persia was an extensive geographical area which had then sovereign authority over the Iraq of today and all the bordering nations included in its large perimeter.

We think that summarizing history as best we can, help us to understand the population which lives in these areas nowadays by throwing light on parts of the past. It also gives some answers about the relationship between Greece and some of the famous cities of the remote barbaric world which produced minds such as Thalis or even Homer.

In 600 B.C. not far away from the location of present day Instabul, Greek colonists built a small city called *Byzantium* which was named after Captain Byzas, the leader of the army.

During the 6th century B.C. many other Greek colonies had been established around the Aegean shores of Asia Minor, like *Militos, Efessos* and *Alicarnassos*. These city states had many connective bonds with the Mother land and they expanded the Greek culture and philosophy as well as their commercial activities.

Starting in the 5th century B.C., Xerxes, the king of the Persians wishing to conquer the world, made a campaign to conquer Greece in the year 490 B.C. He was defeated by the Athenian general Miltiades in *Marathon*. Greece was the strongest nation at that time as it had a dexterously organized army, and contained the famous Athenian navy, which literally ruled all over the Mediterranean.

Ten years later king Xerxes succeeded in ferrying his million strong army across the Straits of the Dardanelles and marched against Athens. On his way he had to go through the pass of *Thermopylae* which was defended by a small select army of Spartans under the leadership of Leonidas. They fought the Persians who tried to break their resistance but in vain, so the King's close advisor Mardonius, who understood the Greek language, suggested to him, after his army had sustained heavy losses, that it would be best to stop and turn back. At this critical juncture a Greek traitor named Ephialtes betrayed the fighting Greeks and, in return for a large sum of money revealed to the Persians a secret mountain pass through which the army of Xerxes could get around the impassable road of Thermopylae. Thus the army gained access through this unexpected pass, reached Athens, and the great Xerxes ordered his soldiers to burn the renowned city to ashes, with all the classical treasures and inimitable beauties which it contained.

This hideous act caused *Alexander the Great* -a student of *Aristotles*- to seek revenge in his renowned expedition against the barbarians of Persia, which enlarged the known world, as we shall see further on.

Although the Persians were defeated by the Greek navy under the leadership of Themistokles at 480 B.C. near the island of Salamina, they never stopped aspiring against Greece and hoping to obtain the gold of the Greek city states in Ionia (the west area of Asia Minor near the coast of Aegean sea).

Around 401 B.C. Cyrus, the prince of the Persian region wanting to fight his brother Artaxerxes and to win the throne, asked the Greek army to help him on the pretext that the invocation for help came from the Greek city states in *Ionia*, in order to fight the cruel oppression of the Persian army.

Ten Greek states responded by sending the urgently needed military help with their ten generals and they appointed Spartan general Clearchos to be responsible for carrying out their unanimous decision. The total number of Greek soldiers was between eleven and thirteen thousand men.

In the great battle which ensued at Kunaxa, the Greek phalanx lined up in the front and confronted the left phalanx of the Persians, which was routed and retreated in a state of great disorder, seeing the danger of being encircled. Cyrus was killed in this critical battle.

At this point Artaxerxes machinated a crafty trap to kill all the Greek leading generals at one fell swap and to leave the Greek army with no military leader.

By means of unarmed messengers he informed the Greek generals that he was willing to make a friendly and solemn accord with them to stop this aimless bloodshed.

The Greeks convened a council to seriously consider, judge the offer and decide. Finally the opinion of Clearchos, the Spartan leader prevailed.

Only one of the ten generals disagreed strongly and stormed out of the conference: the Athenian Xenophon. His distrust was tragically proved right very soon; the other nine generals were treacherously invited to the King's palace where they were treated amicably dined and wined and after they had fallen into a stupor, the Persian soldiers rushed in and killed them all.

Xenophon, the only surviving general, proved to be also an acknowledged and successful historian. He wrote an excellent and detailed narration of the disastrous aftermath. He took under his military disciplinary jurisdiction the whole of the remaining army of 10.000 to 11.000 men. He started to lead this army into a gruelling descent from upper Asia plateau in an attempt to reach the sea.

This descent was gruesome because they had to fight and to repel side attacks carried out by the Persian army. They were also obliged by the circumstances to get everything that the soldiers needed for their survival by stealing, and plundering. They had many adventures with the nations of Inner Persia.

The most characteristic event that the Greek army faced is with the nation of *Carduchi* which offsprings are the progenitors of today's *Kurds*.

The Carduchi were -as Xenophon reveals- hostile and unfriendly to any army considered by them as an enemy. They ruled the only pass that the Greeks had to go through in order to continue their descent towards the sea. The Carduchi impeded the pass by rolling massive boulders down the narrow pass which collided against the stony mountain sides and were shattered to small sharp shells, badly wounding anyone who tried to break through.

Xenophon in order to overpass this hindrance selected a few experienced mountain climbers from among his soldiers and ordered them to climb up the back side of the mountains, as it was seen to be unprotected because of its steep height. They managed to furtively proceed to reach the rear of the defenders, kill them and stay there as a garisson. The rainstorm of sharp stones stopped, and the Greek army passed and continued its way.

Ending this descent, when the soldiers reached the coast of Black sea, an outburst of screaming delirium of joy and happiness could be heard as the entire mass of them cried out «Sea, sea, sea».

The original rendition of all this by the historian Xenophon himself is a very affecting and meticulous narration known as «the mirii» expedition.

Sixty years later in 333 B.C. *Alexander the Great* started his renowned expedition against the «barbarians» of Persia. Before leaving Greece he obtained the Dicta of the Oracle of Delphi. The Dicta - written in the high Greek language of letters - was: *«ΑΡΓΥΡΑΙΣ ΛΟΓΧΕΣΕΙ ΜΑΧΟΥ ΚΑΙ ΠΑΝΤΑ ΘΕΛΕΙΣ ΝΙΚΙΣΕΙ»*. This translates into English thus: *«FIGHT WITH SILVER LANCES AND YOU WILL ALWAYS BE THE WINNER»*. (The Dicta of the Oracle of Delphi were uttered in metaphors. Silver lances in the metaphorical sense of Oracle's Dicta meant silver money).

Alexander the Great followed faithfully the exhortations of the Dicta by distributing silver coins among all the governing heads of the nations which blocked the path of his onward military drive; in this way he neutralized any sporadic resistance encountered in the course of his advance.

In order to secure the completely unhindered and regular supply of badly needed equipment of his army Alexander correctly judged that the most crucial place for this was the centrally located and thriving area of *Ionia* which was almost inhabited with a genuine Hellenic population - its name was changed later to that of *Smyrna*.

In his drive towards the interior of Asia, Alexander came near to the independent dominion of the nation of Carduchia.

He did not fight as Xenophon did, but behaved in a smooth and friendly way to win the confidence and friendship of their king with sumptuous gifts. He also pointed out to him that he intended to fight the enemy that they had in common - the regime of Persia which was trying to subdue and bring all the other Asian nations under its yoke. Therefore the Carduchi showed friendship and trusted Alexander, because he did not give them any sign of enmity and made it clear that he had no intention of depriving the people of the absolute freedom of their kingdom.

Alexander created a renowned regime extended as fas as *India*. His admiral Nearchus explored the Arabian sea and the Persian Gulf. Now the known world included not only the Mediterranean, the northern fringes of Africa and Egypt the coasts of Europe and Britain, but also the huge desert areas of western Asia and parts of India.

Alexander was the first great *explorer* of the ancient world. The knowledge of the world remained almost unchanged for more than 1000 years after his death in 323 B.C. The ensuing *Hellenistic* area lasted three centuries.

The main contribution to the world civilization was the expansion of *Christianity* thanks to the Greek language. Jesus and Apostles' teaching were written in Greek language.

Alexander's successors the «Epigoni» did not manage to keep his empire united and strong. Therefore, most of this part of Asia easily became a region of the Roman Empire. The Romans who built a powerful empire contributed little to exploration.

In 330 A.D. emperor Constantine the Great built a glorious city on the site of the old Byzantium and gave it the name of New Rome. From then on it became the new capital city of the Roman Empire. At the same time Constantine ordered all the government offices and services to be transferred from Rome to his 'New Rome'. A little later the people started calling the city *Constantinople* in honor of its founder.

The new resplended capital city «Capital of the World» remained the capital of the *Byzantine* Empire which bore that name from the first ancient Greek colony, as we have said, until *1453* A.D. when, all this area, fell to the *Ottoman Turks*. So the last king of the regime, Constantine Paleologos was officially named as the last Roman Emperor.

The fall of Constantinople in 1453 A.D. stopped a flourishing culture in Asia and signified the end of time which imparted to the barbarous world the sense of civilization and the intellectual perception of beauty and fine artistry.

BIBLIOGRAPHY

REFERENCE OF PUBLISHED SOURCES

REPORT   Of the «International Commission of Inquiry to Investigate the Treatment of Greek Prisoners in Turkey», Angloellenic Leage, London, 1923.

THREE PUBLICATIONS By the Turks giving their view of Greek atrocities in Turkey, and of the Smyrna's fire. «Copies in U.S.A. National Archives, Files 767.68, 116/36.

«Greek in Asia Minor» Constantinople, 1922.

BRITISH DOCUMENTS: On Foreign Policy 1919-1939, First Series, Vol. XIII, by Woodward, W.L., and Rohan, Butler. (eds) Her Majesty's Stationary Office, London, 1963.

MISSION d' Enquete en Anatolie (12-22 Mai, 1921). Rapport de Maurice Gehri, Delegue du é Comite International de la Croix-Rouge.

BULLETIN PERIODIQUE de la Presse Greque, 1920-1936. France, Ministere des Affairs Entrangere, Paris, Imprimerie National.

BULLETIN PERIODIQUE de la Press Turque, 1920-1936. France, Ministere des Affairs Etrangere. Paris, Imprimerie National.

GRESCOVICH REPORT Commander of the Smyrna Insurance Fire Brigade. Revealing the prearranged fire of Smyrna by the Turks. Constantinople 1922.

BOOKS

ABBOT, G.F. «GREECE AND THE ALLIES», London, 1922.
ALBREHT-CARRIE, RENE «Italy at the Peace Conference». New York, 1938.
BEMIS, S.F. «Diplomatic History of the United States». New York, 1936.
BIERSTADT, EDWARD HALE «The Great Betrayal». New York, 1929.
CHURCHILL, WINSTON «The World Crisis». Vol. «V». New York, 1929
CHURCHILL, WINSTON «Memoirs», London, England.
CUMMING, HENRY HARFORD «Franco-British Rivalry in the Postwar Near East», Oxford, 1938.
DE NOVO, JOHN A. «American Interests and Politics in the Middle East, 1900-1939» U.S.A., Minneapolis, MN, 1963.

DU VEOU, PAUL «La Passion de la Cilicie, 1919-1922». Paris, 1954.

EARLE, EDWARD MEAD «The Great Powers and the Bagdad Railway». New York, 1923.
«Two Faces to the American Position», p.p. 346-348.

EDIB, HALIDE. «The Turkish Ordeal». New York, 1928.

EDIB, HALIDE. «Memoirs of Halide Edib». New York, 1926.

EVANS, LAURENCE. «U.S. Policy and the Partition of Turkey, 1914-1924». U.S.A. Baltimore, MD, 1965.

FISHER, LOUIS. «Oil Imperialism» p. 9: «The British Directed Strategy WITH OIL in Mind». New York, 1926.

FRANGULIS, A.F. «La Grece et la Crise Mondial». Vol. II. Paris, 1926.

GIBB, GEORGE S. AND KNOWLTON, E.H. «History of the Standard Oil Company (New Jersey) «The Resurgent Years 1911-1927». Vol. II. N.Y. 1956.

HOUSEPIAN, MARJORY. «Smyrna Affair», N.Y. 1966. A. thorough and enlightening work.

GIBBONS, HERBERT ADAMS. «The Blackest Page of Modern Turkish History». New York, 1916.

GIBBONS, HERBERT ADAMS. «Europe Since 1918». New York, 1923.

GREY, VISCOUNT. «Twenty-Five Years». Vol. II, New York, 1925.

HARTUNIAN, ABRAHAM H. «Neither to Laugh Nor to Weep». A memoir of the Armenian Genocide. U.S.A. Boston, MA, 1968.

HEMINWAY, ERNEST. «In Our Time». New York, 1930.

HEMINWAY, ERNEST. «The Wild Years». ed. Gene Z. Hanrahan. New York, 1962.

HORTON, GEORGE. «The Blight of Asia». New York, 1926.

HORTON, GEORGE. «Recollections Grave and Gray». New York, 1927.

HOWARD, HARRY N. «The Partition of Turkey». U.S.A. Oklahoma City, 1931.

KEDOURIE, ELIE «England and the Middle East». London, 1956.

KEYNES, JOHN MAYNARD. «The Economic Consequences of Peace». London, 1920.

KINROSS, LORD. «Ataturk». New York, 1965.

KINROSS, LORD «Kemal's Biography», London, England

JACOB, O.E., and SARA JACOB Director of Smyrna's Y.M.C.A., «The Diaries», The Historical Reference Library of Y.M.C.A. in Smyrna, 291. Brodway New York NY.

LADAS, STEPHEN P. «The Exchange of Minorities, Bulgaria, Greece and Turkey». New York, 1932.

LANSING, ROBERT. «The Peace Negotiations». Boston, MA. 1921.

LEPSIUS, JOHANNES. «Le Rapport Secret sur les Massacres D' Arménie». Paris, 1918.

LOCHNER, LOUIS. «What About Germany?». New York, 1942.

LOVEJOY, ESTHER P. «Certain Samaritans». New York, 1927.

MEARS, ELIOT GRINNELL. «Modern Turkey». New York, 1924.

MOHR, ANTON. «The Oil War», New York, 1925.

MORGENTHAU, HENRY. «I Was Sent to Athens». New York, 1929.

NANSEN, FRIDJOF. «Armenia and the Near East». New York, 1928.

NICOLSON, HAROLD. «Curzon, The Last Phases, 1919-1925». Boston, MA., 1934.

OECONOMOS, LYSIMACHOS. «The Martyrdom of Smyrna and Eastern Christendom». London, England, 1922.

PALLIS, A.A. «Greece's Anatolian Venture and After». London, England, 1937.

PSOMIADES, HARRY J. «The Eastern Question: The Last Phase». Institute for Balkan Studies. Salonica, Greece, 1968.

REES, GORONWDY «The Multimillionairs». New York, 1961.

ROSKILL, S. W. «Naval Policy Between the Wars». London, England, 1968.

ROSS, F.A. et ALL. «The Near East and American Philanthropy». New York, 1929.

SFORZA, COUNT CARLO. «Makers of Modern Europe», London, England, 1930.

TAYLOR, A.J.P. «Politics in Wartime» New York, 1965.

THOMAS, LEWIS V. - FRYE, RICHARD N. «The United States and Turkey and Iran». Cambridge, 1952.

TOYNBEE, ARNOLD. «The Western Question in Greece and Turkey». Boston, MA 1922.

TUCHMAN BARBARA. «The Guns of August». New York, 1962.

WALDER, DAVID. «The Chanak Affair». New York, 1969.

WEBSTER, DONALD. «The Turkey of Ataturk». U.S.A. Philadelphia, PA 1939.

WEBSTER, JAMES. «The Diary». New York.

OTHER RELATIVE SOURCES

BUZANSKI, PETER M. «Admiral Mark L. Bristol and Turkish-American Relations, 1919-1922». Ph. D. dissertation, University of California. 1960.

DE NOVO, JOHN A. «Petroleum Diplomacy in the Near East 1908-1928». Ph. D. dissertation, U.S.A. Yale university. 1948.

HARLOW, ELIZABETH. «These are my Sons». Courtesy of Dr. Ralf Harlow, Professor Emeritus, of the American College in Paradise, Smyrna.

SPROUL, JAMES, A. «Who Burned Smyrna?» Islamic Review, August 1923, p.p. 280-284.

TOYNBEE, ARNOLD. «The East After Lausanne», Foreign Affairs, Sept. 15, 1923, p.p. 84-96.

WOODHOUSE, HENRY. «American Oil Claims in Turkey», p. 24 in Current History, March 1922, p.p. 953-959.

THE PAPERS OF MARK L. BRISTOL. The Library of U.S. Congress.

THE PERSONAL PAPERS OF GEORGE HORTON. U.S.A in Custody.

THE DIARIES OF O.E. JACOB. Director of the Smyrna Y.M.C.A. and Mrs Sarah Jacob. «The Historical Reference Library of the Y.M.C.A. # 291 Broadway, New York, N.Y.

THE DIARY OF CHIEF PETTY OFFICER James Webster. U.S.A. in «Custody».

GLASGOW, GEORGE. «The Greeks in Smyrna». The New Europe, March 25, 1920, p.p.253-256.

ELLIS, WILLIAM T. «Jennings of Smyrna». Scribner's, PA. August 1928, p.p. 230-235.

MACKENZIE, ALBERT. «Crimes of Turkish Misrule». Current History, October 1922, p.p. 28-31.

PADU, RENE. «Les Dernier Jours de Smyrne». Societé General d' Imrimerie, Paris, 1923.

RABER, ORAN. «New Light on the Destruction of Smyrna», Current History, May, 1923, p.p. 312-318.

SMYRNA AFFAIR, p. 203 — In a telegram to the State Dept. on October 1923 Bristol strongly suggests that Greece should be kept responsible for the relief and care of the refugees landed in her soil, and not to be expected

America to hold the financial burden: «Let Greece on the frying-pan simmer in her own grease». The State Dept. with its pro-turkish policy and important interests in Turkey, had the same intentions, and it accepted Bristol advice with all heart. He urged instead American relief *«for the Turks left behind»*.

IBID, p. 206.— On March 1923 the American Red-Cross Organization stopped its relief to Greece.

IBID, p. 212.— (excerpt form Adolf Hitler's «Mein Kampf»): In the size of the lie, there is always contained a certain factor of credibility, since the great masses of people will more easily fall victim to a great lie than to a small one».

IBID, p. 216.— Dr. Ralf Harlow, Emeritus Professor of Smith College, and former Professor and Faculty member of MacLachlan American College in Paradise-Smyrna, remembers this experience as the most disillusioning of his life: «THE MISSIONRIES WERE A DISGRACE».

IBID, p. 216.— George A. Plimton (member of the Armenian Atrocities Commitee and later a director of the Near East Relief) together with prominent leaders of the N.E.R. and the Board of Commissioners for Foreign Missions, expressing admiration to Turkey, asked retorically in 1923: WE BELIEVE IN AMERICA FOR THE AMERICANS, WHY NOT TURKEY FOR THE TURKS?».

IBID, p. 212.— According to Standard Oil Company historians, «there were many issues of importance at Lausanne in the Spring 1923 Conference, but *oil usurped the center of the stage»*.

IBID, p. 217.— Child, Washburn Richard, member of the Lausane Conference, had compared *KEMAL TO GEORGE WASHINGTON!*

IBID, 220.— Asa Jennings (according to the book of William Ellis) was turning against Greece (the State Dept had succeeded to buy his conscience with salaries galore, promotions and important positions).

IBID, p. 224.— Until 1927 the State Dept. with the aid of western specialists in the Near East Studies, had succeeded to hideously revise the historical records for the years 1915-1922. (The fire and conflagration of Smyrna was the work of the Greeks not the Turks)!!! And similar distortion all the way.

IBID, p. 154.— George Horton, General Counsel of the U.S.A. in Smyrna, being dragged to safety the last moment and when the Consulate Bldg, was on fire, and started crumbling down, departing from the burning Smyrna at 7.45 p.m. and watching from the destroyer SIMPSON the flames bearing relentlessly down on a human wall nearly two miles long, thought that only the destruction of Carthage by the Romans could compare to the finale of Smyrna in the extent of the horor, savagery, and human suffering. And as the destroyer moved away from the fearful scene, and darkness descended, the flames raging now over vast area grew brighter and brighter presenting an awful and sinister scene, he wrote down: «Yet there was no fleet of Christian battleships at Carthage looking on at a situation for which their goverments were responsible». The Turks had plundered, slaughtered, and now burning the city «*because they had been systematically led to believe that they would not be interfered with.*

«One of the keenest impressions which I brought away with me from Smyrna was a feeling of shame that I belong to the human race».

ROOT, ELIHU. «A Requisite for Success of Popular Diplomacy», Foreign Affairs, September, 15, pp 3-10, 1922, N.Y.

WARD, Dr. MARK, H. «The Deportation in Asia Minor, 1921-1922». Anglo-Ellenic Leage, London 1922.

WILLIAMS, ANEURIN and BRUCE, LORD. «Our Obligations to Armenia». The New Europe, pp. 51-55, July 29, 1920.

BRISTOL DOCUMENTS in «N.A.», Bristol conversation with Suad Bey: Diary 29 October, 1922. He absolves responsibility of the Turks for the atrocities.

BROWN, CONSTANTINE. «A crime was committed yesterday when Turkish soldiery, after finishing pillaging, set this city on fire». Dispatch, in the Chicago Daily News, September, 1922.

CLAYTON, JOHN. Dispatch, «in the Chicago Tribune, 25, September 1922, «The problem of minorities is here solved for all time. No doubt remains as to the origin of the fire. The torch was applied by Turkish regular soldiers».

EINSTEIN, LEWIS. «The Armenian Massacres». The Contemporary Review, April 1917, pp. 486-494.

Dr. LOVEJOY, ESTHER, P. «My confidence in History on account of its great distortion involved in the narration of the true facts has been shaken.. May 28, 1927, in her letter to Horton, in «Horton's Documents», preserved in National Archives; She's alluding to the animaginable distortion of the events of Smyrna's Catastrophe.

MELVIN, JOHNSON. «A shorthand Statement about his eyewitnessing atrocities by the Turks, and the burning of Smyrna by the Turks». U.S.A. 1963-64.

MERRIL, Lt. A.S. «Describes very vividly the unexplicable with words tragic-plight of the burned-up Christian crowds of refugies at the Smyrna's historic conflagration», in September 1919. «Smyrna Affair», pp. 160-161, and 166 in witnessing large detachments of refugees deported to the interior by forced march, to be exterminated as scheduled by Kemal.

MERRILL DIARY. September 16, 1922, in National Archives «WE LOST THE WAR».

PUAUX, RENE. «The Murder of Archbishop Chrysostomos». Les Dernier Jours de Smyrne. Societè General d' Imprimerie National, Paris, 1923.

«TIMES» London: Feature Article on Admiral Mark L. Bristol, 28 August, 1927 outlines his brutish personality.

«U.S.A. Discouraging Private Loans to Greece», FRUS 30 January 1922, Vol. II, p. 456.

«Smyrna Affair» p. 187. N.A. in Bristol's Documents: Declares in a message to the Authorities in Greece that she has the sole responsibility for the relief and care of the refugees landed in her soil, and she should not expect any financial aid and assistance from America. He clearly reveals his hostile predisposition against Greece, and on the contratry his excessively favored the beastly brutish noval nationalistic Turkey's integrity and prosperity. This in order to facilitate all America's expectations for businessmen and its industrialists ventures to rapaciously exploit the supposed unexploited and unlimited -as advertised- chances for quick gains in the noval and newly emerged and regenerated Turkey.

MORGENTHAU, HENRY. «Ambassador Morgenthau's Story», p. 365-367. N.Y., 1918. The Germans suggested Deportation thus eliminating definitely the «Giaours».

IBID: «I was Sent to Athens», N.Y., 1929

Not Published YET

NOT PUBLISHED. «The papers of the American Board Commissioners for Foreign Mission». Reposted in Hoaghton Library, Harvard University. The papers of Mark L. Bristol. The Library of Congress.

ALSO IN U.S.A. NATIONAL ARCHIVES

The personal papers of Clara Van Etten, Director of the Armenian Central Orphanage, Smyrna.

The personal papers of George Horton.

Buzanski, Peter M. «The International Investigation of the Greek Invasion of Smyrna, 1919». «The Historiana», May 1963, p.p. 325-343.

Ward, Dr. Mark H. «The Deportations in Asia Minor» 1921-1922. Anglo-Ellenic Leage, London, 1922.

ADDITIONAL SOURCES

SPECIAL BIBLIOGRAPHY

International Historical Books (in World's Libraries).

Modern Greek History (Greek chroniclers, Larousse, Encyclopedia, Britanica, Et ALL).

«The Italian Dream». Keith W. Stump. «Plain Truth», Vol. 49, pp. 13 - over, U.S.A., 1984.

«History of the Holy-Roman Austro-Hungarian Empire». (Austrian Archives).

«Alexiade». Anna Komnena. Refferchied, Leipzig, Teubner, 1984.

«Encyclopedia Britanica», IX and XI-XII editions (1902-1903, 1910-1911). International Volume XII, pp. 424-530.

«The Catalan Chronicle». Francisco de Moncada. Aragon, Spain, 1620.

«French Financial Records». Earle, pp. 321-322.

«Europe Since 1918». Gibbons Herbert Adams. New York, 1923, p. 452.

«The Blackest Page of Modern Turkish History». Gibbons, H.A., New York, 1916.

Kinross Lord. «Kemal's Biography». pp. 174, 235, 244. New York, 1965.

«Ataturk». Kinross Lord. London, England.

«History». Nicolson. p 260.

«Blight of Asia». Horton, George, 23-24 June 1919, and 9 July 1919, New York, 1926.

«Panic». Latest Results concluded with Scientific Psychanalytical Methods, upon thousands of patients in American and European Hospitals and Clinics.

«D.N.A.» Reference to Genetic Engineering and its sequence, R.N.A., Double Helix, Chromosomes (adenine, cytosine, guanine, and thymine - A, C, G, T.-).

«The Two Faces of American Position» Edward, Mead Earl. pp. 346-348.

«The Great Betrayal». American Economic Imperialism, 1924 (ibid).

«U.S.A. Senate Records». (in U.S.A. National Archives).

«The Smyrna Affair». Marjory Housepian. p. 79, (regarding French planes bombarding Greek positions in the front war-line), New York, 1966.

«N.A.» = «National Archives of the United States». File of the Dept. of State No. 136.72/13199.

«FRUS» = Papers relating to the «FOREIGN RELATIONS of the UNITED STATES», in Supplement 1922 Vol. II., Department of State, Washington, D.C. 1922-1923.

«Louis, Lochner». «What about Germany?» quoting Adolf Hitler declaring his own plans for genocide to his Supreme Commanders on August 22, 1939, in his criminative statement: «WHO, AFTER ALL, SPEAKS TODAY OF THE ANNIHILATION OF THE ARMENIANS BY THE TURKS?». «THE WORLD BELIEVES IN SUCCESS ALONE» (and the entire of his quoting).

GLOSSARIUM

NA = National Archives of U.S.A.

NR = Naval Records Collection, Incorporated into the National Archives of the United States of America; Record Group No. 45, File WT

FRUS = Foreign Records of the United States, Documents related to the Foreign Relations of the U.S.A. from 1915. Supplement 1922 Vol. II, U.S. Department of States, Washington D.C.

NER = Near East Relief

SOC = Standard Oil Company

U.S.A. = United States of America

B.R.F. = BOOKS REVEALING FACTS

GLOSSARIUM = Reveals the capital letters' symbolism of their abbreviated meaning

N.Y. = New York

State Dept. = State Department

CA = California, MA Massachusethes, NY New York, NJ New Jersey

C.F.R. = Council of Foreign Relations

IBID = The Same author

A.G.S. = Army's General Staff

Printed by A. *Triantafillis*
7, Mavromichali str., Athens, 106 79
Tel. 36.36.325 - 36.25.849